The Viking Saint

The Viking Saint

Olaf II of Norway

John Carr

Pen & Sword
MILITARY

First published in Great Britain in 2022 by
Pen & Sword Military
An imprint of
Pen & Sword Books Ltd
Yorkshire – Philadelphia

Copyright © John Carr 2022

ISBN 978 1 39908 781 0

A CIP catalogue record for this book is
available from the British Library.

Typeset by Mac Style
Printed and bound in the UK by CPI Group (UK) Ltd,
Croydon, CR0 4YY.

Pen & Sword Books Limited incorporates the imprints of Atlas,
Archaeology, Aviation, Discovery, Family History, Fiction, History,
Maritime, Military, Military Classics, Politics, Select, Transport,
True Crime, Air World, Frontline Publishing, Leo Cooper, Remember
When, Seaforth Publishing, The Praetorian Press, Wharncliffe
Local History, Wharncliffe Transport, Wharncliffe True Crime
and White Owl.

For a complete list of Pen & Sword titles please contact

PEN & SWORD BOOKS LIMITED
47 Church Street, Barnsley, South Yorkshire, S70 2AS, England
E-mail: enquiries@pen-and-sword.co.uk
Website: www.pen-and-sword.co.uk

Or

PEN AND SWORD BOOKS
1950 Lawrence Rd, Havertown, PA 19083, USA
E-mail: Uspen-and-sword@casematepublishers.com
Website: www.penandswordbooks.com

Contents

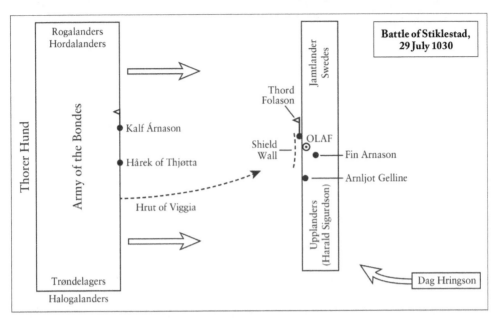

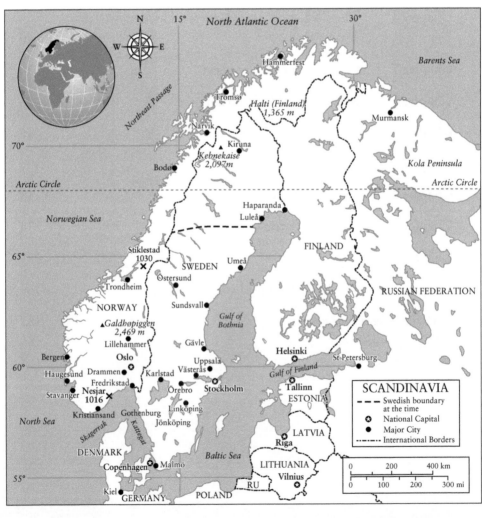

Prologue

Hagiography in this secular age is not one of the more fashionable genres in the non-fiction field. The main reason is that the term itself has come to be misleading; in our era hagiography is equated with fairy-tale propaganda, the whitewashing or blatant promotion of a person or institution, likened to what many still believe are fanciful concoctions, devoid of critical content and fit only for the naïve or, in the case of saints, the 'religious'.

But that is not the dictionary definition. The term hagiography derives from the Greek *haghios*, saintly or holy, and *graphe*, written text. The connotations of propaganda and insincerity are later accretions. A hagiography can be penetratingly candid and quite historical. A great many, it is true, contain something of the implausible, but that alone does not automatically consign them to the historian's recycle bin. Even the most subjective and 'hagiographical' of saints' lives are not without a hard kernel of truth. It is the task of whoever has the temerity to write about the life of a saint – especially one who lived a thousand years ago – not so much to separate 'fact' from 'fiction' (impossible in most cases) as to present all that we know of the subject and let the reader's own conscience decide.

History does not come down to us in neat, labelled particles which we can analyse under a microscope and pronounce on their authenticity. All non-fictional narration, in fact, including that of daily journalism and in the vast wasteland of social media, suffers from the same problematic, hence the recent insoluble issue of what does or does not constitute 'fake news'.

Sainthood itself is a subject extremely fraught with such difficulty. The worldly and the divine combine and clash in ways that cannot be unravelled. The subject cannot be treated in the usual dry reportorial manner of a television documentary, even of a docu-drama. History is not a set of algorithms or mathematical functions where inputs A and B must inevitably result in X and Y; most of the time we don't even know what A and B really are, and must resort to speculative intuition, aware that a so-far unknown C or D may be lurking in the shadows. One reads not only with the coldly rational mind but with the heart also.

Olaf II Haraldsson (or, as it is variously spelled, Óláfr in Old Norse, Olav or Olave) was born around 995 in a noble household with connections to the Danish Norwegian royal line. In the accounts we have, he showed remarkable precocity at a very early age, going enthusiastically on Viking raids before quite getting into his teens. He did not live very long – he was killed in battle when he was thirty-five – but the story of his young adult years bears similarities to that of Saul in the New Testament, who from 'breathing out threatenings and slaughter against the disciples of the Lord', (Acts 9:1) experienced that momentous conversion on the road to Damascus that at one stroke turned him into the pre-eminent Christian apostle of all time. Olaf too had his warlike and violent early life, until his conversion in Rouen which set him on a diametrically opposite course to become Norway's patron saint.

The main source for the life of St Olaf is the monumental history of Norway's kings, the *Heimskringla*, of Snorri Sturluson, an Icelandic annalist of the thirteenth century. Snorri marshals his entire history, including the lives and exploits of kings before Olaf, into a definite Christian framework replete with dramatic scenes and seat-edge accounts. The work has been criticized as historically unreliable in places, though we have no corresponding standard of what 'reliable' means in this case. Of course it contains flaws, and where these are detectable they are mentioned, but to try to decide on arbitrary grounds which elements are pious tales and which have what is vaguely called 'the ring of truth', and separate the one from the other, would be a waste of time. The modern chronicler is simply not qualified to make the distinction; a pious tale to one reader may be an entirely authentic divine revelation to another.

In cases such as the *Heimskringla*, as with other such seminal sagas as Homer's *Iliad*, the conscientious historian is faced with an insoluble dilemma. I suggest dealing with this conundrum by taking what I would call a 'half-empty or half-full' approach. Either the *Heimskringla* can be considered 'by and large' legendary (half-empty), or 'by and large' truthful (half-full). Out of respect and tribute to my subject, I have chosen the latter course.

Olaf II Haraldsson was not made a saint lightly; no saint is. Was he simply a capable man who unified Norway and made it Christian – or was he someone who transcended mere power politics and joined the company of saints by the divine power released in him? Thus the central problem in examining the story of St Olaf is squaring his earthly record with his subsequent sainthood. Some authorities have implicitly cast a certain doubt over whether he deserved to be a 'true' saint. There certainly is a contrast between Olaf's saintly status and some of his distinctly un-saintly actions while he was king of Norway. Such implied criticism, though understandable, makes the historical mistake of judging past events (or what we are told of past events) by today's standards. Olaf Haraldsson acted on the old Roman dictum of *dura lex, sed lex* – the law is harsh, but it's the law. The alternative would have been a continuation of the Old Norse heathen cults of blood and violence, which had to be extinguished by all possible means.

A second source of historical fallacy lies in the uncomfortable fact that, as with any historical event, we simply have too few facts to go on. What we know of St Olaf, largely through Snorri Sturluson and other sources, must be infinitesimal compared to what actually happened through his brief but extraordinarily full life. From this standpoint, judgements on saintliness or otherwise would be meaningless.

The fact today, however, is that Olaf is a fully-fledged saint in the Protestant, Catholic and Orthodox churches, and it cannot be an accident that he is. Divine criteria are not human ones. Saints are people too, with their faults and flaws: 'Judge not, that thou be not judged.' I present St Olaf's story here as it has been transmitted by the basic sources and, apart from some incidental commentary in the text, leave the ultimate verdict to the reader.

Thanks go to Gro Reistad for helping me with a few obscure Old Norse and Norwegian terms, and providing back-up help in the linguistics department, and to Philip Sidnell of Pen & Sword who offered some valuable suggestions on how to write a better book than the one I had started out writing, and encouraging me through the lockdown months when *tedium vitae* threatened to engulf any creative effort. Thanks to Janet Wood for copy-editing the manuscript.

At the outset of this project I was aware, sometimes uncomfortably, that in deciding to write about a Norwegian warrior and saint I was stepping into alien territory well outside my usual subjects of Greece and the Mediterranean. But I take as my guide the American literary scholar Morris Bishop's dictum: 'If you want to find out about something of which you know nothing, write a book about it.'

Chapter 1

London Bridge Fell Down

In August 1012 a Danish Viking chieftain, Thorkell the Tall, descended on Canterbury with a large force as part of a Viking attempt to conquer England. It was the latest of several such attempts over the past couple of hundred years, which had seen eastern England regularly inundated with Norse soldiery, with no apparent end in sight. It wasn't the first time that Thorkell had threatened Canterbury; a similar attempt three years before had been averted by the payment to him of large amounts of protection money. This time, however, the treachery of an abbot enabled Thorkell's Danes to seize the city. One of those taken into custody was Archbishop Alphege, who was led to Thorkell's ships despite the fact that fifteen years before he had overseen the baptism of another leading Viking, Norwegian King Olaf I Tryggvason.

Thorkell, however, was a heathen and part of his success so far was attributed to the relative docility of Christianized Anglo-Saxons of England, whom he found to be pretty much a walkover. People such as Archbishop Alphege were seen as fair game, weak religious folk who deserved to be ground down by the stronger Vikings who had no spiritual compunctions. The Danes, already accustomed to blackmailing huge sums out of the intimidated English, demanded a hefty ransom for Alphege, who replied sadly that his see was simply too poor to pay it. At Thorkell's camp at Greenwich Alphege suffered the full wrath of his captors; after a dinner, when many of the men were drunk, the unhappy prelate was pelted with bones (including cattle skulls) and stones and blocks of wood so savagely that in the end, barely alive, he was despatched with an axe-blow to the head. The fate of St Alphege, as he subsequently became, would have seemed to the English to fulfil the worst doom-laden forecasts of a new millennium, now in its twelfth year.

So far London had been spared Thorkell's attacks. 'Praise be to God,' wrote the author of the *Anglo-Saxon Chronicle*, 'that it still stands sound, and [the Vikings] always fared badly there.' The Danes' chief foe, King

Ethelred the Redeless, had never given up resisting them, however ineffectually, but in 1010 his army had suffered a crippling defeat at Ringmere in East Anglia. In the following year Ethelred sued for peace, offering yet more tribute to Thorkell, who accepted it as *heregeld*, or army-money and, on the surface at least, agreed to become Ethelred's ally. Therefore when Danish King Svein Forkbeard invaded Britain again in 1013, he came upon Ethelred and Thorkell defending London together.

One of the nobles in Thorkell's army was a young Norwegian of royal lineage, Olaf Haraldsson. Not yet out of his teens, he had already displayed his mettle in several campaigns in Scandinavia. It is almost certain that Olaf was in Thorkell's army at the time, the same army which martyred St Alphege. We have, of course, no way of knowing whether he was present at that particular event, but according to the bard Ottar the Black, Olaf did participate in the taking and sacking of Canterbury and inevitably would have enriched himself considerably from Ethelred's bountiful supply of *heregeld*.

After Canterbury the stage was set for Olaf Haraldsson's most famous early exploit, the destruction of London Bridge. Frustratingly, however, some historical confusion surrounds the exact date. It is often dated to 1009, though Snorri Sturluson places it immediately after the death of Svein Forkbeard, who ruled Viking Britain, but before the killing of St Alphege at Canterbury. It was when Olaf was about to sail to Britain from raiding Friesland, or after he had already arrived, that Svein Forkbeard had died unexpectedly, and peacefully in bed, on 3 February 1014. As such a calm demise was not what any self-respecting Viking wished for himself, there were whisperings that the spirit of the martyred Christian St Edmund (of whom more later) had done it; among the learned there were parallels with the death of East Roman pagan Emperor Julian the Apostate, killed in battle in 363 by a mysterious arrow said to have been shot by Christian Saint Mercurius in the guise of a soldier.

As Thorkell (and his underling Olaf) were now formally allied to Ethelred's English, his ships sailed into the Thames to try to reduce a strong Danish fortification on the north bank of the river. A wide bridge 'able to take two wagons' abreast connected the fort with a flourishing trading post at Southwark (Sudvirke). The bridge itself was stoutly defended by men behind parapets and towers. Ethelred called a conference of commanders to consider what action to take; Olaf had a specific and ingenious plan: to make large wooden (or wicker) platforms out of the roofs of old houses and place them atop his vessels, allowing the men enough room to fight while under shelter. As these ingenious armoured ships sidled up to the bridge they came under heavy attack from stones, arrows, spears and other missiles hurled from the parapets, causing some damage to the flotilla. The crews tied strong ropes around the wooden piles of the bridge; with the ropes in place the crews were ordered to row downriver with all their strength. The piles gave way and the over-weighted bridge collapsed with many men on it. Southwark was soon taken, and shortly afterwards the Danes north of the river capitulated.

Ottar the Black exulted:

> London Bridge is broken down,
> Gold is won, and bright renown…
> At London Bridge stout Olaf gave
> Odin's law to his war-men brave –
> 'To win or to die!' And the foemen fly.
> Some by the dyke-side refuge gain –
> Some in the tents on Southwark plain!

There has been understandable speculation that Ottar's verse may have been the origin of the English nursery rhyme 'London Bridge Is Falling Down', and there could be some merit to that theory. The reference to Odin indicates that Olaf was still a heathen at the time, and would not have taken the compliment amiss. The destroyed bridge was one of several that had spanned the Thames at that point, going back to at least AD 50 or so, after the Romans landed. The earliest bridge may have been a victim of Boudicca's revolt in AD 60, when much of Londinium was burned, but if it was, it was quickly rebuilt, and remained in place until the Romans left about 410. We hear of a second bridge built around 944 after a severe storm destroyed hundreds of houses, though it was constantly vulnerable to fire or surging tides. It was this one, more than likely, that Olaf pulled down.

Who was this precocious Norwegian adolescent whose tactical talents had shown themselves at such an early age? Olaf Haraldsson was old enough to remember his namesake Olaf Tryggvason (Olaf I), who had tried to Christianize Norway, sometimes by violent methods (see Chapter 4 below). But after the latter's death in battle it seemed as if his efforts had been in vain. The Danes seized back control of southern Norway in collaboration with the aggressively independent Lade earls of Trondheim. In the words of the *Ágrip*, a twelfth-century history of Norway, 'as much pain and effort as Olaf Tryggvason had put into forwarding Christianity – and he spared nothing which was to the honour of God and the strengthening of the Christian faith – so [his successors] put all their strength into quelling it.' According to Theodoricus Monachus (Tjodric Munk in his native Norwegian), many Christians at this time were swayed by the revived heathenism and fell away from the faith.

One of those vassals, or 'minor kings' under the Danish King Harald Bluetooth (the father of Svein Forkbeard, who was eventually to depose him), was Gudrod Bjornson, who had a son named Harald, born sometime in the mid-950s. While Harald was still a boy, for some unknown reason but very likely to keep him away from harm at Danish hands, Gudrod sent him to be fostered by a noble in the snowy wastes of Greenland; there he grew up with his host's own son as a foster-brother, earning the cognomen Grenske, or Greenlander. Though the record here is confused and hazy, with at least a couple more Haralds appearing briefly on the stage and disappearing, at some point Gudrod was toppled, and Harald Grenske was forced to flee to the Scandinavian peninsula.

Barely out of boyhood, Harald joined a band of Viking raiders who, in Snorri's felicitous phrasing, 'went out a-cruising to gather property'. Proving quite competent in that department, he joined the company of the renowned warrior Skoglar-Toste on his regular summer raiding excursions. During one of the winters he spent at Skoglar-Toste's house, Harald Grenske took a liking to his host's daughter Sigrid, 'young and handsome'. On the downside, she was also 'proud and high-minded' and preferred to become the spouse of King Eirik the Victorious of Sweden rather than of an obscure minor noble.

Sometime in the 970s we find Harald joining the forces of Danish King Harald Gormsson who had gathered together those Norwegians who had lost their lands under the persecution of Eirik Bloodaxe's widow Gunnhild and her sons. Leading 600 ships, Harald Gormsson sailed to Viken, where he received an enthusiastic welcome. The Danish king seems to have had little trouble in reinstating indigenous rule over most of Norway; Harald Grenske, for his contribution to the campaign was given a sizeable chunk of territory where his ancestors had ruled. His claim was based on his descent from his great-grandfather Harald Haarfager (or Finehair) who made the first moves to unify Norway and was thus the pedigree that Olaf Haraldsson himself would employ when his turn came to do the same.

While still only eighteen years old or slightly more, Harald Grenske made his base in Vestfold and married Åsta Gudbrandsdottir. In the summer of 994 Harald set out on another 'property-gathering excursion' to the Baltic and touched at Sweden; there he found that the high-minded girl he had once wanted and who in the meantime had become Queen Sigrid of Sweden, was a widow. 'When she heard,' says Snorri, 'that her foster-brother was come to the country a short distance from her, she sent men to invite him to a feast.' The details of that feast are not known, but we are told that Harald Grenske was smitten once again with Sigrid, and back home during the winter he was 'very silent and cast down'.

The following summer he took ship and sailed directly for Sweden intending to have it out with Sigrid. It would prove a fatal decision. She rode down to the waterfront to meet him, and during the initial talk he blurted out a proposal. At first Sigrid laughed; was he not already well-married? And besides, she had learned that his wife Åsta was pregnant, so what was he doing courting another woman? 'Åsta,' Harald replied, 'is a good and clever woman, but she is not so well born as I am.' Sigrid was not to be taken in by Harald's infatuated excuses; shortly after this frosty exchange she rode off.

Harald had no intention of swallowing the snub, and rode with his considerable entourage to Sigrid's house, where he found a rival suitor in the person of King Vissalvald (Vsevolod?) of Kiev. Both men and their companies got drunk that evening, and when they were all insensible Sigrid ordered flaming torches to be put to the large outbuilding in which they were all asleep; any who escaped the flames were cut down by the sword. Thus perished Harald Grenske. As a measure of Sigrid's inner hardness (and what today might be considered rather extreme feminism), she said she was thoroughly tired of 'small kings' coming to woo her, and saw no more effective way of deterring future suitors than to burn them all. She well lived up to her sobriquet the Haughty (Storråde).

At about that time, Harald Grenske's wife (or widow) Åsta must have had their son Olaf Haralddsson, who was either just born or anything up to about five years old. The date of Olaf's birth is problematic; the most common estimate is about 995, though the historical evidence for his early exploits may argue for some years earlier. A birth year of 995, for example, would make him hardly old enough for the military adventures he is said to have engaged in towards the end of the first decade of the eleventh century. His mother Åsta presently remarried; the offspring of her and her second husband, a minor Norwegian noble named Sigurd Syr, was another Harald, Olaf's half-brother and future king Harald Hardraada.

Almost nothing is known of the circumstances of Olaf's birth, except that it took place at Ringerike in Oppland, in the home of Åsta's father Gudbrand, and that according to Snorri's saga, 'water was poured over him'. This would not have been a reference to the occasion in 998, when Olaf Tryggvason met the boy who was destined to outshine him in history. Olaf, now at least three years old, Åsta and her second husband Sigurd Syr were living on Åsta's farm when Olaf Tryggvason offered to be the boy's godfather; in fact, all three of the household were reportedly baptized together. Sigurd Syr was a stern but fair taskmaster; Snorri relates that one day Sigurd looked for a farmhand to saddle his horse, couldn't find anyone and asked Olaf to do it. Seeing the chance for a practical joke on his stepfather (and almost certainly resenting being ordered to do a servant's task), Olaf found the biggest billy-goat on the farm and put the saddle on it. Though annoyed at such spirited disobedience, Sigurd by his reaction seems to have become resigned to the boy's character: 'It is easy to see that you will little regard my orders', Sigurd said. 'You are far more proud than I am.' Olaf merely laughed.

Stories of adolescent defiance of dull authority are common in biographies of historic personalities, and are used invariably to build up a consistent portrait that too often lies in the imagination of the writer or bard; Snorri's story may or may not be true, though from the physical description of Olaf that we are given, it sounds quite credible. On his mother's farm Olaf grew up to be a strapping lad, tall and well-built, with blond hair and a roseate complexion. His eyes were reported to be his most remarkable feature, blazing alarmingly when he was angry. He was an all-rounder, good at athletics and all physical tasks, especially swimming – and ambitious, always wanting to be first in everything.

While trying to unravel the mixture of fact and fiction regarding Olaf's early life is an impossible task, what we do know is that at a remarkably young age we find him a full-fledged Viking raider in the Baltic Sea at the improbable (but not impossible) age of twelve. He got there thanks to the initiative of his mother; what we don't know is whose decision it was, hers or his – the latter seems more likely. Olaf entered the service of one Hrane, who seems to have been an experienced professional raider and received Åsta's authority (how exactly, we are not told) to command a warship with her son in it. Though extremely young and a rookie, Olaf was given the nominal rank of 'king' merely because of his royal pedigree, and the rough-hewn crews seem to have accepted it; to keep his crewmates' allegiance, however, he is believed to have put in some time on the rowers' benches. (A more recent parallel can be found in the late Duke of Edinburgh, who as Prince Philip of Greece served in Britain's Royal Navy during the Second World War and carried the title of prince even before his commissioning.)

Olaf's first tour of duty, as it were, took him to the Danish coast, from where Hrane's ship sailed into the Baltic to attack targets in Sweden. Olaf particularly relished this campaign, as it would enable him to get his revenge on the Swedes, who in the person of Sigrid the Haughty had murdered his father. In the words of the skald Ottar Svarte (the Black): 'Across the Baltic foam is dancing, shields and spears and helmets glancing!' At Sotasker in Sweden Olaf may have had his first real baptism of combat. The reference in the *Heimskringla* to 'his men' and 'his ships' might raise eyebrows, but the phraseology is likely a reference to his official royal status and not to any actual command, for which he would be quite inexperienced at that age. The fleet to which Olaf belonged captured several Swedish vessels by throwing out grapnels and pulling them in, to be boarded and cleared of men.

We next hear of Olaf sailing farther up the Swedish coast to land at Sigtuna on the Maelar Lake. But Swedish King Olof Sköttkonung, the son of Sigrid the Haughty and quite her equal in obduracy, had chains placed across the narrow channel at Stoksund (present-day Stockholm), blocking the Norwegians' only exit from the Maelar Lake. Olaf's force countered this by digging a diversionary canal which, swollen by heavy rain, enabled his ships to escape to sea; the rudders had been taken off and the sails fully hoisted, and with remarkable seamanship the Norwegian oarsmen successfully negotiated the canal. The Swedes' tactics here are uncertain; according to Snorri, some of them rushed to block the canal, but such was the volume of rushing water that the canal's bank collapsed and drowned many. The Swedes, on the other hand, denied that anything like that had happened. We can believe, however, that Olof Sköttkonung flew into a rage, which he tried to assuage by raiding the large island of Gotland in the Baltic, though the Gotlanders bribed him to leave them alone before he could do any real damage.

Olaf next encountered resistance at Eysyssel to the east, where he defeated a force sent against him. From there the Norwegian ships sailed to Finland, driving the local people from their homes and looting whatever they could. While Olaf's men were walking back to their ships one evening through Herdaler Wood, they came under surprise attack from a strong local force; Olaf ordered the men to cover themselves with their shields, but such was the ferocity of the attack that casualties were heavy. Olaf and what was left of his men straggled back to the ships late at night in the midst of a storm which Snorri attributes to 'the Finlanders' witchcraft.' The ships sailed despite the storm, hugging the coast, but the Finns shadowed them by land, and eventually the Norwegians had to give up the campaign.

At some point after this Olaf found himself in Thorkell's expedition to England, having gone to Denmark after the Finnish expedition in search, presumably, of more military employment and its concomitant possibility of becoming rich. The famous destruction of London Bridge was Olaf's sixth battle, and the one that seems to have made his initial reputation. He later helped King Ethelred and his successor in other battles, some fifteen in all.

There is evidence that probably after the London Bridge exploit Olaf Haraldsson joined an ambitious Viking expedition to the Iberian peninsula – in fact, one of a long series of them that began about 1008 and lasted some thirty years, on and off. Olaf seems to have played an active part in sailing up the Miño River in Galicia, burning a town and seizing a local bishop who was presumably held hostage. This involvement appears to have been covered up later, as Snorri (almost certainly intentionally) makes no mention of it, though court skalds do.

Chapter 2

'Never was such an atrocity seen'

To better understand the story of Olaf Haraldsson and his sainthood, and the remarkable transformation of Viking culture that resulted, we need to go back a couple of hundred years before he was born, to the era when the very terms Viking and Norseman had become a terror to the people of the British Isles. In the late eighth century most of Britain had been Christian for at least half a millennium. After the Anglo-Saxon invasions of the fifth century, life in Britain had settled down to normal around the foci of a handful of kingdoms.

Human history is replete with examples of sudden, unexpected disaster that can strike a society without warning. As the event comes as a complete surprise, right out of the blue, the victims have generally not thought to protect themselves beforehand, which makes the final toll all the greater. The most recent example that comes to mind is the multiple terrorist attack of 11 September 2001 in the United States. In 793 something of the sort struck the idyllically peaceful monastic island of Lindisfarne, off the Northumbrian English coast. So momentous was this event that it has been defined as the starting point for a whole age of history.

Lindisfarne was the site of a monastery that already had a serious history of devotion and scholarship. Within its walls was kept the illuminated Gospel Book of Lindisfarne, written sixty years before by Irish monks who sought in the bleak surroundings the peace and isolation they required. Lindisfarne was just one of several devout centres of learning in the north-east of England, such as Hexham and Whitby, which flourished in the centuries after the conversion of the Anglo-Saxons to Christianity, and did much to ameliorate the semi-barbarity of their previous customs and morals.

In the eighth century, Northumbria (or Northanhymbre in Old English) was one of the more settled areas of the British Isles, a major centre of culture and learning. Much of this security was underpinned by a capable military establishment set up under kings Edwin (616–632),

Oswald (633–641) and Oswin (641–670), who set Northumbria on a par with the Anglo-Saxon kingdoms of Mercia and Wessex to the south. Those kings had built on the legacy of Edwin's immediate predecessor, King Aethelfrith of Bernicia, who had combined his realm with a smaller one called Deira to create Northumbria.

By the late eighth century the people of Northumbria could well boast of living in a golden age of spiritual and artistic achievement enjoying the security of an effective administration. Around 660 a clergyman named Benedict Biscop (whose name very likely came from the Greek *episkopos*, or bishop, from which we derive our terms episcopal and Episcopalian) had set up a monastic school at Monkwearmouth, across the River Wear from a similar monastery at Jarrow. One of its students was a precocious youngster named Bede, born in 673 and made a deacon at nineteen. The Venerable Bede, as he became known, penned his still-acclaimed *Ecclesiastical History of England*, which is one of our prime sources of knowledge for that period. When Bede died in 735, Northumbria stood at its apex. Less than sixty years later, with awful suddenness, it all came crashing down.

The monastery on the 'holy island' of Lindisfarne was established around the mid-seventh century by Aidan, an Irish monk, as a main centre for proselytism and conversion through the Anglo-Saxon world. He had gone at the request of King Oswald of Northumbria, who was concerned that the faith among his people, for various reasons, might be slipping. One monk, Cuthbert, became known for his prophetic and healing powers and was appointed the bishop of Lindisfarne in 685. His tomb became a proper pilgrimage destination, with many healings reported. This reputation gained Lindisfarne considerable wealth, as grateful pilgrims donated what they could in thanks for, or in hope of, healing. Many of these donations were in the form of precious liturgical objects – all temptations to plunder.

The monks at Lindisfarne probably suspected what was about to happen when they sighted the ships descending on them from out of the North Sea 'on the sixth day before the ides of January' (according to the *Anglo-Saxon Chronicle*) of 793. They would have heard reports of earlier landings of 'Northmen', such as the three vessels that arrived on the coast of Wessex in 787, 'the first ships of the Danish men that sought land of Engle folk'. The crews murdered the local reeve when he came, presumably in good faith, to take them to King Bertric. The rulers of Mercia, north of Wessex, were concerned enough to put in place defensive measures in 792.

And there were more mysterious worries. According to the *Anglo-Saxon Chronicle*, 'dreadful forewarnings' had appeared in Northumbria itself. These included 'amazing sheets of lightning and whirlwinds,' which may be attributed to extreme weather events; but not so for the 'fiery dragons... flying in the sky' that were seen by some, followed by 'a great famine'. Leaving aside for the moment the issue of the validity of such observations, we are told that all these unsettling signs appeared in 793 before the Lindisfarne raid; therefore the *Chronicle*'s assertion that the raid occurred 'on the sixth day before the ides of January' – that is 8 January – would appear to be in error, as allowing too short an interval between the omens and the raid. A revised date of 8 June is now generally accepted, mainly on climatic grounds, as a Norse fleet might have found it hard going in the depths of winter.

Therefore the green and pleasant shores of England in early summer would have been a strong attraction to the invaders. Of the raid itself we know very little. We know neither the number of Norse ships that took part nor how many men were in their crews. We don't know whether the raiders landed all at once or in waves. What we do know is that it was a brutal and bloody business. The *Anglo-Saxon Chronicle* mentions only that the church was destroyed, treasures were seized and 'blood was shed'.

That last bare piece of description was considerably dressed up in later accounts. The earliest (and presumably most authentic) was that of Alcuin, a Northumbrian scholar educated at York. At the time of the raid Alcuin had been residing at the court of the Frankish King Charlemagne for eleven years; indeed, the reason he had moved to France was that he sought a safer environment as 'the Danes' were already causing trouble in the English realms. Living the pleasant life with thousands of serfs (if we are to believe the anti-ecclesiastic Voltaire) to support it, he would have fervently thanked God he had fled England when he did.

What Alcuin learned (from an unknown source) about Lindisfarne was that it was a stupendous calamity. He was familiar with the place and knew some of its monks well. The church of Saint Cuthbert, he wrote to King Ethelred of Northumbria, 'was spattered with the blood of the priests of God' and the raiders 'trampled on the bodies of the saints in the temple of God, like dung in the street'. He reflected that 'never before has such an atrocity been seen in Britain as we have now suffered at the hands of a pagan people'. It was truly a day of infamy in every sense.

A much later account, written by Simeon of Durham in the twelfth century, adds that the raiders not only destroyed the sacred buildings and objects and 'trampled the holy places with polluted steps', but dragged many hapless monks away in fetters, 'naked and loaded with insults', and drowned them in the sea. 'Like fearful wolves [they] robbed, tore and slaughtered not only beasts of burden… but even priests and deacons, and companies of monks and nuns.' Given the more than three centuries between the raid and Simeon's account (which Viking-era scholar Robert Ferguson speculates could have been based on an earlier lost work), we may allow for a certain degree of distortion, perhaps even of exaggeration. But the basic savagery of the event is never in doubt.

We have a single pictorial record of the raid, or something like it, in the so-called Lindisfarne Stone, a crudely-sculpted relief of seven men in a line attacking what seems to be a building. Though the detail is very vague, the energy of the attackers, their swords and axes raised, comes through clearly. The Norsemen are wearing what seem to be padded tunics, but we see no shields or any other defensive equipment (no stereotypical horned helmets!). The raiders were obviously not expecting any kind of armed resistance. Not much can be historically deduced from this single work of relief sculpture, but its roughness and lack of finished artistry indicate that someone was in haste to tell posterity in pictorial form of the terrible thing that had happened.

What motivated these invaders from across the northern seas? The answer is by no means clear-cut. It would be logical to assume that unsettled conditions in the Scandinavian peninsula drove bands of Norsemen and their families to seek a more fertile and warmer climate in the isles to the southwest. Traders and others would have told the folks back home of conditions there, adding that the natives were generally peaceable and adhered to a curiously docile religion. Norway and its rugged, ragged coast has never had much lush living space; the very name of the country derives from *Nordvegr*, which is translatable as 'North Way'. Therefore the Norway of the early Viking age was not a defined country but essentially a sea-route along the northern shore of the Scandinavian peninsula. The sea and the rocky coast were the home of the Norse, whose living must have been precarious at the best of times. Add a few poor harvests, possibly some natural disasters, and we see the Norse following the example of the Angles and Saxons a few centuries earlier (not to mention the Goths and Vandals surging westwards) in search of a land they would have believed offered a better living than their own.

This may explain the migrations themselves, but it fails to explain the violence with which they were conducted. Two factors have been mooted as possible motivations: poverty-induced greed and religious conditioning. We may comfortably dispense with the school-image stereotypes of horned helmets, grizzled red beards, wild eyes and battle-axes wreaking havoc, though there was some of that element. The Viking incursions of Britain, France, Ireland and Russia were never simple, unthinking raids. All were the result of planning, followed by accurate navigation and formidable seamanship. Wherever the Norsemen landed, after the initial violence they invariably settled down to become an administrative part of the places they had conquered and carved out. Possession, it is often said, is nine-tenths of the law.

Yet the hapless monks of Lindisfarne, one feels, would have taken cold comfort from such a forecast. The gold and silver of their church (or at least some of it) would have been carted off back to Norway to boost its slender economic resources, much as the English plundered the South American gold from the Spanish galleons in the sixteenth century. As for religious impulses, the Norse followed a muscular pagan religion in which personal prowess and the use of force played a large role. In the Viking mind-set, the placid Christians of Britain – especially the contemplative, prayerful monks – were losers, full stop. They deserved what was coming to them.

The very same conclusion, oddly enough, was drawn by Christian commentators before the shock-waves of the Lindisfarne raid had subsided. In the inevitable agonized search for causes, one theory stood out above all: the slaughter was divine punishment for the sinful easy life many Anglo-Saxon clergy had fallen into. In Alcuin's view, the Norse raiders served as a hammer of God brought down on the laxity of English Christians. He was no doubt aware of other events in Northumbria that same year, when Siega, a nobleman, had led a conspiracy against King Aelfwald, who was killed. Siega had later committed suicide, further darkening the political skies. Was this, Alcuin could have thought, the way a Christian kingdom should be run?

'Truly it has not happened by chance', Alcuin wrote, 'but it is a sign that it was well merited by someone. But now, you who are left, stand manfully, fight bravely, defend the camp of God.' Alcuin warned pointedly that phenomena such as 'the dress, the way of wearing the hair, the luxurious habits of the princes and the people' could well be to blame for the sudden disaster that befell them.

Not surprisingly, such a historical interpretation as Alcuin's has come in for severe criticism, if not outright ridicule, in our secular-minded age. As a consequence, the sticky finger of revisionism has made itself felt here, too. The old fearful saying *A furore normanorum, libera nos domine* ('From the Norsemen's fury, deliver us, Lord') has been downgraded by some scholars to a mere piece of anti-Viking propaganda bearing little relation to reality. It appears to be part of a general anti-Christian animus in the academic world, to the point at which Anglo-Saxon Britain's early Christian heritage is downplayed more than is historically justifiable.

There is no doubt that morals in the Britain of the late first millennium were on the loose side, among clergy as well as laity. A wet climate promoted the habits of immoderate feasting and drinking. In the eighth century the Anglo-Saxon missionary Winfrid, a native of Devon later canonized as Saint Boniface, had occasion to lambaste both the pagans and Christians of his country as 'refusing to have legitimate wives, and continuing to live in lechery and adultery after the manner of neighing horses and braying asses'. In 756 King Ethelbald of Mercia came in for a stinging rebuke from Boniface: 'You wallow in luxury, and even in adultery with nuns... we have heard that almost all the nobles of Mercia follow your example, desert their lawful wives, and live in guilty intercourse with adulteresses and nuns', was a criticism recorded by William of Malmesbury in his *Chronicle of the Kings of England*. The condemnation came with a warning: 'If the nation of the Angles... gives free indulgence to adultery, a race ignoble and scorning God must necessarily issue from such unions.' This picture of widespread laxity and licence was somewhat ameliorated about twenty years after Saint Boniface's blast by the Synod of Hertford that gradually raised morals, along with the status of women.

The belief that savage alien attacks were a form of divine punishment was not a new one; this was an age of faith, after all, and every natural and man-made occurrence was interpreted within the framework of sin versus virtue, and how neglect of the latter could have catastrophic consequences. Three centuries before Lindisfarne, the British monk Gildas had seen the Anglo-Saxon invasions of Britain in precisely the same light, as a corrective for a decline in Christian morals even then. Now, lamented Alcuin, dinner halls echoed to recitations of the pagan poem *Beowulf*, which praised the doings of 'fair women and brave men' on the muscular model of the Homeric epics, with hardly a Christian stanza in it.

It is this relatively restrained reaction to the early Viking raids on Britain, in a spirit of Christian humility, that undoubtedly helped the Anglo-Saxon and Viking ethnic elements, after a period of initial friction, to fuse into a single nationality within a few centuries. It may not be too much to argue that the underlying Christian faith of the inhabitants of the British Isles served as a yeast for the conversion of the Scandinavians and the emergence of figures such as Saint Olaf.

> Wake early if you want another man's life or land.
> No lamb for the lazy wolf.
> No battle's won in bed.
>   The *Hávamál* (The Wisdom of the North)

This advice from the *Hávamál*, a collection of Viking sayings at least a millennium old, encapsulates the basic survival philosophy of Norse culture in the Viking era. Another maxim from this widely-known Eddaic work warns us that when passing a door-post, 'watch as you walk on, inspect as you enter. It is uncertain where enemies lurk or crouch in a dark corner.'

There is much in the myths and practices of Norse Heathendom that is reminiscent of the Homeric Greek so-called 'Heroic Age'. Both set great store by individual acts of extreme courage, heroism and – inevitably – great brutality and barbarity. In the *Ragnarök* we read of the giant wolf Fenrir that wants to swallow the sun – an understandable concern under the leaden skies of the north. There are frost-giants who sail on a ship made of the fingernails of the dead. In line after grim line, monstrous protagonists slay one another in an endless massacre. Little progress seems to have been made in European metaphysical thought since the eighth century BC, when the Greek shepherd Hesiod – probably Europe's earliest known poet after Homer – sang of similar monsters.

There is here an almost fatalistic acceptance of the evils with which we are always surrounded; but the message goes on to convey the idea that since that is the way the world was put together, we must make our way through an evil world the best way we can. An actual cultural connection between the Homeric and Norse worlds is, however, historically highly unlikely. It is conceivable that northern traders venturing into the Mediterranean picked up some of the Greek lore; those in contact with Roman Britain might well have done so. But the structural completeness of the Norse pagan beliefs strongly suggests that they developed indigenously and over a long time, conditioned by geographic and social conditions.

Yet there is one tantalizing clue at a possible direct connection. The Icelandic poet and chronicler Snorri Sturluson (with whom we will have much to do) in one of his works makes a startling suggestion that the god Odin might have been a real person and the Aesir – the Norse divine family – a real tribe, living around the Black Sea in the days of the Roman Empire. This tribe, with Odin as its chief and priest, is said to have migrated north through what is now Ukraine and Russia to the south coast of Sweden, where it was able to cultivate new lands. If there is any truth to this legend, it would indicate that any people living around the Black Sea in Byzantine times could have played the role of cultural conduit. But that is as far as we can go.

Stripped to its bare bones, the essence of Norse heathenism was the doctrine that out of an initial chaos (shades of Hesiod) there arose a generation of brutal giants, out of which Odin built some kind of order by tearing to pieces his predecessor. As narrated by Snorri Sturluson, a sort of divine residence – an Olympus of sorts – called Asgard was the home of the Aesir. These gods represented various forces of nature, including the earth's fertility and female sexual power. (Odin also represented hanged men, thereby giving execution victims some post-mortem justification. The idea was eerily similar to that prevailing later in Anglo-Saxon Britain, where an executed person through his ordeal was deemed to have earned some divine pardon.) The world was round and flat, and the heavens were held up by a gigantic tree, Yggdrasil, beneath whose roots three other-worldly women were constantly busy spinning out the fates of everyone on earth – an uncanny similarity to the Three Fates of the Greeks. The dark nether regions (the Greeks'

Hades) went by the name of Utgard, as distinct to Midgard, or the sphere of human life.

One of Odin's chief characteristic was his insatiable thirst to learn new things, an unquenchable curiosity about the world. His main desire was actually to penetrate the mystery of death, that inescapable, all-devouring foe of human endeavour. (Here he has a more than passing resemblance to Gilgamesh, the subject of the eponymous Sumerian epic of about 1800 BC, probably the first known epic poem in human history. The superhuman Gilgamesh was tormented by the same urges and fears, though as what has survived of the epic is incomplete, we don't know how the issue was resolved.) There are intrigues and scandals galore in Aesir, on a par with the nefarious doings on Mount Olympus. The darker side also included human sacrifice. Burials of eminent people were very elaborate, sometimes in large Viking ships.

The use of human sacrifice to earn the gods' favour is illustrated in both Norse and Greek legend. The story of how Håkon the Bad, the Norwegian Earl of Lade (Trondheim) in 986 sacrificed his nine-year-old son Erling to get a favourable wind for his ships fighting the Battle of Hjórungavág almost exactly parallels the case of King Agamemnon of the Achaians, who was said to have sacrificed his twelve-year-old daughter Iphigenia to get a good wind to enable his fleet to sail for Troy. In both instances, naval considerations played a crucial role, with the winds so vital to success deemed to be under the gods' control alone. They also perfectly illustrate the extremes to which the lust for power and conquest can drag leaders into, violating even the sacred laws of family and kinship. In societies where action in all its forms was held up as the natural end of man, there was no moral brake on such atrocities.

In his concise analysis of Norse pagan beliefs, Scandinavianist Robert Ferguson makes the cogent point that they 'underscore[d] Midgard's perception that social and technological advances could only be advanced by risk-taking' – which by and large remains true. All the myths, in fact, contain a strong element of risk that is sometimes rewarded, sometimes not. They are didactic tales warning against timidity and dilatoriness. The valuable secrets of beer and writing (especially the former!) were in fact said to have been stolen from Utgard thanks to Odin's trickery. Odin himself, however, was never immortal; in fact, according to Snorri

Sturluson, he died peacefully in his bed, which at once raises questions about just how godlike a figure he was regarded as.

The Norse version of heathenism was not a philosophy that encouraged contemplation or the belief that a supernatural power could help you when the chips were down. The Norse gods, like those of the Greeks, were simply fallible and imperfect human beings writ large. Odin was to be feared and where possible propitiated; he could be influenced and even bribed outright, but for that reason could never be loved, in the way that Christianity would later preach that God above all is love. The element of faith was entirely absent. The Norse religion was essentially a cold, mechanical system of thought and belief, based on a constant jockeying for advantage; there was not the slightest hint of a concerned and loving God to mitigate the world's effects on the human psyche.

The poet-bards of the Viking world were called skalds. 'There were skalds in Harald's court', writes Snorri Sturluson, 'whose poems the people knew of best even at the present day.' The Harald was Harald Haarfager, the son of Norway's first king, Halfdan the Black, who ruled out of Trondheim. Harald held his long (860–933) rule together by seeing off a succession of attempts to topple him. When he wanted to marry Gyda, presumably a high-born woman, she told him coolly she would only consent if he conquered all of Norway; for the next ten years he set about with grim determination to do just that, vowing never to cut his hair until the job was done. When it was, he cut his hair which by then must have attained a prodigious length, married Gyda (and nine other women besides) and sired a multitude of children. The one who succeeded him, Håkon the Good, we will meet again.

In the period of relative peace presided over by Harald Haarfager in his later reign and by his son, the skalds were busy in the royal and noble halls singing 'in praise of the chiefs themselves and their sons' (not unlike modern politicians and their media). The peace was too much for some of the bolder spirits. Snorri quotes one grizzled warrior as fearing that his long unemployment would condemn him to die ingloriously 'of old age, within doors on a bed'. Meanwhile, however, events across the sea in Britain were evolving in such a way as to meld the Anglo-Saxon and Viking elements together into a society where Christianity would find favourable ground to grow, and in the process influence the kings of Norway in the same direction, culminating in Saint Olaf.

An explanation of the implacable nature of Norse mysticism has been sought in the cold climate of Scandinavia, where the weather, on land or sea, can be unforgiving – and hence, human survival had to employ equally unforgiving methods enshrined in the local religious practices. This is a point made in *The Passion and Miracles of the Blessed Óláfr*: 'Living in a region close to the north, it was that same north from which comes every evil over the whole face of the earth, that had gripped [the people] all the more firmly in the ice of unbelief.'

Saint Olaf, in this narrative, was the instrument of God: 'Who scattered the rigours of the north with the mild wind of the south and at last softened the stubborn and fierce hearts of savage peoples with the warmth of faith.'

What we might call the individualistic excesses in Norse civilization can be reduced to a basic factor: the sheer power of the human ego, which stems from insecurity. Human beings seem always to have been engaged in an implacable contest with the forces of nature, a zero-sum struggle. It has been the great driving force behind all the achievements of the mind, from religion and philosophy to technology and digitization. But on the negative side it has tended to bring out the worst in humanity as well; history's great dictators and tyrants have one thing in common: their overwhelming need to dominate the world's affairs so completely that no room is left for the vagaries of nature or the human condition. Ambiguity is anathema to them. It's insecurity writ large – *après moi le deluge*. Yet the deluge always wins in the end.

In the early Norse sagas (like the Greek) what counts above all is power. The men (and less often women) who make a name for themselves do so through acts which demonstrate their raw ability to impose themselves. In this, we must admit, they are little different from other ages, especially our own. But as the sub-text of this book is the specific replacement of pure heathen power-seeking by the Christian way in the specific territory of Norway, we need to emphasize the role that power, and the desire for it, played in that particular culture at that particular time.

Alfred Adler, the psychologist and disciple of Sigmund Freud, posited that all human relationships (and by extension all human history) are driven by the urge for power and personal accomplishment. This, he says, is a compensation for deep-seated feelings of inferiority. Since Adler's time, of course, this view has been considerably modified by the behaviourists and neo-Freudians, among others, but it still serves as an explanation for much of human history, politics, war and family and professional relationships. It's not enough to keep up with the Joneses; we must surpass them. As for death, it has meaning only when one's individual fame can echo through posterity.

On a more practical level we may quote Edward Gibbon: 'Cold, poverty and a life of danger and fatigue fortify the strength and courage of barbarians. In every age they have oppressed the polite and peaceful nations... who neglected, and still neglect, to counterbalance those natural powers by the resources of military art.' Having as a background this soberly realistic assessment, valid to this day, we can trace the gradual Christianization of Norway and the figures who by contributing to it were Saint Olaf's precursors.

Chapter 3

The Precursors I: St Anskar to Athelstan

The West European scene at the turn of the eighth to the ninth century was overshadowed by one man: Charlemagne, the King of the Franks. Born in 742, he was the younger son of Pepin III (the Short), whose capable and practical reign transformed his land from the erstwhile Roman province of Gaul to what served as the foundation of modern France. Pepin enjoyed the active support of the popes of Rome, who enjoined the Franks to choose their kings only from Pepin's progeny as a way of maintaining the church's control over that large territory to the northwest of Italy from which invaders could, and did, too often come. Pepin's elder son Carloman I had died three years after his accession, leaving the Frankish throne to his younger brother Charles, who would soon earn his better-known name of Charlemagne.

Twenty-nine years old when he mounted the throne, Charlemagne was more German than French, in manners and outlook as well as blood and speech. He wasn't much for book-learning and preferred active living, though we may assume that he had enough instruction as a prince for him to be able to speak Old Teutonic and Latin and understand Greek, yet oddly enough he never managed to learn to write. But what he lacked in formal education he more than made up for in sheer leadership ability on the military front. Barely had he become king than he embarked enthusiastically on dozens of campaigns designed to eject the invading Lombards from the papal lands, Christianize Bavaria and Saxony, build up defences against the Moors of Spain and even shield Italy from Saracen raids.

The year of Lindisfarne, 793, found him in the middle of taming the unruly Saxons. It was a fierce and unforgiving task. After one battle Charlemagne gave the defeated Saxons the choice of baptism or death; some 4,500 of them chose the latter and were beheaded in a single day. At home, however, he was a more than competent, humane and far-seeing administrator. As we have seen, he lured Alcuin from York to teach in the palace at Aachen, while, according to William of Malmesbury, 'the Danes... were laying [England] desolate, and dishonouring the monasteries with adultery'.

Charlemagne's supreme moment came on Christmas Day 800, when, kneeling before Saint Peter's altar in Rome, he felt a jewelled crown descending slowly onto his head. The crown was held by Pope Leo III, an unpopular pontiff who had several charges of misdeeds hanging over his head and wished to cultivate Charlemagne in this crudely obvious way. The congregation obediently cried out: 'Hail to Charles the Augustus, crowned by God the great and peace-bringing Emperor of the Romans!' Charlemagne had now been suddenly upgraded to 'Roman Emperor'. Technically and legally, the motion was absurd. There already was a legitimate sovereign of the Romans in Constantinople in the person of Byzantine Empress Irene, the forty-second of a long line of rulers running unbroken from Roman Emperor Constantine I. Pope Leo's move was by any measure totally illegal. But few in Western Europe knew or cared enough to point out that fact, though Charlemagne himself unquestionably did, and therefore with more than a little dishonesty he could pose as the champion of Christianity in the north of the continent.

Charlemagne was now, according to one recent authority, 'strong enough in body and nerves to bear a thousand responsibilities, perils and crises... He could vision large purposes... He could lead an army, persuade an assembly, humour the nobility, dominate the clergy, rule a harem.' Yet even this larger-than-life man had to pass on, which he did after a fever in 814, aged seventy-two. One of his great aims had been left undone: the conquest and Christianization of the Scandinavian lands. For this purpose he had groomed the Church at Hamburg as a fountainhead for the conversion of the north, a task inherited by his son and successor Louis I (the Pious).

First on the list were the Danes. It is unclear how many earlier attempts had been made at Danish conversion. They and other Norse peoples would already have been familiar with Christianity through their raiding contacts with Britain and the Frankish lands, and it is reasonable to suppose that some individual conversions occurred. Frodo VI of Denmark (who may have been a tribal chief rather than a full-rank king) was said to have been baptized in England after what seems to have been a typical career of marauding. The date of this alleged event is uncertain, though

Saxo Grammaticus writes that Frodo sent envoys to 'Pope Agapetus' in Rome asking him to despatch missionaries to Denmark; the envoys died before they could reach their destination. If this refers to Pope Agapetus I, who died in 536, it would be extraordinarily early for such a development. Pope Agapetus II, on the other hand, occupied the throne of Saint Peter from 946 to 955, by which time the conversion of the Danes was more or less complete, and almost certainly this is the one mentioned by Saxo.

Willehad, the first bishop of Bremen, claimed to have preached to the peoples north of the River Elbe shortly after the middle of the eighth century. At about the same time Willibald, the bishop of Eichstadt, according to the *Centuriatores Magdeburgenses*, 'won for Christ a certain number of Danes'. Willibrord, an Anglo-Saxon missionary, had attempted to convert Danish King Angantyr (sometimes referred to as Orgendus) around 720, without much success. Described as 'more savage than any beast and harder than stone', Angantyr nevertheless allowed Willibrord to carry out his work unhindered and reportedly treated him and his associates well. We know of a church at Meldorf on the North Sea coast, midway between Hamburg and the present Danish border; sometime in the latter half of the eighth century this church was destroyed by the Saxons.

In the first decades of the ninth century a dynastic struggle broke out. King Godfrid of Denmark, an ambitious ruler who sought to subjugate much of Germany including Charlemagne's headquarters at Aachen, was assassinated before he could carry out his plans. Claiming the succession were two brothers, Klak-Harald and Reginfrid, who probably served as regents after Godfrid's death, but the late king's sons disputed that claim. While Klak-Harald and his brother were unwisely absent in northern Norway, probably trying to secure tribute, Godfrid's son had amassed a large army; when Klak-Harald and Reginfrid returned in 814, the latter was killed in battle. This left Klak-Harald the sole pretender to the Danish throne; incidentally, that year also saw the demise of Charlemagne, plunging much of northern and central Europe into gradual chaos.

There followed a confused period when Klak-Harald appeared to secure the backing of Louis the Pious, who through the Dane saw his chance to Christianize Denmark. Somehow – we are not sure how – Klak-Harald maintained contact with Godfrid's sons (who are never named in the sources), and in 819 we find him actually joining the sons on the throne in a royal triumvirate. As might have been expected, the arrangement soon broke down; four years later, according to the *Vita Anskarii*, Klak-Harald fled back to Louis, who had a brilliant idea. Why not, he told the Dane, become a Christian? That way the alliance with Louis would become more durable 'and a Christian people would more readily come to his aid... if both peoples were worshippers of the same God'. Thus on 24 June 825 Klak-Harald was baptized in Saint Alban's in Mainz, in the presence of his wife, brother and a large retinue.

Was Klak-Harald's conversion genuine? There is no way of knowing. As an added reward he was given a piece of territory on the Friesian coast between the Ems and Aller rivers, to serve as a refuge and a base. The location would also be convenient from which to launch seaborne expeditions on Scandinavia. On the downside, the Franks tended to look down on the less-sophisticated Danes, who were bound by a formal agreement to obey Louis 'always and everywhere and in all matters'. Naturally, a certain amount of resentment set in; many Danes agreed to be baptized merely for the arms and luxurious new clothes given to every convert. But Louis the Pious appears to have had firm faith in Klak-Harald, whom he despatched to Denmark. Accompanying him as spiritual adviser – and perhaps to ensure that he remained on the Christian path – was a young monk named Anskar.

Born in 801, Anskar (sometimes rendered Ansgar) entered the monastery at Corbey near Amiens. When he was twenty-one or shortly thereafter, he moved to the newly-founded New Corbey monastery (still standing) near Höxter in the Weserbergland. Though the monastic life in Europe at the time, we are told, was becoming somewhat lax, New Corbey tried to maintain a high spiritual standard. Anskar was detailed to run the monastic school and preach to the public, which indicates a high degree of trust in his abilities at a young age.

Bishop Rimbert, in his *Vita Anskarii*, credits Anskar with having had visions and portentous dreams since he was five years old. He was just thirteen when he entered holy orders, possibly right after the death of Charlemagne, and the mystic messages continued to arrive. Rimbert quotes Anskar as describing to him having been brought 'into the presence of the unending light, where the majesty of almighty God was revealed to me without the need for anyone to explain'. He went on to tell of 'a most sweet voice, the sound of which was more distinct than all other sounds and which seemed to me to fill the whole world... addressed me and said: "Go and return to Me crowned with martyrdom"'.

Anskar took the divine injunction very seriously, 'both terrified and comforted'. It wasn't long before Louis the Pious learned of Anskar's spiritual qualities via a favourable report from Wala, the abbot of New Corbey. Anskar jumped at the king's proposal that he go with Klak-Harald and preach to the northern heathens. Of course, he was apprehensive at the same time, and appears to have had periodic doubts. 'Lord, what wilt Thou have me do?' he is reported as asking, and hearing in reply a voice saying, 'Go and declare the word of God to the nations.' Most of his fellow-monks were horrified that he had decided to place himself in danger like this; to the ordinary perils of the voyage would be added the very real risk of being killed by the heathens. They tried to argue him out of it, but he was adamant, with a military dedication to duty: if he sought 'the crown of martyrdom', this was the way. In the end only one monk named Authbert proved brave enough to set out with him.

Anskar arrived in Denmark in 826, setting up a seminary at Hedeby in Schleswig. Rimbert tells us that his first twelve students were 'either purchased by Anskar or presented to him by the king'. The term 'purchase' is an odd one, suggesting the purchase of slaves. But as we cannot attribute any such practice to Anskar, what Rimbert probably means is that Anskar may have had to pay some compensation to the boys' families for taking them away from a productive life. On the other hand, Klak-Harald could have simply recruited them for the seminary at Hedeby. Either way, the school got going, but we are given to understand that it achieved no great result. Three years later Anskar was forced to leave. Klak-Harald was also compelled to leave his kingdom after meeting stiff resistance to his Christianization drive, a resistance that could have stalled whatever success the Hedeby evangelization school could achieve.

Louis' reaction to the news was to suggest to Anskar that he give up the stubborn Danes as a bad job and go and preach to the Swedes instead. The Frankish king had received ambassadors from Sweden who had said 'there were many in their nation' who wished to embrace Christianity. The Swedes had no doubt made some acquaintance with the faith through traders, and Louis saw a renewed chance to increase his standing among the Scandinavians. It was abbot Wala of New Corbey who suggested to Louis that Anskar was the man for the job. Leaving the monk Gislema to run Hedeby, in about 829 Anskar left for his new mission with a companion named Witmar.

Sweden at the time had a highly organized pagan religious system centred on the figure of Odin. The main element in this was a form of ancestor-worship. Writes Rimbert: 'As the king was the national priest so every father of a family was regarded as a priest in his own household.' Family members were buried near their house, the graves being places where the head of the family would sit for hours, 'no doubt to hold converse with the spirits of the departed'. These sessions, Rimbert believed, were attempts to peer into an uncertain future.

The Swedes themselves were the descendants of the old Teutonic tribe of Siones (according to the Roman annalist Tacitus); several of its early kings were named Sweyn, or Svein. Pliny the Elder, on the other hand, called the territory Skane (or Scandia) – the origin of the term Scandinavia. But, in the words of one popular historian: 'the fertility of women, or the imagination of men, outran the fertility of the soil.' Therefore, like their neighbours the Norwegians and Danes, they sought new territories; while the Norwegians and Danes flowed towards the British Isles and France, the Swedes sought land and resources in Russia. They lived alongside the Goths and shared with them a single king based at Uppsala. This king was considered a direct descendant of Odin, an office confirmed with great ceremony every nine years. In these circumstances it would seem that Anskar faced another uphill battle.

The first hurdle appeared while Anskar was still at sea, in the form of a Viking pirate attack that relieved him of some or all of his possessions. Touching land in Sweden, he arrived at Birka, a flourishing port on the small island of Björkö about 20 kilometres west of what is now Stockholm. Birka's position in the calm coastal estuary gave it access to Russia, five days' voyage away, and thence to the great Russian rivers leading to the Black Sea and Constantinople. As by that very fact it was also a tempting target for pirates, Birka was strongly fortified: a stout stone wall has been found under the water, as well as the remains of wooden stakes that were driven into the seabed to force incoming ships into a narrow and easily defensible approach.

Making Anskar's task somewhat easier was the authorization given him by King Björn in nearby Uppsala to preach freely. Rimbert says that the king made his decision after 'consulting his people', indicating that there was a general consensus in high places that Christianity was not a serious threat to the established order. This, however, was a time when Uppsala itself was adorned with 'the bodies of men and animals that had been sacrificed to the gods' left hanging from the trees in a 'sacred wood' surrounding the chief heathen temple. It strongly suggests that King Björn, as the keeper of the old religion, saw Anskar's mission not so much in spiritual terms as a means whereby he could channel into harmless avenues any discontent felt by the Christian elements, among whom were many slaves.

It was among the Christian slaves brought to Birka by the trading ships, earning colossal profits for the traders, that the arrival of Anskar had its first effect. They came mainly from the Slavic regions of Eastern and South-Central Europe. (It was apparently from this time that the term 'Slav' morphed into the word 'slave' in several European languages: e.g. Italian *schiavo*, French *esclave*, Spanish *esclavo*, German *sklave*, colloquial modern Greek *sklavos*, Norwegian *slave*, *slavekvinne*, etc.) Others were shipped in from Britain. The former had received their faith from the Byzantine Empire, and the latter from the Anglo-Saxon church. The slaves of Birka were overjoyed to be able to practise their religion unhindered, and Anskar may have been able to purchase freedom for some of them. Anskar remained at Birka for 'two winters', after which he returned to Louis' court to report on his progress. He must have said that there was still considerable work to be done in that region, as Louis decided to upgrade the bishopric of Hamburg into an archbishopric as a hub for missionary work in Scandinavia and appoint Anskar as archbishop, the city's first.

Anskar did not have much time to settle into his new duties. In 840 Louis the Pious died. His final years had been clouded by the rebellion of his sons, who mistreated him and packed him off to a monastery. He was succeeded by his fourth and favourite son, Charles I (the Bald). Charles' constant struggle against his brothers' intrigues left him little time for ruling France effectively, with the result that the Norse raiders found a fresh opportunity to turn Western Europe upside down. Barely had Anskar time to consecrate his nephew Gautbert as bishop of the church in Sweden than he faced overwhelming problems at home. In 845 King Eirik of Jutland led a heathen force that ravaged Hamburg, razed almost all its Christian churches and sent Anskar himself fleeing. In that same year Gautbert was driven out of Sweden by what appears to have been a well-organized heathen mob which killed his chaplain Nithard and several others, robbed Gautbert himself and drove him out of the country with 'insults and abuse'. Rimbert is careful to point out that the action was carried out not by any royal command but was 'a plot devised by the people'. For a few years Anskar wandered over his shattered diocese, trying to pick up the pieces.

His fortunes turned around in 849, when Bremen replaced Hamburg as the base from which the conversion of Scandinavia could continue and Charles made him archbishop of Bremen. He had not completely given up on Sweden, as he sent Ardgar to continue where Gautbert had left off; Ardgar, we are told, 'laboured for ten years' at his missionary work, with unclear results. Anskar, meanwhile, experienced another vision in which the late abbot of Corbey urged him not to falter in his work of carrying 'salvation even to the ends of the earth'. So in 853 he set out for Sweden again.

What he found on his return to Birka cannot have been encouraging. The king and his people were in the middle of a debate over whether or not they should honour a new pagan deity – apparently the old order was proving somewhat unsatisfactory. Anskar asked to be allowed to preach the Christian faith as before. In response, the king held a pagan ritual involving the drawing of lots in the open air; the results proved favourable, whereupon Anskar was called to put his proposal before a general popular assembly. After a great deal of debate the assembly granted Anskar his request, and he stayed in Sweden for a year, returning to Hamburg in 854 and leaving Gautbert's nephew Erimbert in charge of the Birka mission.

By now Anskar was a relatively young fifty-three years old, but prematurely worn out by his vicissitudes. He had hoped from an early age to die a martyr's death on duty, in the process of spreading the faith, but so far it had been denied him. Rimbert tells us, however, that in a vision he was assured that it was no fault of his own. The narrative strongly implies that his friends were concerned that his health was breaking down. He died peacefully on 3 February 865 and was canonized a few years later.

While he lived, Saint Anskar could never be completely sure that his exertions for the faith in Scandinavia would have any lasting result. Later commentators, however, would have laid his concerns to rest. He accomplished more than he could imagine. Adam of Bremen two centuries later wrote that '[if] amid so great changes of kingdoms or inroads of barbarians some small part of Christianity that had been planted by Anskar had remained, the whole had not failed.' According to Charles H. Robinson, who translated the *Vita Anskarii* into English, '[h]is zeal, his heroism, his faith, his far-reaching designs and above all his saintly life... contributed not a little to the establishment of the Christian Church throughout Northern Europe.' (The *Vita* itself was believed lost until it was rediscovered in the middle of the seventeenth century.) Ferguson thinks it very probable that Anskar's activity 'prepared the ground in the Scandinavian homelands for a coming sea-change in religious belief'.

A few years after the death of Saint Anskar, another figure arose to foreshadow the eventual conversion of the Vikings, though, as in the case of Anskar, it was far from apparent at the time. This was Edmund, crowned king of East Anglia at the age of fifteen on 25 December 855 and reputed to have been a model monarch in all respects. Regrettably, nothing is known about his early life as the Danes who overran the east of Britain in the ninth century obliterated all the records of his life that they could find. We are not far off the mark, however, (according to later scholarship) to say that he was most probably related to King Aethelstan of Kent. He may have been the successor to King Aethelward of East Anglia, but that is as far as the identification effort can proceed. All extant sources insist that Edmund was no interloper but descended from a long line of nobility.

In the year of Edmund's coronation a Viking force landed on the Isle of Sheppey in the Thames estuary, sparking a new wave of destructive raids. It is enough to peruse the *Anglo-Saxon Chronicle* for a depressing list of such events almost every year. There was a major clash at Hingston Down in 838, where King Egbert of Wessex trounced a combined Viking and Cornish force on the River Tamar. Three years later a Viking fleet of thirty-three ships was smashed off Southampton. But often the result went the other way: Danish Vikings carried out 'great slaughter' in London and Rochester in 842, while a Viking fleet triumphed in the Bristol Channel a year later.

Those encounters, however, paled before the onslaught of the Great Heathen Army (as termed by the *Anglo-Saxon Chronicle*) onto the shores of East Anglia in 865. About 100 years later Abbo of Fleury would write of 'a ship-army, harrying and slaying widely throughout the land, as is their custom'. Led by the brothers Halfdan and Ingvar, the force swept through the Humber estuary and into what is now Yorkshire, using horses taken from the local population. York was taken; its two defending leaders – until then at each others' throats – were killed. A few years later Nottingham fell, becoming a southern buffer for the new Viking kingdom of York.

Before the appearance of the Great Heathen Army, King Edmund ruled East Anglia by all accounts justly. 'He was humble and virtuous', writes Abbo, 'and remained so resolute that he would not turn to shameful vices, nor would he bend his morality in any way.' He was said to live by the principle: 'As a ruler, don't puff yourself up, but be among men just like one of them.' According to Abbo, Edmund's reign was noted for its charity to poor people and widows, and keeping arrogant nobles on a tight leash. At some point during his fifteen-year reign he shut himself away in the royal tower at Hunstanton, overlooking The Wash, for a year, spending much of the time in prayer and memorizing the Psalms. Yet when he was still only about twenty-five or so, it must have seemed to Edmund as if the very demons of hell were about to devour his domain.

The Ingvar cited by Abbo of Fleury as one of the leaders of the Great Heathen Army is almost certainly identified with Ivar the Boneless, a son of the Danish chieftain Ragnar Lodbrok who in 845 had mounted an audacious attack up the River Seine, threatening Paris and according to a local annalist 'laying waste everything on every side'. Lodbrok, bought off by Charles the Bald with a large amount of silver, had returned the way he had come, looting and burning as before. As for Ivar the Boneless, his curious sobriquet has been the subject of much fascinated speculation. According to one Viking saga, he was unable to walk because of some infirmity and had to be carried around; there is a theory that he suffered from brittle bone disease. Another is that the word 'boneless' was an indelicate term for sexual impotence. Yet another suggests that the word was intended as a synonym for snake, which would accord well with his well-documented cruelty. If he was indeed afflicted with major debility, it might not have done much for his disposition. In the words of Adam of Bremen he was 'the most gruesome of all the Danish petty kings'.

Ivar the Boneless landed in East Anglia, according to Abbo, 'just like a wolf, and slew the people, men and women and innocent children, and ignominiously harassed innocent Christians'. In Abbo's narrative (the only one we have) he lost no time in sending an envoy to King Edmund with the uncompromising message:

> Ivar, our king, bold and victorious on sea and on land... has now come to this country to take up winter quarters with his men. He commands that you share your hidden gold-hordes and your ancestral possessions with him straightaway, and that you become his vassal-king, if you want to stay alive.

The 'winter quarters,' of course, was a mere excuse; Ivar just wanted the 'gold-hordes' and no other king around to challenge him. He also most probably had heard of Edmund's gentle piety and figured that he would submit without trouble.

Edmund showed the undiplomatic message to 'a certain bishop with whom he was most intimate' and asked for his advice. The bishop counselled submission: too strong an army was arrayed against the king, who might well not survive if he resisted. Abbo relates that Edmund was silent for some time, looking at the ground. 'Alas, bishop,' the king said at length, 'the poor people of this country are already shamefully afflicted. I would rather die fighting so that my people might continue to possess their native land.'

The bishop pointed out that a good many of Edmund's people had already perished. 'You do not have the troops for fighting. Save your life by flight, or save yourself by submitting to [Ivar].' Edmund's reply to that was essentially: what use would I be alive after my people were dead? 'It was never my way to flee. I would rather die for my country if need be. Almighty God knows that I will not ever turn from worship of Him... If I die, I live.'

Edmund then turned to Ivar's messenger and informed him that he was lucky not to be executed on the spot. His return message to the Dane was: 'Never in this life will Edmund submit to Ivar the heathen war-leader, unless he submit first to the belief in the Saviour Christ which exists in this country.' It was a bold, even foolhardy message, yet Edmund courageously stood up not only for his kingdom of East Anglia but for the Christian faith of the entire Anglo-Saxon domain. As was to be expected, Ivar the Boneless erupted in rage, ordering his men to seize this aggressively independent king.

On 20 November 869 (some sources say 870) Ivar marched against Edmund's palace – believed to have been near the Norfolk village of Hoxne – and confronted him in the hall. Edmund was deliberately unarmed, in emulation of Christ. Abbo relates what followed:

> The impious one [Ivar] then bound Edmund and insulted him ignominiously, and beat him with rods, [and bound him to a tree]. In between the whip lashes, Edmund called out with true belief in the Saviour Christ… They then shot spears at him… until he was entirely covered with their missiles, like the bristles of a hedgehog (just like St. Sebastian was). When Ivar the impious pirate saw that the noble king would not forsake Christ, but with resolute faith called after Him, he ordered Edmund beheaded… While Edmund still called out to Christ, the heathen dragged the holy man to his death, and with one stroke struck off his head, and his soul journeyed happily to Christ.

Edmund was at most thirty years old.

The Danes seem to have left the headless body where it was, and hidden the head in the undergrowth of a wood. Grieving local people searched for Edmund's head, which according to legend was guarded by a wolf. As a search party combed the wood, they heard a voice calling out 'Here, here, here'. Reaching the spot the searchers found the grey wolf 'who watched over the head, and had the head clasped between his two paws'. Though the wolf was hungry, Abbo adds, it did not harm the head but protected it against other predators. The people took the head and 'the wolf followed along with the head as if he was tame, until they came to the settlement, and then the wolf turned back to the woods.' Edmund's head was rejoined to his body, which was quickly buried.

When peace returned to East Anglia years later, the local people built a church over Edmund's grave, as miracles at the site had been reported often. In a prefiguring of what would happen to the body of Saint Olaf a century and a half later, when they exhumed the body to transfer it to the church proper they found that Edmund 'was as sound as when he was alive, with a clean body, and his neck, which previously was severed, was healed'. The only trace of the beheading was a line like 'a red silken thread around his neck'. But the holy king still had some power in him.

We are told of a widow named Oswyn who prayed and fasted at Edmund's tomb for many years, and cut the saint's hair and nails regularly. A bishop, Theodred, encouraged the faithful to deposit gold and silver offerings at the tomb – which of course attracted robbers. Always according to Abbo, a well-equipped band of them attempted to break into the church one night; but 'the saint miraculously bound them stiffly', with the result that they were discovered in the morning, paralysed in the act. The furious Theodred ordered them to be hanged on high gallows, but he soon repented of his harshness, as it was a clerical canon of the time that 'it is not fitting for those who are chosen for the service of God to consent to any man's death'. The principle was phrased in Latin: *Eos qui ducuntur ad mortem eruere ne cesses* – always redeem those whom man condemns to death. The good bishop bitterly regretted his decision for the rest of his days.

Of course, there were those who disbelieved the entire story of an undecayed saintly corpse, as there would be in Saint Olaf's case. One Leofstan, 'rich in worldly things but ignorant of God', insisted 'with exceeding arrogance' on seeing the body for himself. Many others, too, had seen it, but it seems Leofstan's negative and scornful attitude ensured that 'as soon as he saw the saint's body he went mad, and raged cruelly, and ended wretchedly in an evil death'. Twenty years after Edmund's death, when Abbo wrote his *Passio Sancti Eadmundi*, the cult was already growing. At about that time, the kingdom of Wessex absorbed East Anglia; the saint's relics appeared to be safe in the church at Bury St Edmunds, but we read that in 1010 they were taken to London for three years for safekeeping against Viking attacks. They were supposedly last seen in 1198, still apparently uncorrupted.

In the fifteenth century Henry VIII unwittingly completed the work of Ivar the Boneless when he suppressed the monasteries of England and the shrine at Bury St Edmunds was destroyed. In France, however, the Basilica of Saint-Sernin in Toulouse was said to have housed the remains of St Edmund; he is believed to have saved the city from bubonic plague between 1628 and 1631, when the epidemic raged across central Europe. Fast forward to 1901, when the Archbishop of Westminster, Herbert Vaughan, received some relics from Saint-Sernin, supposedly including the remains of the saint. Pope Leo XIII gave permission for them to be housed in Arundel Castle, where they remain to the present day –

although, inevitably perhaps, scientific doubts have been raised about their authenticity.

Can Abbo of Fleury's narrative be trusted? It was written just over a century after the events it relates, which leaves room for a certain expected amount of distortion and embellishment. In a preface to the Anglo-Saxon version of the story by Aelfric of Eynsham, Aelfric writes that the story was first told by Edmund's sword-bearer to King Athelstan of East Anglia (924–939). From there it was relayed by Archbishop Dunstan to Abbo who 'came over the sea from the south'. Issues of reliability therefore arise. That, however, begs the question of what 'reliability' really means. The absolute historical truth is impossible to get at, as is the case with all history. Therefore it is in the spiritual rather than the secular realm that the significance lies.

In a secular age it is natural to dismiss stories of the supernatural, of divine intervention, of saintly bodies that remain intact, of miracles at shrines, as pious fantasy. But is that a fair treatment of the past? The history of Christendom, east and west, is full of such accounts rendered with great seriousness by highly intelligent men and women. We are on a slippery slope indeed if we get into the habit of 'censoring' our sources simply because what they say does not accord with the secular values of a later age. As Abbo of Fleury is our sole major source for Saint Edmund, it would be historically irresponsible to arbitrarily erase some of his conclusions simply because they sound implausible to us. In an age when fake news runs rife, we are yet hardly in a position to judge.

The King Athelstan to whom St Edmund's sword-bearer told the story of the martyrdom began life as a Danish Viking chieftain named Guthrum, cited as one of the Viking leaders in the turbulent decade of the 870s. Guthrum, a nephew of Horik II of Denmark, had unsuccessfully contended for that country's throne, and in April 871 had taken a command under Halfdan in the Great Summer Army that renewed the Danish attacks on Britain just after Saint Edmund's death. He joined the main force at Reading, where Halfdan's army had wintered. When the Great Summer Army moved on Wessex, King Ethelred and his brother Alfred marched to meet it; there were some fierce battles at Ashdown, Basing and Englefield, where the Danes suffered losses but remained unbeaten. Only at Ashdown did Ethelred and Alfred score a distinct victory; later at Merton, Ethelred was mortally wounded and the English fled.

Alfred mounted the throne of Wessex at twenty-two, already a battle-hardened veteran. Yet Guthrum's Danes proved too strong for even his considerable talents, and at Wilton his force was so badly trounced that he had to buy peace from the enemy. The deal bought perhaps a couple of years of valuable breathing space for Alfred, who used the interval to establish control over Mercia in the Midlands, strengthening his defences against the Danes based in East Britain. The Great Summer Army was distracted by a revolt in Danish-controlled Northumbria, but returned in 874 to claw back Mercia from Alfred. Threats from the Picts and Britons of Strathclyde dragged Halfdan with half of his army northwards again, while Guthrum's half continued south to settle accounts with Wessex and Alfred.

At first Guthrum evaded Alfred's forces at Cambridge, slipping down to Wareham in Dorset. Here it appears that the two leaders judged it prudent to reach some kind of truce; on Guthrum's part, however, it must have been a ruse to gain time, for hardly had the Danish leader sworn solemnly 'on a holy ring' to quit Wessex and leave behind hostages to boot, he and his army slipped away by night to Exeter. Alfred caught up with him there; new 'oaths' were sworn and more breathing space gained by Guthrum.

Guthrum opened his next offensive with a surprise night attack on Alfred at Chippenham on 6 January 878; that it was the feast of the Epiphany was very likely a factor in the timing of the attack, as the Dane would have figured that the English might have let their guard down on that holy day. Some suspicion swirls around Wulfhere, the Ealdorman of Wiltshire, whom the *Anglo-Saxon Chronicle* implicitly blames for either negligence or collusion in the Danish plans. The Danes were joined by Ubbi, a brother of Ivar the Boneless, who had wintered in South Wales, with twenty-three ships.

Alfred had no choice but to flee for his life, first to Athelney in Somerset, and then, according to his Welsh biographer Asser, to hide 'amid the woody and marshy places' of the county. Here, at the nadir of his fortunes, Alfred gathered together a guerilla force which by May had included men from Somerset, Wiltshire and Hampshire, numerous and determined enough to inflict a stinging defeat on Guthrum at Edington. In addition to the resolve of the guerrillas, Guthrum and his own army could have lost some of their original impetus. Throughout the late winter and spring of 878 Alfred's bands had sniped at the Viking forces, and viewed in the light of what happened later, Guthrum himself would have been having his doubts about the chances of subduing the English in Wessex.

After Edington Guthrum and his army withdrew to Chippenham, pursued by Alfred. After a two-week siege Guthrum saw that the game was up and offered to capitulate. Alfred was in a lenient mood, taking a number of Danish hostages but refraining from reprisals. Guthrum agreed to leave Wessex at once, but Alfred, having been deceived this way before, insisted on a further condition: that Guthrum undergo Christian baptism – by Alfred himself. The demand was a canny one. In addition to making Guthrum a technical ally of the English, the solemnity of the promise would presumably be a deterrent to any more hostilities.

The *Anglo-Saxon Chronicle* describes how after three weeks, during which Guthrum presumably thought out the issue, he and thirty of his leading men came to Alfred near Athelney. After the ritual, 'King Alfred raised [Guthrum] from the holy font of baptism, receiving him as his adoptive son.' Eight days later 'the chrism was unbound', that is, the holy oil used in baptism was deemed to have done its consecratory work and its recipient could be considered completely accepted into the community of the faithful. The *Chronicle*'s account concludes that for the following twelve nights, Alfred 'freely bestowed many excellent treasure[s] on [Guthrum] and all his men'.

Guthrum, in fact, got up from the font with a new name – Athelstan, which Ferguson considers an example of successful 'cultural and conversion diplomacy'. In Guthrum/Athelstan's case, we may be reasonably sure that, notwithstanding the treasure he received as an earthly reward, his conversion was more or less genuine. Culture, too, probably played a part; we have seen how the Viking and Danish newcomers did not take very long to gradually assimilate with the native English, and we can speculate that Guthrum's experiences in Britain might have helped mould his own attitudes as well.

By the Treaty of Wedmore, where Guthrum became Athelstan, he agreed to permanently leave Wessex. Another pact, known as the Treaty of Alfred and Guthrum, firmed the boundaries between the English and Danish territories and included a trade agreement. Athelstan ruled East Anglia as a Christian king for twelve years. Yet the Viking threat to England was far from over. Alfred's relations with Athelstan were not always smooth; Alfred found he had to seize London in 886 to deal with Viking incursions into the Thames. Yet the basic terms of the treaty were kept by both sides. Athelstan died in 890 and was buried at Hadleigh, Suffolk. Just twenty years earlier, Saint Edmund's gruesome death had not boded well for the future of Christianity in East Anglia, but by the end of the ninth century the picture had changed radically. Edward's martyrdom had triggered another stage in the course towards the Christianization of the Vikings.

The tenth century was a period of general decline. After Alfred the Great's death in 899, the drive to repossess the Danish-occupied lands faltered. Alfred's son and successor, Edward, had to fend off a challenge from a cousin, Aethelwold, who sought the help of the East Anglia Danes but died in the attempt at Holme. The boundary agreement fixed between Alfred and Guthrum/Athelstan was now seriously threatened. Edward joined forces with Queen Ethelfled of Mercia to oust Viking-led forces from Stafford and Derby while Edward seized Oxford and London. The year 917 was a crucial one, with decisive victories by the English, so that by 920 Edward was in undisputed control over all Britain south of the Mersey and Humber. (The imposing Queen Ethelfled railway bridge over the Mersey Estuary at Runcorn is an eloquent tribute to the power of the warrior queen.)

In 924 Edward was succeeded by his brother Athelstan, who proved to be a wise and capable ruler. True to his beliefs, Athelstan nursed an ambition to be the sole ruler of the English 'and of all of the nations round about', and came close to doing so; he issued coins to that effect and seems to have taken as his role model the emperors of Byzantium by using the Greek term for king, *basileus*. That claim was disputed first of all by King Constantine II of Scotland, who joined Olaf Guthfrithson of Northumbria and Ireland and the Welsh rulers of Strathclyde to thwart Athelstan's ambitions. In 937 Athelstan marched north to meet the threat; the two sides clashed fiercely at Brunanburh (most likely Bromborough in the Wirral on the south side of the Mersey estuary).

The *Anglo-Saxon Chronicle* records Brunanburh as the decisive event of Athelstan's reign, where he 'won by the sword's edge undying glory'. For a whole day the king and his brother Edmund hurled their men, including mounted detachments, against the enemy. According to the account, 'five young kings... and seven [Norse] earls' perished; the Norsemen, like the vanquished Persians at Marathon, fled to their ships and sailed to Ireland. It was said that Oda, the Bishop of Ramsbury in Wiltshire, was present at the battle and credited with 'miraculously restoring Athelstan's sword'. In short, according to the *Chronicle*, it was a one-sided encounter in which Athelstan and Edmund slaughtered their enemies wholesale.

A rather different account of the battle comes from the *Saga* of the Viking poet Egil Skallagrimsson, who says that Athelstan took his time to march to Brunanburh, and when he got there the size of the force opposing him stopped him in his tracks and compelled him to withdraw. He then ranged through the country gathering men, and when he deemed he had enough he sent a message to Olaf Guthfrithson formally offering battle at an agreed date and place. Olaf and his army turned up on the agreed day but while the English army was there, Athelstan himself was not. The king, at a distance, negotiated with Olaf, offering him money to withdraw; Olaf gradually raised his demands, unwittingly allowing Athelstan to play for time and when the king of Wessex was finally ready his final message to Olaf was that he should 'go back to Scotland with his army and... pay back all that money which he has unlawfully seized in the [English] realm'. Moreover, Athelstan added, Olaf should agree to be his vassal. Athelstan must have known that no self-respecting Viking leader would accede to such humiliating terms, and battle was joined.

Egil Skallagrimsson himself fought on Athelstan's side at Brunanburh as a mercenary. In his own account, during the celebratory feast after the battle his fierce demeanour and his habit of playing with the hilt of his sword, as if ready at any moment to use it, disconcerted a number of people present until Athelstan offered Egil his ring and defused the atmosphere. As for Constantine of Scotland, already elderly at the time, he lost his son in the battle and afterwards the fight went out of him; six years later he abdicated his throne and lived out the remaining nine years of his life in a monastery.

Athelstan did not long survive Brunanburh, dying two years afterwards. His brother Edmund took the helm, to be faced with attempts by Olaf Guthfrithson to claw back what he had lost to Wessex. Though Olaf managed to seize York, his death in 941 put paid to his grander plans. Three years later the Danes of York ousted their leader in favour of Eirik Bloodaxe. Eirik's brother Håkon had been sent by their father Harald

Haarfager to Athelstan's court at Wessex to be brought up in the way of the Christian faith. While still in his teens Håkon, displaying an apparent youthful prowess common in high-born Viking youths, had driven out Eirik with Athelstan's help and had been proclaimed king of Norway, where we will hear more of him.

Bishop Oda of Ramsbury, who had fought at Brunanburh, was an example of how Christianity had seeped into the Viking elements in Britain in the middle of the tenth century, as he himself was said to be the son of a heathen Danish Viking. Not the slightest discrimination, however, seems to have attached to Oda's origins; he had joined the church in his youth and, impressed by visits to Rome and the disciplined cloister at Fleury in France, wore a monk's habit for the rest of his life. In 938, possibly in gratitude for his presence at Brunanburh, Athelstan named him Archbishop of Canterbury. He served the Wessex throne ably as a diplomat, legislator and administrator. In East Anglia, where Oda very likely was born, he re-established the bishopric at Elmham. As a reward he received the estate of Ely but died (958) before he could carry out the monastic reforms he planned. (Byrhtferth of Ramsey, in the tenth-century *Life of St. Oswald*, suggests that Oda's clerical zeal could have been an attempt to make up for his forebears' violence against the Christians.) At any rate, he was one more stone in the plinth on which Saint Olaf would eventually rise.

Chapter 4

The Precursors II: Håkon the Good and Olaf Tryggvason

H arald Haarfager, the strong-willed and rather eccentric Norwegian king who refused to have his hair cut until he could gain the woman of his dreams, enjoyed a largely peaceful reign that straddled the last decades of the ninth century and first ones of the tenth. But he was generally not well-liked. Ruling from Avaldsnes in south-west Norway, he hadn't much of a solid territory to rule over. As we have seen, Norway at the time was scarcely more than a geographical expression – roughly 1,000 kilometres of coastline east of the North Sea and Arctic Ocean and little of the hinterland including what is now the Trøndelag, the district around Trondheim.

Harald began consolidating his rule after winning a sea-battle over his rivals off Stavanger in 879. At the outset he aimed to make himself king over all of Norway, or as much of it as he could manage to control. His firm ways lent a feeling of security to those nobles who formed a sort of aristocracy around him, though his general taxation was by no means popular. Snorri Sturluson, our main source, indicates that the respect accorded Harald Haarfager was based more on fear than affection. Harald's attempts to include Iceland in his realm accomplished nothing except to make the Icelanders aware of their potentially precarious position, motivating them to take steps to create a stronger government of their own.

Harald Haarfager had more than one son by more than one wife, but it was his youngest, Håkon, who would make his name in the history books. His mother, Thora Mosterstang, seems to have taken good care of him, as he is reported by the Catholic Encyclopedia to have been 'a beautiful youth, in every respect like his father'. The 'every respect' referred most likely to a physical resemblance, as in character he would prove to be very different. Håkon appears to have been his father's favourite as well, as we are told that his elder half-brothers had little love for him and according to Snorri sought to do away with him, in the biblical manner of Joseph and his brothers. There were also economic reasons for the enmity, as Harald had already divided most of his realm among his sons, and the two elder ones apparently wanted to gobble up Håkon's share.

When Håkon was still very young, the threat to his well-being was deemed serious enough for Harald to send the boy for safekeeping to King Athelstan of Wessex in England (not to be confused with the Athelstan, formerly Guthrum, of East Anglia of two generations before). The exact nature of the relations between Harald Haarfager and Athelstan is not known; what we are told, however, is that in the court at Wessex Håkon received the best education of his time and was baptized a Christian. In 934 Harald Haarfager died after a seventy-year reign. At once the young Håkon, still only about fifteen, realized that he would have to head back to Norway, with men and ships supplied by Athelstan in case he had to fight.

At Trondheim Håkon found an ally in Sigurd, the Earl of Hlader, 'known as the ablest man in Norway', and promised him a key position in the state as a reward for his support. Håkon's youth and good intentions rewarded him with considerable popularity; he promised land to those without, and more rights for the general populace than his father had allowed. After the people of Trondheim made him king, the impression that he was going to right his father's wrongs 'flew, like fire in dry grass, through the whole land'. Yet, still barely out of his teens, he had a great deal to do before he could pragmatically make good his claim to be the king of Norway. One of his half-brothers, the fearsomely-named Eirik Bloodaxe, controlled territory in the south and needed to be neutralized.

In spring 935 Håkon fitted out a fleet and army at Trondheim, arriving at Vik near the Oslo fjord, where Eirik tried unsuccessfully to stop him. Eirik and his forces sailed off to Britain to seek land there, seizing it by raids when necessary; his father's ties of friendship with Athelstan of Wessex enabled him to rule from York, but in 941 Athelstan's successor Edmund marched against Eirik Bloodaxe. In a major encounter Eirik and five of his chieftains fell; on the other side, according to Snorri, 'for one [Englishman] who fell, came three in his place out of the country behind'. Eirik's family and sons quit Northumbria for Orkney; lamented the bard Glum Geirason:

The hero's blade dips red with gore,
Staining the green sward on the shore.

With Eirik out of the way, Håkon from his base at Vik attacked the Danes in Jutland, overcoming spirited resistance – 'he went forward with his banner without helmet or coat of mail.' He sank eleven Viking ships in the Eyrarsund and ravaged the coast of southern Sweden, retiring to Vik in 966 to winter. There he set up Trygve Olafson as a vassal king and returned to Trondheim. Trygve, however, would have his hands full battling the Danes off Vik for some time.

We have a portrait of Håkon, who now must have been in his mid-twenties, as a man 'of a remarkably cheerful disposition, clear in words, and very condescending. He was a man of great understanding also, and bestowed attention on law-giving.' If the term 'condescending' (as it appears in the English translation of the *Heimskringla*) seems at variance with the other positive traits described, we probably can interpret it as a lack of hauteur or snobbishness, a readiness to listen to anyone. But there were still potential traps for him where his Christian faith was concerned, and in 950 he narrowly missed falling into one.

Håkon was well aware, of course, that 'the whole country was heathen, with much heathenish sacrifice, and [that] many great people, as well as the favour of the common people, were to be conciliated.' Snorri describes some of the pagan rituals in terms uncannily reminiscent of the ancient Jewish rituals in the Old Testament: 'The whole of the altar and temple walls, both outside and inside, were sprinkled over' with the blood of horses and cattle, 'and also the people were sprinkled with the blood'. Yet Håkon's own example of character led several of his chief ministers to be baptized by a bishop brought over from England. A crucial moment came when the king decided to publicize his faith, at which point the leading men of Trondheim called a general province-wide meeting to consider the implications.

In the Norse world such an assembly was called a *thing*; that convened by the influential men of Trondheim is known to history as the Frosta-thing, at which the king urged the assembled people to 'believe in one God, and in Christ the Son of Mary, and… keep holy the seventh day'. Was this asking too much of those who had been sprinkled with horses' blood? An ominous murmuring spread through the crowd; many workers and slaves feared their livelihoods would be at risk if the old religion were swept away. (One is reminded of the riot at Ephesos when Saint Paul wanted to do away with the local idol industry.) One Asbjorn of Medalhus spoke up to give cautious approval to the king's proposals, but implored him to 'use some moderation towards us'. Håkon might well have taken a hint from the *Hávamál*, a collection of Norse folk-wisdom: 'A prudent man wields his power in modest measure. With brave men he finds that none is foremost or excels in all things.' Håkon decided that prudence in this case would be the best course.

Asbjorn, however, was probably in a minority. According to the old heathen custom the king was not only a temporal ruler but also the high priest of the people; if anyone was obliged to keep strictly to the rituals it was he, otherwise he faced deposition or worse. The Norse kings, after all, were supposed to be of divine descent. A Christian king was a truly revolutionary idea, and small wonder that the nobles of the Trøndelag ended up banding together to force Håkon to either toe the heathen line or abdicate. When he was informed of this at the Frosta-thing, he withdrew, keeping company with only a few of his Christian entourage.

Håkon did a slow burn until the next autumn sacrificial feast, which he attended grudgingly, seating himself on the High Seat only with the utmost reluctance. When Earl Sigurd of Hlader – always careful to keep relations between the king and his subjects at a functional level – toasted Odin over the first drink, Håkon responded by making the sign of the cross over it. 'What does that mean?' said Kar of Gryting, no doubt with some concern.

'He's making the sign of the hammer,' Sigurd said quickly. The hammer was the symbol of Thor. But Håkon was in no mood for humouring the heathens; when horse meat and its soup were offered him, he declined. The assembly was horrified – this was rank sacrilege. The horse had sacred status among the Norse – perhaps a relic from possible Asiatic origins. Sigurd covered that one up by proposing a compromise that ultimately satisfied no-one: the king agreed to open his mouth over the soup bowl and simply pretend to eat.

Kar of Gryting was one of four chieftains who had resolved to root out all traces of this new heresy called Christianity in Norway. They met Håkon again at the next feast at Møre, where the king was persuaded to taste bits of horse meat. He may well have regretted his lapse; furious at himself, he resolved to leave Trondheim and winter at Møre, where he could raise an army with which he could wreak his vengeance.

But at this time, about 951, the chiefs of the Trøndelag seem to have had a change of heart. It was more or less confirmed when Guthorm Eirikson, the son of Håkon's late half-brother Eirik, drove out Trygve Olafson from his domain. Håkon appealed to Trondheim for help, and Earl Sigurd sailed south with an army containing men who had grumbled about the king's Christianity. Now that an external threat had appeared, however, the religious differences were buried. The fleets of Håkon and Guthorm put ashore at Ogvaldsnes, where the armies clashed. In Snorri's account, Håkon and Guthorm met in single combat; Guthorm was killed, after which his army fled back to its ships. Håkon attempted a pursuit by sea, but broke it off.

Back at Trondheim Håkon busied himself with security, setting up an elaborate early-warning system with the use of fire-beacons. In fact it was this beacon system that was almost the king's undoing. When the late Eirik's remaining sons assembled a fleet for another crack at Norway in 954, Håkon at first refused to believe the news of the fleet's approach as there had been too many false alarms in the past. But when this time he was assured that the threat was genuine he debated, as was his habit, with his nobles about what to do. Then up spoke an old warrior named Egil Ulserk who had been most unhappy at spending his declining years in ignoble peace; he was the one who, in an earlier chapter, we saw as hating the idea of a peaceful death in bed, fit only for cowards and weaklings. Egil, we are told, urged the king to stand and fight. 'Now may it so turn out in the end as I wished it to be.'

It so turned out. Håkon's army and the invaders commanded by Eirik's son Gamle faced off at Fredarberg, on a large flat field overlooked by a ridge. Håkon, his force somewhat outnumbered, drew up the men in a long line to avoid being outflanked. According to Snorri's account, it was Egil Ulserk who decided the battle by a brave show of banners that gave the enemy behind the ridge the impression of an overpowering force. Gamle's army dissolved in retreat, though Gamle himself tried to make a stand and a counter-attack. Egil personally took him on, only to fall and meet his devoutly wished-for end. Gamle, wounded, resumed the retreat but found that most of his ships had already sailed; trying to swim out to them, he drowned. Egil Ulserk and his fallen comrades were given an elaborate Viking ship-burial on the field at Fredarberg.

Six years later, in 960, Håkon was enjoying a feast with nobles and peasants on Stord Island, one of the many studding the Bjørnafjorden south of Bergen, when a courier ran in with news of a large fleet approaching. 'Up king! The avengers are at hand! Eirik's bold sons approach the land!' Håkon, again, dismissed the news as a false alarm until he went out and saw for himself. At first irresolute, he was talked into staying and fighting. 'The king put on his armour, and girded on his sword Quernbite, and put a gilt helmet upon his head, and took a spear in his hand....'

The leader of the Danish force this time was Eirik's son Harald, whose army outnumbered that of Håkon six to one. Nonetheless, when the two armies approached one another, Håkon threw off his armour and waded into the battle. As his shiny helmet was quite conspicuous, a Dane named Eyvind Finson mockingly slipped a hat over it. Håkon lifted Quernbite and 'hewed Eyvind through helm and head, and clove him down to the shoulders'. But as Harald's forces dissolved in rout, a stray arrow caught Håkon in the upper arm.

Bleeding profusely, the king was taken on board his ship to sail home, but his weakening condition forced the crew to put ashore sooner than they planned. Håkon, in a remarkable display of conciliation, asked that a message be sent to Eirik's surviving sons that they could have the kingdom of Norway. If he survived his wound, he said, he wished to retire to a Christian country where he could penance for his many sins (he was certainly thinking of his past heathen practices performed under duress). But shortly afterwards he expired.

This somewhat idealized view of Håkon in Snorri's *Heimskringla* has been qualified by another source, the *Ágrip*, written by an unknown author more than 200 years later. This work claims that the reason Håkon was sometimes conciliatory to the heathens was that his wife was a heathen. Another source, the *Historia Norwegie*, flatly asserts that his death in battle was divine retribution for his supposed backsliding, and that the arrow that killed him was shot by a relatively young boy because he had 'dared to renounce the Christ-child'. However, in view of what we know of Håkon, he emerges as a realistic figure, all too human in his conflicting impulses, but when the chips were down, fighting fearlessly for his faith to the end.

He was buried in full armour beneath a mound at Saeheim. The bard Eyvind Skaldaspiller would ensure that Håkon the Good would be long remembered:

> Happy the day when men are born
> Like Håkon, who all base things scorn,
> Win from the brave an honoured name,
> And die amidst an endless fame.

Harald Gráfeldr (Greycloak), against whose army Håkon fell, ruled most of Norway competently enough until about 974, when he was killed in battle against rebellious subjects. Before that, however, he had offered an alliance to the son of that faithful Earl Sigurd who had backed Håkon the Good throughout his career; this son, also called Håkon, thus almost by default became the king of Norway. Here arose an anomaly: while this Håkon was a dedicated heathen, Harald was an equally dedicated Christian. So why did the two form a bond, with the former agreeing to pay the latter an annual sum in tribute, and to send forces to help Harald Greycloak whenever he might need them?

The answer must be that religion was not necessarily the defining issue in rivalries and power relationships in the Viking world. It made little difference to either Harald or Håkon what the other's faith was, as long as each could prove diplomatically and militarily useful to the other. The era of devastating religious wars in Europe was still several centuries away. Yet they were foreshadowed by the start, in 974, of the drive by Holy Roman Emperor Otto II to forcibly Christianize the Danes, who had recently staged raids.

Otto II had succeeded to the imperial throne in 973 aged eighteen. He had already married a Byzantine princess, Theophano, so his mission had the backing of both eastern and western Christianity. When Otto invaded Denmark Harald appealed to Håkon for aid, but was unable to stem the German advance; Otto aimed to seize the Danewirke, a long defensive fortification near Hedeby, but it proved too strong, so Otto sailed round it to Jutland, where he won a victory and compelled Harald Greycloak (perhaps superficially) and Håkon (totally superficially) to embrace Christianity. After this defeat Håkon returned to Norway.

Meanwhile, Trygve Olafson, Håkon the Good's southern vassal who had been driven out by the Danes, had married Astrid Eiriksdottir, who was pregnant when Trygve was assassinated in 963. Their son Olaf was born either in the Orkneys or on an island in one of Norway's myriad lakes; in either case, Astrid was at the time hiding from her husband's Danish killers who apparently were ordered by Eirik Bloodaxe's redoubtable widow Gunnhild to track down her and her son, who many said was the great-grandson of Harald Haarfager.

The story of the flight of Olaf and his mother, told dramatically by Snorri, has come in for serious criticism on the grounds of accuracy. To some scholars it sounds just too much of a fairy tale, perhaps blatantly modelled on the biblical account of the flight into Egypt. We of course are in no position to pronounce absolutely on the actual details as they have come down to us. But we can on the other hand be reasonably sure that the birth of Olaf presented a dynastic threat to Gunnhild and her own sons, and that she would be expected to take steps to mitigate or eliminate that threat. It is in this light that Snorri's account may be read.

According to the saga Astrid and young Olaf secured a temporary sanctuary in her father's house. Gunnhild's men tracked them down there, but not before Astrid's father had seen them coming and Astrid and Olaf escaped in peasant disguise. Eventually both found safety of sorts in Sweden. A Danish mission demanded that the Swedish King, Håkon the Old, send the infant back to Gunnhild; the king initially agreed, but Astrid and others physically resisted the Danish mission, which had to leave empty-handed. Mother and son stayed two years with Håkon the Old, after which she considered they would be safer with her brother Sigurd who was in the service of Prince Vladimir I of Russia at Novgorod. At some point Olaf acquired a foster-father named Thorolf. On the voyage across the Baltic Sea the ship was waylaid by Estonian pirates; Thorolf was murdered and young Olaf, separated from his mother, was sold into slavery, to find his way into a household in Eistland (possibly Estonia) where he remained for six years.

In the detailed and fascinating *Heimskringla* narrative Sigurd, in Eistland on a tax-collecting mission, happened to notice 'a remarkably handsome boy' in a marketplace. On being asked who he was, Olaf revealed his identity; Sigurd (who was actually his uncle) bought him off his owners and took him to Novgorod (other sources say Kiev). Vladimir (or Valdemar in the Norse tongue) became Olaf's protector. Snorri tells us that in the marketplace of Novgorod one day Olaf recognized the man who had killed his foster-father Thorolf, whereupon he 'clove [his] skull down to the brain' with a hand-axe he happened to have on him. A mob chased him through the streets to the palace, where Princess Allogia

(Olga?) bribed the pursuers to leave the boy alone. This can be said to have been Olaf's first act as a genuine Viking. Under the care of Vladimir and Allogia, Olaf grew up into 'the handsomest of men, stout and strong'. (Stout, in this case, almost certainly meaning well-built.)

Olaf as a young man must have had outstanding qualities, as barely out of his teens we find him commander of the king's guard. Though popular with his men, his exalted position at such an early age inevitably aroused jealousy at court, and as the years passed, even Vladimir began to treat him with distinct coolness; besides fearing that Olaf might stage a coup with the guard, Vladimir paid heed to whisperers who claimed the young commander was eyeing the queen. Whatever the truth, the atmosphere must have been uncomfortable. After nine years in Russia, Olaf considered it prudent to leave and expend his considerable energies on the beloved Viking pastime of overseas raiding. His first raids were against the Baltic island of Bornholm, where he looted and killed with the best of them.

In 982 Olaf wintered in Vindland. When his ships first appeared in the main port the local ruler, Queen Geira, sent an invitation to him and his men to attend a banquet. It took just a few days' stay for Olaf and Geira to form something more than a mere social relationship, and it wasn't long before they were married. At one point Geira complained that some towns in Vindland were rebelling against her rule; Olaf promptly went out and brought them once more under her control.

After three happy years Queen Geira died – a severe emotional blow for Olaf. What happened next is unclear. Contradictory traditions have him either returning to Russia or going on major raiding expeditions to the west, including Britain. In 988 on an expedition to Britain he married Gyda, an Irish earl's widow who was looking for a new husband. Even though he was in his 'bad weather clothes' when he arrived for Gyda's inspection, he won out over the other suitors in their finery.

According to the *Anglo-Saxon Chronicle* in 991 Olaf was in command of a massive fleet of ninety-three Viking ships that ravaged Kent and proceeded north to Sussex, where he came ashore at Maldon at the mouth of the River Blackwater to take on an opposing English army. In the words of a long poem by an unknown bard, Olaf in no uncertain terms demanded tribute from the English leader, Byrhtnoth. 'You shall not win tribute so easily,' Byrhtnoth is reported as saying, 'but spear and sword must first decide between us, the grim sport of war, before we pay tribute to you.'

To get at their opponents the Vikings needed to cross a slender isthmus that connected the south bank of the Blackwater with their base on Northey Island. The first Viking to try it was shot down. Then Byrhtnoth, perhaps overconfident in his position, allowed the Viking force to cross over. In the resulting battle the English were trounced, forcing King Ethelred the Unready to promise Olaf a hefty sum of tribute to keep the 'Viking terror' away. An attempt by Ethelred to raise a large fleet at London fizzled out thanks to the treachery of an earl, Aelfric. In 994 Olaf made an attempt on London; after trying but failing to consign the city to the flames, he set out to devastate the southern counties as far as Southampton, where he wintered.

From there it was a short distance to the Scilly Isles, where we find him in the early 990s. It was on those islands that, according to the chroniclers, Olaf was impressed by a seer who told him: 'Thou wilt become a renowned king, and do celebrated deeds. Many men wilt thou bring to faith and baptism.' The seer (whom some scholars identify with Saint Lide) also foresaw that Olaf would be severely wounded in battle, 'yet after seven days thou shalt be well of thy wounds, and immediately thou shalt let thyself be baptized'.

That came to pass almost immediately afterwards, when some of Olaf's men mutinied and grievously wounded him. In Snorri's account, when he recovered he remembered the seer's words and consented to become a Christian. There is some dispute, however, over where and when that event occurred; one story claims Olaf was baptized near Andover by Bishop Aelfeah of Canterbury in 994, but that is generally discounted by other sources, who say that the Andover event merely confirmed his new faith and was part of a treaty by which he agreed to stop raiding in England.

We must, for the sake of completeness, mention Snorri's account which has Olaf going to Russia after Geira's death and having a dream in which God spoke to him to the effect that as Olaf never apparently had much use for the Norse gods, he had thus put himself on the side of righteousness. 'Still,' the voice of God warned, 'you are very deficient in those qualities that would allow you to be in these regions... because you do not know your Creator and you do not know who the true God is.'

By whichever process Olaf Tryggvason was converted, there is no doubt that he took his new faith very seriously. After marrying Gyda he spent about half of his time in Ireland. Word of Olaf's military and marital achievements reached Norway; a spy told Håkon, Earl Sigurd's son who now ruled Norway, that Olaf Tryggvason was indeed in Ireland and by all appearances a serious contender for the Norwegian crown. By now Olaf almost certainly considered himself as such. In the words of Robert Ferguson: 'His new monotheistic religion gave him the moral, military and intellectual justification he needed to set about imposing himself as the sole ruler of the Norwegians in the name of Christianity.' This position, however, is ambiguous; did Olaf view his Christianity as a mere 'justification' for seeking power, a convenient excuse? Or was he driven by genuine missionary zeal? The evidence favours the latter view; and true to form, he set about his mission with the vigour and occasional ruthlessness he had displayed with such talent as a Viking warrior.

When Olaf reached Norway he found heathen Håkon to be deeply unpopular because of his misrule; we are told that Håkon and his slave hid in a hole underneath a pigsty to avoid being taken. In a dramatic sequence Snorri recounts how they overheard Olaf outside promising a great reward for the slayer of Håkon, how Håkon suspected that his slave might be tempted by the offer, and how his fears were proved right when his slave cut off his head when at some point he had to sleep. But far from getting his reward, the slave's own head was lopped off at Olaf's orders: regicide, even of an enemy, was not to be tolerated.

In 997 Olaf Tryggvason set up his seat of government in Trondheim. He went about enforcing Christianity in a typical Viking way – no holds barred. Theodoricus Monachus, a Norwegian Benedictine monk writing in the twelfth century, records that when Olaf stopped at the Orkneys on his way to Norway he threatened to kill the three-year-old son of a noted earl if the latter did not accept baptism forthwith. The earl had little choice, Theodoric notes, but to go along. Once in the Trøndelag, Olaf terrorized the remaining heathens; at one point he gathered up eighty male and female heathen priests and to drive home his point had them all burned in a temple, along with all their heathen images. Almost overnight the Trøndelag turned – at least nominally – Christian.

The far north of Norway was a particularly difficult place to convert. Far from the coastal districts influenced by traders and travellers, it hewed strongly to the ancient ways. Snorri recounts in blood-curdling detail the fate of Raud, a fiercely anti-Christian chieftain of Hålgoland, who was captured and brought before Olaf. The king explained that he didn't want money or property – all he wanted was for Raud to be baptized and be his friend. Raud replied with a string of defiant curses. Olaf, enraged, informed him that he was about to suffer 'the worst death imaginable':

He had him tied with his back to a pole, then put a piece of wood between his teeth to wedge his mouth open. He took a snake and tried to force it into Raud's mouth, but Raud blew at it and the snake wouldn't go in. Then the king took a hollow stalk of angelica and put it in Raud's mouth and put the snake into the angelica (some people say he used his horn). He drove it through the angelica with a red-hot iron, and the snake passed into Raud's mouth, down his neck, and bored its way out through his side: Raud lost his life.

Olaf then helped himself to all Raud's treasures and forced his followers to be baptized. 'Those who refused he killed or tortured.' Similar treatment was meted out to 'sorcerers' at Tønsberg, where he called a number of them together in a feasting hall, and when they were good and inebriated he burned them all.

This narrative has inevitably raised questions about how 'Christian' Olaf actually was, when he did not hesitate to employ the most brutal methods in enforcing the faith in Norway. To be fair, some modern commentators all but dismiss some of Snorri's more hair-raising reports as figments of an overactive imagination. But the violence attending Olaf's mission to Christianize the Norwegians is never in doubt. Snorri, himself a committed Christian, could have preserved the gruesome stories to show readers that Olaf still had the toughness of a Viking leader (always valued in Norse culture) despite his own conversion. We must also consider the mentalities of Olaf's time: there was no liberal academic and media establishment ready to theorize about democracy or human rights. Such notions were unknown. In the eyes of Olaf (and other Christian leaders in subsequent years, including Olaf Haraldsson) Christianity was simply too vitally important to be left to the whims of individuals or individual tribes. There was no such thing as 'freedom of conscience', nor would there be in Europe for seven more centuries. To Olaf the only way to make his nation Christian was to coerce it, and if the stubborn heathens suffered frightful punishments, they just had it coming to them. It was payback time for Lindisfarne.

The liberal mind will likely not be satisfied with this explanation. Therefore we need to add that in the tenth century Christianity and politics were not separate. A unified kingdom such as Olaf Tryggvason wanted to make out of Norway required a solid, unquestioned religious doctrine. Cohesive statehood required nothing less. It could be argued that Olaf's motives for what he did were as much practically political as personally spiritual, and at the time – unlike today's fashionable separation of church and state – both were indistinguishable.

Of Olaf's final years we know little. Snorri recounts an incident at Avaldsnes where Olaf was having dinner when a curious visitor turned up, a one-eyed 'old man who wore a broad-brimmed hat'. This man proved to be a pleasant and talkative dining companion, displaying a formidable knowledge of old local history and legend. It was getting late when a clergyman told Olaf it was time to get to bed, but so fascinated was Olaf by the old man's stories that even though he was in bed, he wanted to hear more tales from the visitor who sat on a stool at the foot of the bed. The clergyman then apparently peeped in and advised the king he had better get some sleep. The visitor duly retired, but Olaf, unable to sleep, called for him again, but he was nowhere to be found.

The next morning Olaf called his cook and wine keeper and asked them if they had seen any strange person around. Yes, they replied.

As they were making ready the meat a man came to them, and observed that they were cooking very poor meat for the King's table; whereupon he gave them two thick and fat pieces of beef, which they boiled with the rest of the meat.

Olaf was most disconcerted at this, and ordered all the meat to be thrown away; the steaks actually must have been horsemeat rather than beef, and as there was a strict ban on eating horsemeat, the King had no choice but to throw the stuff away. In the story Olaf interpreted the incident as identifying the curious one-eyed storyteller with the old god Odin in disguise, who had tried to trick him into eating what was forbidden to a Christian.

Legends aside, Olaf Tryggvason reigned for just five years, during which he tried to Christianize the rest of Scandinavia and Denmark in the teeth of a persistently strong heathen element. He is reported to have made an offer of marriage to Queen Sigrid the Haughty, after his third wife Gudrun Skeggesdatter abortively tried to murder him in his sleep, and left him. Olaf's motive was not so much romance as a desire to bring Sweden into the Christian fold. This was vividly illustrated when he met her to discuss the marriage and insisted that she be baptized in the process. No doubt remembering the failed suit of Harald Grenske, she refused in no uncertain terms. Then the mask fell. Olaf, enraged, cried, 'Why should I care to have thee, one old faded woman, and a heathen jade?' and slapped her with his glove. Her feminine and royal pride stung beyond endurance, Sigrid the Haughty said to Olaf as he left, 'This may some day be thy death.'

Olaf then turned to Tyra, the sister of King Sweyn I of Denmark. This next wife proved to be the fatal one, because it was as Olaf was on a campaign to wrest lands from Tyra's heathen brother that he met his end.

By now Olaf's aggressive conversion campaign had amassed against him a redoubtable array of foes – Swedes and Danes and the sons of the Håkon who was eliminated in the pigsty. His fleet and theirs collided on the island of Svolder in one of Norway's fjords. Olaf fought bravely on his flagship, the *Ormrinn Langi* (Long Serpent) but what happened then remains obscure. Tradition holds that as he saw he was being overcome he leapt from his ship into the sea and was seen no more. It was the year 1000 and Olaf Tryggvason was not yet forty years old.

As with many exalted figures whose death is cloaked in mystery, many believed that Olaf did not perish at sea but was murdered ashore by a farmer after the battle at Svolder had ended. According to the *Morkinskinna* chronicle, many years later Harald Hardraada, the king of Norway, learned that Olaf's killer was still alive, got a confession out of him and hanged him. Other legends abounded, such as the story that Olaf survived and was seen at various times in Rome, Jerusalem and other points in Europe as late as 1046. It was said that King Ethelred the Unready of England and Olaf's sister Astrid received gifts from the presumed long-dead Olaf. Whatever the truth or otherwise of these tales, his lasting legacy was that he laid the Christian foundations of Norway to be ready for the advent of Saint Olaf II Haraldsson.

Chapter 5

Conversion and Conquest

The European picture on the eve of Olaf's kingship was a complicated one. When in 1009 Thorkell the Tall was preparing his first expedition to bolster the Danes' presence in Britain against the refractory English kingdoms, he could not be confident that the Danelaw (the name for the Viking-controlled section of Britain) was quite secure. King Ethelred the Unready (more accurately Unraed, or Without Counsel) ultimately proved unable to motivate the English to do decisive battle with the Danes, and his own efforts came to nought, partly through the treacherous doings of Earl Eadric Streona. Since their victory at Maldon in 991, the Danes were well aware that the Anglo-Saxon realms were weak and divided. Towards the end of that decade King Svein Forkbeard of Denmark sent armies continuously across the North Sea to raid England at will, Kent and the Isle of Wight being the most afflicted districts.

The sense of crisis in Ethelred's court peaked in 1002, when Huna, one of his commanders, warned him that the Danes were plotting to assassinate him and grab his kingdom. In the narrative of the *Anglo-Saxon Chronicle*, Ethelred panicked, lost all restraint and ordered a mass murder of 'all the Danish men who were in England' on 13 November 1002 – the St Brice's Day Massacre. Other accounts speak of Danish Vikings fleeing for their lives before enraged English mobs – no doubt seen by many as a well-deserved turning of the tables. A group of frightened Danes broke into a church to seek sanctuary there, but their pursuers burned the church and everyone inside. Ethelred had no regrets about his brutal order, considering that as 'the Danes had sprung up in this island, sprouting like cockle among the wheat, [they] were to be destroyed by a most just extermination.'

Norse sources, naturally, treat the massacre with outrage. William of Jumièges, for example, claimed that Danish women were buried naked up to waist so that dogs could maul their breasts and Danish infants had their brains beaten out. Svein Forkbeard's sister Gunnhild, she who tried to hunt down the infant Olaf Tryggvason, and who happened to be a Christian, was one high-born victim of the pogrom. All the Viking sources admit that Ethelred's savage blow came as a complete surprise. Svein accordingly avenged himself on Britain in 1003, ravaging Exeter, and burning Norwich the following year. A severe famine in Denmark temporarily held up the annual raiding programme, but in 1006 the unhappy regions of Wessex and Mercia witnessed again the spectacle of booty-laden Vikings marching back to their ships through a landscape of burning houses and devastated fields. Ethelred's attempts at a counter-offensive were undermined by defeatism and treachery, so that by 1011 the Danes were in possession of almost all southern and eastern England.

The Danes' king was now Svein Forkbeard's capable son Cnut, who in 1015 sailed to Britain with a large fleet, landing on the south coast and ravaging at least three counties. He was joined by Thorkell the Tall, who made his second switch of the campaign – back to the Danish side. Ethelred was now ailing and even more incapable than before of putting up an effective fight. Figuratively stabbing him in the back was his son-in-law Eadric Streona, an alderman of Mercia and thoroughly unscrupulous traitor to his king and countrymen whose talents included organizing gangland-style murders of political rivals. It was Eadric who in 1009, as Ethelred had surrounded Thorkell's Danes, abandoned the fight and disrupted Ethelred's strategy. For six more years Eadric played the field with both sides as the opportunities presented themselves to him, until in 1016 he openly allied with Cnut.

By now, however, a change had come over the English. More than 200 years of the Vikings' presence in the British Isles had made them a familiar, if unpredictable, element in national life. In many places, especially the east and north of the country, it was impossible to say where Anglo-Saxon features, language and culture ended and Viking began. Both elements had begun to blend. By the time Ethelred the Unready died on 23 April 1016, English fighting men must have been wondering just who the 'enemy' was and why he was being fought. 'By now,' writes Ferguson, 'everyone was a Viking.'

In the east, the Prince Vladimir whom the young Olaf Tryggvason served ably for nine years could himself claim to have Norse roots. As the fifth 'Grand Duke of Kiev' he ruled what was commonly called Rus from

972 to 1015. According to an old Russian tradition three Scandinavian brothers – Rurik, Sineus and Truvor – had travelled to the Novgorod region to settle chronic social and political unrest that in the middle of the ninth century appeared to be threatening trade stability. Rurik then is said to have sent two aides named Askold and Dir to seize Constantinople, though one might legitimately wonder how they proposed to overcome Byzantium's large and efficient imperial army.

On the way Askold and Dir stopped at Kiev, which they figured offered them more chances of actual rule, whereupon they stayed there and declared themselves independent of Rurik at Novgorod. Kiev, conveniently situated on the Dnieper River for trade with the Black Sea area, quickly grew prosperous; Askold's second successor at the helm was Prince Igor, whose redoubtable widow Olga and her son Svyatoslav expanded the realm until it took in most of what is now Ukraine and much of Russia west of the Urals. But Constantinople remained the overriding goal; between 860 and 1043 the principality of Kiev made no fewer than six futile attempts to seize Constantinople, the first of many such drives over subsequent centuries, and not quite abandoned even in our own day.

Svyatoslav's son and successor, Vladimir, thought he saw his chance when in 989 Byzantine Emperor Basil II (known as the Bulgar-slayer from his propensities in that direction) was trying to fend off the ambitions of a would-be-usurper. Basil sought help from Vladimir, who agreed to send 6,000 Norse Varangians (as the Scandinavo-Russians were now called) – in return for the hand of Basil's sister, Princess Anna. Basil accepted – on condition that Vladimir be baptized.

Vladimir's Norsemen, with the Greek Emperor at their head, attacked the forces of Basil's rival, Bardas Phokas, after a night crossing of the Bosporus. As the Byzantine navy shot salvoes of the deadly Greek Fire from its flame-throwing ships, the Norsemen waded into the enemy, battle-axes dripping with blood. On 13 April 989, in a memorable encounter witnessed by the Vikings, Bardas Phokas on horseback charged Basil alone only to topple from his horse, dead of an apparent stroke, when he was just a few metres away from where the Emperor Basil was waiting, sword at the ready.

Now the main deal had to be implemented: Basil would give his sister to the pagan prince, who in turn would embrace Christianity. It must not have been an easy decision, even for someone renowned as a slayer of Bulgars. For the fly in the ointment was that Vladimir did not have a good reputation; it was reported, perhaps reliably, that he kept several hundred women for his personal use, and that his seven official wives included his brother's widow. He gave every appearance of being an enthusiastic heathen, setting up images of the old gods near his palace. The *Russian Primary Chronicle* records that when one of his Norse soldiers returned from Constantinople a newly-converted Christian, Vladimir ordered the man's young son sacrificed. And this was whom Anna, a devout Christian princess, was to be given to? Well might she, and many of her compatriots, shudder.

They need not have worried. Vladimir's grandmother Olga had been a devout and saintly Christian, and so might her son Svyatoslav have been had he not feared ridicule from the majority of his subjects. Yet many of the Norse inhabitants of Kiev had converted, and it is likely that by 988 Vladimir saw which way the wind was blowing; he at first viewed the major religions as a marketplace of ideas, and decided to try out each before deciding which to officially adopt. Well before receiving the request from help from Basil II he had summoned representatives of Roman and Greek Christianity (the two churches were still technically one; the final irreconcilable schism would not take place until 1054), Judaism and Islam to make their respective cases before him. He didn't like the Muslim ban on alcohol and pork, was not impressed by the condition of Europe's Jews who had no home, frowned at the fasting rules of Rome, and in the end opted for the Orthodox Christianity of Constantinople.

Poor Princess Anna cried when she had to leave her family for the bleak unknown before her. According to the *Russian Primary Chronicle* her brother comforted her: 'Through your agency God turns the land of Rus to repentance, and you will relieve Greece from the danger of grievous war.' With Anna present, Vladimir had himself baptized in February 988. Almost overnight he was a changed man. Down went the wooden statues of the old gods, dragged behind horses to the Dnieper and beaten with sticks on the way for good measure; then he ordered a mass baptism in the river for the next day, threatening that whoever refused, 'rich or poor, lowly or slave, he shall be my enemy'. This was not mere window-dressing, as most astounding of all, Vladimir is reported to have given up his licentious ways and become a model husband for Anna;

he refused thenceforth to take life, built many churches and provided for the poor of Kiev. The modern state of Russia was born.

In the year 1000 the Byzantine, or East Roman, Empire was at its zenith. Its capital Constantinople outshone Rome, Alexandria and Baghdad; its commercial influence reached far and wide, especially up the great Russian rivers to Kiev, Novgorod and Scandinavia. Not many years would pass before a trickle of Vikings would make their way to 'Micklegarth' (as Constantinople was known, while Kiev was called 'Gardarike') in search of adventure and wealth in the service of the Byzantine emperors. One of them was St Olaf's half-brother, Harald Hardraada, who was destined for an adventure-filled career in Byzantium (see below) before returning to become Norway's king.

The image of Byzantium was in strong contrast to that of Rome, governed at the turn of the millennium by Pope Sylvester II. He was one of a series of short-lived pontiffs who were essentially prisoners of a corrupt aristocracy and the ever-distrustful Roman mob, not to mention the Holy Roman emperors who intervened in Roman affairs at will and literally sold the papacy to the highest bidder. We might mention Pope Benedict IX (1032–45), who was crowned at the age of twelve and led such a scandalous life that the people temporarily drove him out; he ended by selling the papal office to Gregory VI (who was a rather better character) for sackfuls of gold. Church reform, long overdue, was on the way, but would not arrive for another half-century.

Germany, in the meantime, had been put into some kind of order by King Otto I, known as the Great. Soon after his accession in 936, this strong-willed Christian monarch brought the bumptiously independent dukes under his thumb, despite undermining efforts by his younger brother Henry. Otto gave senior military commands to his bishops, who thus had a direct stake in the preservation of the establishment; this also marks the beginning of the German church's gradual alienation from Rome. Otto made vigorous attempts to control the chaotic situation in Italy, with meagre success. Before his death in 973, Otto made sure that his son and successor, Otto II, married the Byzantine Princess Theophano, momentarily raising the possibility of a unified German-Byzantine Empire.

It was not to be. Otto II died young trying to add southern Italy to the German realm; his son Otto III grew up to revive the German-Byzantine dream, only to perish at the age of twenty-two by poison at the hands of his Roman mistress, whose husband he had executed for rebellion. Henry II, the last of the Saxon line of German kings, continued the generally futile efforts of his line to subdue Italy and to make enemies of the popes.

Neighbouring France had fallen a long way since the genius of Charlemagne. When the last of his successors, Louis V, died childless in 987, the French nobles and clergy turned to one of those families that had demonstrated its power and resilience in the past resistance against the Norsemen. The most powerful French noble at the close of the tenth century was Hugh Capet, who with little ado, and at the promptings of the clergy, was crowned king of France. Capet, who died in 996, made the final break from that vague entity known as the Holy Roman Empire and gave promise of a renaissance for France. His son and successor Robert the Pious, as his sobriquet suggests, had little taste for war and politics but was hugely popular with the people, protecting the weak and the poor.

Normandy, meanwhile, had become the most enterprising and prosperous duchy in France, barely a century after the Norsemen took control. Midway between Paris and England, Normandy was now stoutly Christian, and ruled with a vigour and capability largely absent in the rest of France. 'The progeny of the Vikings', writes Will Durant, 'made strong governors, not too finicky about their morals, nor palsied with scruples, but able to rule with a firm hand a turbulent population.' Duke Robert I took as mistress the daughter of a tanner; she gave birth to William the Bastard – or as he is better known to history, William the Conqueror. Said Robert of his son before departing on a pilgrimage to Jerusalem: 'That he was not born in wedlock matters little to you; he will be none the less able in battle.' Which, in 1066 at the age of thirty-nine, he would prove to be.

Against this backdrop, and while Cnut was in the process of converting Britain into a unified Christian realm, Olaf Haraldsson had undergone a key conversion of his own. After Etheldred's death, as we have seen, he had continued his career as essentially a warlord, doing battle against recalcitrant elements wherever he could, and enriching himself considerably in the process. Snorri relates that after a dozen or so successful battles Olaf steered his fleet into the English Channel and down the coasts of France, Spain and Portugal, 'intending to sail... on to the land of Jerusalem'. Just why he would have that destination in mind is unclear; it is probable that he had no other motive than seizing some of the wealth of that fabled city, yet as he waited for a favourable wind, he is reported to have had a dream:

> There came to him a great and important man, but of a terrible appearance withal, who spoke to him, and told him to give up his purpose of proceeding to [Jerusalem]. 'Return to thy [land], for thou shalt be king over Norway for ever.'

The effect of this dream on him may not have been immediate. But he seems to have taken it seriously enough; such things generally were – after all, the dream promised that he would be king of Norway. He abandoned plans for Jerusalem and moved back into France, where he fought his fifteenth battle in Poitou. Normandy, having been under Viking control for several generations, was friendly territory, ruled by Earls William and Robert. In 1013 Olaf arrived, and spent what must have been an unusually peaceful winter on the banks of the Seine. Here he was able to assess the situation in Norway, the land he had been mystically promised in his dream.

That situation was chronically unstable. Several powerful men vied for control, including the Earls Eirik and Svein, and a newcomer called Einar Tambaskelfer, who had taken advantage of the fall of Olaf I Tryggvason to carve out considerable influence. Einar was renowned as an archer and all-round man of action, aided by his wealth and family connections. Given Olaf Tryggvason's daughter as wife, he was probably the most powerful man in the Trøndelag. Another leading figure was Erling Skialgsson, whose sister was Sigrid the Haughty's niece. A man whom few cared to tangle with, Erling 'never went to sea with less than a full-manned ship of twenty benches of oars' – or at least two hundred men. He was known to manage his farmstead well and allowed his slaves to buy their freedom whenever they could afford it.

In the Norman court of Duke Richard II, himself an ardent Christian, all this would have been well known. Cnut was busy putting England in order while fighting off a Norwegian challenger, Eirik Håkonarson (or Håkonson), the Earl of Lade. It would have been natural for Olaf and Richard in the winter of 1013 to consider the possibility of restoring the unified kingdom of Norway, whose last king, Olaf I Tryggvason, had perished trying to forge it. Was his Christianizing influence in the end to mean nothing? Sometime in early 1014 (at the latest) the decision would have been made: Olaf Haraldsson would return to Norway, and in accord with his dream, be its Christian king. Geostrategic and spiritual motives here coincided nicely. Olaf's next step was to be formally baptized in the Notre Dame Cathedral in Rouen by Archbishop Robert the Dane, who was Duke Richard's brother.

However, two issues of chronology arise here. The first has to do with when Olaf was actually baptized, as Snorri's account, as we have seen, asserts that Olaf Tryggvason himself baptized the three-year-old Olaf in Norway, which would be in about 998. Though baptism for anyone remains valid throughout life, it is reasonable to suppose that Olaf let himself fall away from the faith during his tumultuous and combat-filled youth; in which case, when he matured and was old enough to make a conscious spiritual decision, he would have sought more a confirmation than a re-baptism (which would have been most anti-canonical), and the ceremony at Rouen could well be seen in that light. But whatever the formalities, Rouen was the great turning-point in Olaf's life, when he began to turn from his worldly Viking ways.

Our sources give us no dramatic Paul-type flashing revelation as described in gripping detail in the New Testament. Most likely the inner conversion was gradual, a cumulative process from his time in England. But the event in Rouen undoubtedly was the key turning point in Olaf's life. It is intriguing that Snorri Sturluson, though writing in a Christian context, makes no such mention of Olaf's spirituality at this time. Indeed, in his subsequent account of Olaf's assumption of power, and the means he employed to attain it, he seems to be at pains to downplay the spiritual side. Both accounts together, however, help us form a more rounded picture of him.

The second chronology issue concerns just when the Rouen confirmation occurred. Our extant accounts leave us in some confusion, with some dating the event to 1010 and asserting that it was as a confirmed Christian that Olaf took part in Thorkell the Tall's campaigns in Britain. This might help explain his decision to fight on the side of Ethelred. Most opinion, however, centres on 1014, after a stay of several months in Normandy, where Olaf would have had the chance in a peaceful environment to reflect on what he really wanted to do. Reinforcing this view is the reasonable assumption that if Olaf had become confirmed in 1010, he would not have remained silent at the murder of St Alphege by the army to which he belonged.

In 1013 Cnut, who was still struggling for control of England, sought help from his brother-in-law Eirik Håkonarson, the Earl of Lade. Eirik at the time was the most powerful man in Norway, having earned his reputation fighting the Jomsborg Vikings and Olaf Tryggvason, whose Christian reforms he set about systematically nullifying. Flattered by the invitation, Eirik sailed forthwith for England, leaving his lands in the care of his son Håkon and Eirik Tambaskelfer. The somewhat confused evidence points to Håkonarson's using the campaign to seize territory and a castle in London from Cnut. Snorri adds the curious detail that Eirik was planning a 'pilgrimage' to Rome, but died of a severe gastro-intestinal ailment before he could do it. This does not sound like the plan of a man whose record consisted of trying to erase Christianity in Norway and restore heathenism. Eirik's real motives must therefore remain in the realm of speculation.

In Normandy Olaf Haraldsson conferred with Ethelred's surviving sons on how the Danes could be driven out of Britain; he was promised Northumbria if he could help pull it off. At this point Hrane, Olaf's foster-father and the man who led the raids in which the boy cut his fighting teeth, makes an unexpected reappearance. We have seen how, even at age twelve, Olaf was formally considered a 'king' by the men who campaigned with Hrane, who appears now to be in a subordinate role. Olaf sent Hrane to England to gather men and money; many English nobles, eager to see the back of the Danes, responded enthusiastically, 'as the people of the country would rather have a native king over them'.

Olaf, however, would have seen an attempt on England as a preliminary to his real mission, which was to return to Norway as its king. But for that he would need a plentiful supply of men and money, and the only way to obtain them was by traditional Viking methods. Olaf's forces landed at Jungufurda, an unknown location on the south-east coast of England, where they were overwhelmed by a Danish force. But whereas Olaf's allies returned to France, Olaf himself sailed to Northumbria, where he won a battle at another now-unknown location called Valde and seized considerable treasure with which he could now fund his main aim.

In 1014 the west coast of Norway was particularly vulnerable to an incursion, as Cnut was preoccupied in England. Olaf's initial operation, however, seems curiously low-key, as he took just two merchant ships and a couple of hundred 'well-armed and picked' men to land on the tiny island of Selja, southwest of the coastal town of Ålesund, which they reached intact after negotiating a severe storm. If the feebleness of the force is puzzling, so is the response by Earl Håkon of Lade, the late Eirik Håkonarson's son, who sailed out to confront Olaf with a single ship. The conclusion to be drawn is that Olaf didn't wish to appear overly aggressive and to give the impression of an invader in what, after all, was his own country; likewise Håkon, still very young and unsure of his powers, felt that an overt conflict would likely prove disastrous.

While walking ashore on Selja, Olaf slipped in the mud but managed to avoid falling. Olaf feared that it might be a portent of bad luck, but Hrane reassured him: 'You didn't fall, King, but set your foot fast in the soil.' The stay on Selja, however, was brief; Olaf and his men took a short sail south into the Ulfasund (present-day Nordfjord) where at a particularly narrow point he placed his two ships on either side and stretched a thick cable between them. When Håkon's solitary vessel approached, the submerged cable was winched up, pitching the ship stern-up and its occupants into the water. Håkon and some of his men were fished out, while others drowned or were picked off by Olaf's men. Snorri gives us an account of what happened next, though some authorities claim the dialogue must be invented. (It may, however, be 'invented' in the Thucydidean sense, where the essence of what was said by and large rings true, though the actual words spoken may be unknown.)

Earl Håkon, who must have been still in his teens, cut an impressive figure as he was led before Olaf. His long, fine hair was tied to his head by a gold headband, and from what we are told of the subsequent conversation, he had a degree of maturity belying his years.

'Your land has deserted you', Olaf remarked, in a possible sly dig at the paucity of Håkon's force.

'Success is changeable', Håkon replied philosophically. 'I'm a little beyond childhood, so we couldn't have defended ourselves.' He hinted, however, that they could have a chance to settle accounts later.

'Don't you realize it might be all over for you?' Olaf said.

'Only you, King, can decide that.'

Olaf would have had some rueful admiration for the dignity of the young earl's responses. Here, he must have thought, was a possible ally.

'What will you give me if I let you go free?'

'What will you take?' Håkon asked in turn.

'Nothing,' Olaf said. 'Just leave this territory, stop claiming a kingdom and swear that you will never go into battle against me.'

Håkon swore on the spot, took his ship (which seems to have been little the worse for its upending) and departed. Håkon's destination was England, where he told his uncle Cnut what had happened and settled down to a comfortable sinecure in the court.

Olaf proceeded up country to Vestfold to meet his stepfather Sigurd Syr and presumably discuss plans. He arrived at Sigurd's house early one morning, taking the household by surprise. His mother Åsta, on being told of his approach by servants, ordered the main room to be prettied up and all present to don their best clothes; manservants brought up plenty of beer and food. Leading people of the country round about were hurriedly invited, and all preparations were made for a great welcoming feast. At that moment Sigurd Syr himself was overseeing the grain harvest when one his farm servants arrived with news of Olaf's arrival and a change of clothes for Sigurd. 'Åsta told us', said the servants, showing him the finery they had brought with them, 'that on this occasion you ought to behave like a great man.' Sigurd Syr, not one to put on airs, was not overly impressed by this typically wifely advice. After some grumbling about Åsta's habitual fussiness, he expressed some doubts about the wisdom of her maternal enthusiasm.

'This man, King Olaf', Snorri has him saying, 'goes against greatly superior power', and if he were so rash as to defy the power of the Danish and Swedish kings he would bring them down on him. But he heeded Åsta's advice and sat down to change his clothes as befitted the stepfather of a prospective king, 'with a scarlet cloak over all; girded on his sword, set a gilded helmet upon his head, and mounted his horse'. When he and thirty retainers approached the house they saw the banners of Olaf's hundred men fluttering in the near distance. Neighbours gathered on the rooftops to view the spectacle.

With aristocratic and manly self-restraint Sigurd Syr saluted Olaf while still on horseback and (rather formally, one might imagine) invited him and his men inside to 'drink a cup' with him. Åsta, of course, made a point of warmly kissing her son and offering him all her land and the workers on it. She led Olaf to one of the seats of honour; Sigurd took the other 'and the feast was made with the greatest splendour'.

Homecoming was sweet, but Olaf was not there for nostalgia; he had not travelled to Norway to savour the joys of farm life; he had a job to do – to impose his rule over a country – and shortly after his arrival he called together Åsta, Sigurd Syr and Hrane to discuss how he was to do it. 'Foreigners', he said, echoing a common grievance, 'are now sitting in the possessions which my father, his father, and their forefathers owned for many generations.' The time to remedy this state of affairs was now, and it would be vain to seek the aid of the Danish or Swedish kings, as they would most likely support the usurpers of Harald Haarfager's heritage. Olaf told the assemblage that he had decided to fight for his heritage 'with battle-axe and sword' to avenge the death of his predecessor Olaf I Tryggvason. He said he was well aware that the majority of Norwegian people were of like mind and would flock to his support, especially after the example he made of Earl Håkon.

Sigurd, in his thoughtful manner, advised Olaf to think carefully about the formidable task he had set himself and not to give in to 'hasty pride'. However, he knew Olaf well enough from his early years and precocious displays of spirit and leadership qualities, and was convinced that Olaf would go ahead regardless. He urged Olaf to wait until he, Sigurd, could sound out the other noble family heads; if he detected interest, he pledged that all his property and effort would go into the campaign. But Cnut in England and King Olof Sköttkonung of Sweden would be powerful adversaries, he warned, and reminded his hearers that Olaf Tryggvason, too, had landed in Norway to enthusiastic popular support, but in the end he had not lasted very long.

Åsta, for her part, did not mince words. 'I rejoice at your arrival, but much more at your advancing your honour', she said. 'I'd rather you be the supreme king of Norway, even if you don't sit on the throne any longer than Olaf Tryggvason did.' With that, Snorri writes, the meeting broke up and Sigurd Syr prepared to journey to Uppland (modern Oppland) to sound out the nobles there, many of whom were of Harald Haarfager's kin and therefore likely to be allies. Olaf had made clear early in the discussion that he required more resources than he had at the time.

Two of those nobles, the brothers Hrorek and Ring, at first appeared sympathetic to Sigurd's proposals, but sounded a note of caution that to Olaf by now must have been familiar: true, it was a sad thing that Harald Haarfager's heritage had dwindled and decayed and was in alien hands, but recent events in Norway were not encouraging; either there were foreign rulers (Gunnhild's sons) who cared little for the people, or local nobles who arrogated power to themselves and were worse than the foreigners. They cited the tragic examples of Håkon the Good and Olaf Tryggvason whose good intentions in the end had been defeated by hostile powers. Yet there was a general sentiment among the Norwegians that a native king was needed to restore the country's honour, and on that nucleus Olaf could act.

But Hrorek brought up another issue that must have troubled Olaf; they had, they said, unhappy memories of Olaf Tryggvason, who had behaved autocratically, not allowing 'any man to believe in what god he pleased'. Hrorek concluded by saying that he had yet to see what benefits Olaf would confer on the country, where he, Hrorek, was at present quite well off, with no complaints to make. Yet the underlying sentiment seemed favourable. Hrorek's brother Ring added that Olaf would be well advised to cultivate the friendship of the powerful men in the regions; in short, Olaf would first have to prove himself. 'If he be the honourable man I believe him to be… therefore let us join the adventure and bind ourselves in friendship with him.' There were other leading men present at the meeting, and most of them agreed with Ring. Olaf thereupon promised he would do all that was expected of him and confirmed the pledge with an oath.

The next step was to convene a Thing, or general assembly of Norwegian realms. Olaf addressed it circumspectly, promising to keep his hands off the chieftains' local laws and jealously-guarded right to act individually to defend their lands from any external threats. Snorri tells us that Olaf's address was long and earnest, but that it was the aforementioned pledge that won over the regional leaders. Then and there they elected him King Olaf II Haraldsson. At once, with 300 men-at-arms, he made what turned out to be a triumphal tour around Hadaland and parts of the north; supporters flocked to him from all quarters. Conscious that his large entourage might exhaust the slender provisions of the areas he went through, Olaf made sure he never stayed in any one place too long, to the point of preferring to take a hard route over a mountain than eat up the food of a lowland community.

Olaf did not find support everywhere. At Melaldal he convened a Thing, but his hearers appear not to have trusted him; they accepted him as king merely because 'they had no strength to oppose' him, but once he left they sent secret word of Olaf's progress to Einar Tambaskelfer. On hearing the news Einar cut a battle arrow into four pieces and sent them to the four points of the compass as a token message to his vassals to gather together men to resist Olaf's advance and assemble them at Gaulardal in the Trøndelag, north of Trondheim.

At Einar Tambaskelfer's urging the locals of Orkadal managed to pull together about 700 men to block Olaf's path. Probably because Einar himself seems not to have been with them, this force was disorganized and without a command structure. Olaf himself proceeded 'in all peace and gentleness', unwilling to force a fight, but when over the crest of a ridge he spied Einar's force he hesitated. Olaf sent an aide, Thorer Gudbrandson, to suggest to his opponents to select twelve men known to sympathize with Olaf's cause. The twelve thus selected proceeded to the top of the ridge to meet the king, who told them: 'You have heard already that [Earl] Håkon [of Lade] has given me all the land of Norway. I offer you peace and law, the same as Olaf Tryggvason offered you before. I offer you a choice: join me or fight me.'

That last phrase was an honest and forthright challenge that any Viking would recognize. Olaf must have presented an impressive figure, as the twelve went away to deliver the ultimatum. After much debate the leaders of Einar's force accepted the former and more reasonable alternative. Much feasting accompanied the king's progress through the Trøndelag, where he obtained four longships, and probably their crews as well, to add to the handful he already had. With these, just before Yuletide 1015, he sailed into the long and tortuous fjord of Trondheim.

Einar Tambaskelfer informed his brother-in-law Earl Svein Håkonarson of Lade, the leading local noble, by sending messengers in a boat up the fjord to Steinkjer, a commercial town about 120 kilometres north of Trondheim, where Svein was preparing for the Yule festival. When the news reached him in the evening, under cover of darkness he loaded his longship with ample supplies of food, drink and clothing and sailed out; when dawn broke he spotted Olaf's flotilla and steered his ship into a concealed spot by the fjord's bank at Masarvik. Hiding his vessel behind a screen of felled trees, Svein watched as Olaf's ships sailed unwittingly by. Once they were out of sight, he continued down the fjord to Frosta, to be closer to his seat of administration. From there Svein messaged Einar that the time had come to contest Olaf's progress.

Einar, knowing Olaf's abilities, took a cautious line, advising Earl Svein to keep an eye on Olaf as he apparently intended to spend the Yule season at Steinkjer where presumably he would be off his guard. Assembling a force against him would have to be done as quietly as possible. Svein set up quarters at Stjørdal, east of Trondheim (now near the site of Trondheim airport), to await developments. But Olaf had no intention of remaining idle at Steinkjer; he loaded festive provisions on his ships and sailed down the fjord to Nidaros, where Olaf Tryggvason had built a mansion, intending it to grow into a commercial town; on the contrary, Eirik Håkonarson had built up his own entrepot at nearby Lade, leaving Nidaros to crumble. Olaf set men to work to repair the buildings, after which he held a Yuletide feast with the provisions he had brought with him. The plot by Einar and Svein to ambush Olaf at Steinkjer thus never got a chance to operate.

At this point a young and talented Icelander named Sigvat Thordarson, whose father Thord was with Olaf's forces, sailed into the Trondheim fjord on a merchantman. Sigvat apparently only just then learned that his father was in the vicinity and sought out the king. Sigvat's outstanding skill was that of skald, or bard-poet, and once with Olaf he wrote a ballad in his honour and proposed to sing it to him. Olaf modestly dismissed the suggestion, saying he didn't care much for poems written about him and didn't really understand what the skalds' efforts were all about anyway. The exchange, recorded by Snorri, could suggest that Olaf's spirituality was already developing and that he wished to avoid the subtle sin of believing himself to be someone special. But Sigvat went ahead and sang anyway:

> Rider of dark blue ocean's steeds!
> Allow one skald to sing they deeds;
> And listen to the song of one
> Who can sing well, if any can.

Even a saint may occasionally feel flattered, and Olaf rewarded the young poet with a heavy gold ring and a position in the king's entourage. Whereupon Sigvat enthusiastically continued:

> I trust that I shall ever be
> Worthy the sword received from thee.
> A faithful follower thou hast bound –
> A generous master I have found.

Olaf had a job for his new courtier. He had been demanding tax arrears due to Norway from Icelandic merchants, but the Icelanders claimed their payments had been quite regular. They petitioned Olaf and suggested that Sigvat, himself an Icelander, should plead their case in verse:

> It is not right that these poor men
> Their harbour dues should pay again.
> That they paid once, I know is true;
> Remit, great king, what scarce is due.

Frustratingly, we are not told whether the appeal worked; Snorri's subsequent silence on the subject gives us no clue, though judging from what we know of Olaf's character, we may surmise that he did as the Icelanders wished; he could not afford to make enemies needlessly at this stage.

Olaf had little time to enjoy his sojourn at Nidaros, which still was not finished when the king's scouts noticed a large force advancing on Gaulardal; this was the army of Earl Svein, amounting to about 2,000 men, mobilized in a final effort by him and Einar Tambaskelfer to block Olaf's plans for good. The two men had support from a number of local heathen potentates, who feared losing their power and privileges to a national king, and a Christian king at that. The messengers rushed to Nidaros in the middle of the night, rousing Olaf, who at once ordered all his people to take to the ships with their weapons and belongings. They were just in time: as the ships pulled out, those on board would have seen the flames as Svein's men turned up and put the new settlement to the torch. Olaf and his flotilla sailed up the fjord to Orkadal, where they left the ships and struck inland to the mountains flanking the Gudbrandsdal valley.

The present-day border with Sweden crosses this inhospitable region, though in Olaf's time the frontier was not clear-cut. Probably Olaf and his force entered Swedish territory at Jamtland. It would have been dangerous to do so, as this was Svein Håkonarson's territory, but Svein's campaign against his suzerain Olaf cannot be considered a strictly national one. There was no clear-set distinction at the time between Swede and Norwegian, as there is today; both ethnic groups were heir to the Norse traditions and tongue and many parts of the Scandinavian hinterland were a mixture of both. While Svein's chief motive was most probably to prevent the Norwegian Olaf from penetrating into Sweden as well, the Norwegian nobles who were with Svein had the rather less exalted motive of preserving their aggressive independence and feudal privileges.

It may be asked why Olaf decided to go south over the mountains rather than by sea down the west coast and around the southern end of the Scandinavian peninsula. Firstly, the latter would probably take considerable time, and as it was winter, all sea voyages were more hazardous than usual. Also, he would surely have been pursued by enemy vessels. Secondly, he was undoubtedly taken by surprise at Nidaros, and the first thing he required was reinforcements. These were only available inland under his foster-father Sigurd Syr. An overland march in the snow-clad mountains, too, had its risks, but such was the urgency that he had to risk it. After receiving men from Sigurd Syr he stayed put over mid-winter. In the early spring of 1016 when the snows were beginning to melt, Olaf resumed his southward progress, ending up at Viken, on the fjord on which Oslo now stands.

If we assume that Olaf had spies in his service, he would have known that his foes were hot on his heels, driving down the west coast of Norway by sea. To await them he assembled a fleet at Tønsberg near the mouth of the fjord. By April Svein and his strong force which he had put together at Trondheim with the help of several wealthy nobles (including some who had recently sworn allegiance to Olaf) had arrived at Rogaland (Stavanger region), to be joined by a local opportunist, Erling Skialgsson. On Palm Sunday Svein's fleet had neared Viken, where Olaf was waiting for him. On reaching the south coast Olaf had assembled a fleet. He rowed out to meet Svein at Nesjar, a village on the narrow Langesundfjorden in the region of Larvik.

As is the case in many pivotal encounters in world history, hard facts about the Battle of Nesjar are thin on the ground. We must, with the requisite degree of caution, necessarily depend on Snorri Sturluson's saga for the great bulk of the narrative. But since there is nothing intrinsically unlikely in that account, we may take its framework as more or less historical, even with the Thucydidean presumed dialogue placed in the mouths of Olaf and others.

It is uncertain just when Olaf learned of the arrival of Svein's fleet; Snorri says that Olaf had already deployed his own ships when he received the news, so he must have had some forewarning. On Palm Sunday, we are told, Olaf rose and dressed on his flagship *Carl's Head*, distinguished by a carved wooden king's head, which he is said to have made himself, on the prow. He left his ship and went ashore, where he called together the army and informed it of an impending clash. 'Let the people arm', are the words attributed to him, 'and every man be at the post that has been appointed him.' He admitted that as he had no precise knowledge of where Svein's fleet actually was, his own ships needed to exit cautiously in tight formation, none too far ahead or behind, to avoid being surprised. He advised his men to avoid an early clash and to conserve their weapons and ammunition, 'so that we do not cast them into the sea, or shoot them away into the air to no purpose', but when the fight really got underway, 'let each man show what is in him of manly spirit'.

These words, if accurate, show Olaf to have been a capable tactician. His confidence may well have been a result of his faith, which he was proud to display on his men's helmets and shields in the form of a conspicuous cross. The 100 or so men of the *Carl's Head* wore what Snorri describes as 'foreign helmets' – perhaps Russian or Byzantine – with the cross on their front. His own banner featured a kind of dragon. After assembling the army, Olaf ordered a service to be read, then boarded his ship with instructions to the men to fortify themselves with food and drink (though, one hopes, not too much of the latter). Then these northern crusaders – a full eighty years before the First Crusade set out for the Holy Land – would be ready.

Olaf's ships advanced, battle-horns sounding, to seek Svein holed up in the Langesundfjorden; Svein seems to have been surprised by the appearance of Olaf's fleet, as he was probably about to sail himself in search of his adversary. Svein ordered his ships to be bound together in the standard naval defensive tactic of the time, to enable the complement of any ship to easily rush to the aid of another if necessary without touching water. Olaf ordered his rowers to speed up. The eager skald Sigvat threw himself into the fray while Olaf made for Svein's flagship that was either still in harbour or just putting out. 'Then was the conflict exceedingly sharp', says Snorri, 'and it was long before it could be seen how it was to go in the end.' Casualties on both sides were heavy. Svein appears to have had the larger force, but according to Snorri, Olaf's own chain-mail-armoured crew and their metal helmets gradually prevailed.

When Olaf saw the enemy ranks thinning he flourished his dragon banner and made for Svein's ship, intending to board it. In the lay that Sigvat composed afterwards:

> On, steel-clad men! and storm the deck,
> Slippery with blood and strewed with wreck…
> Into the ship our brave lads spring –
> On shield and helm their red blades ring.

Svein's army put up a stout fight and for some time the issue appeared to be in doubt. But as Svein's losses appeared to exceed Olaf's, the men on the *Carl's Head* succeeded in boarding Svein's ship. There followed a desperate struggle in which Svein ordered his crew to cut the cables tying his ship to the others, to try to make a break for it, but Olaf's men threw grapnels over the wooden gunwales of Svein's vessel; Svein's answer was to chop off the gunwales and their timber supports, and free his ship once more. Einar Tambaskelfer rowed up alongside Svein and had his anchor thrown over the bows of the ship and successfully towed it out of harm's way. But seeing Svein apparently in flight, his force gave up the battle and followed him down the fjord.

Snorri gives us a curious vignette of this closing phase of the battle: one of Svein's skalds, a handsome and well-regarded fellow called Berse Torfason, 'always well-equipped in clothes and arms' – a veritable Viking cavalier – stood on the forecastle of Svein's ship as it was retreating, and when it was close enough to Olaf's ship Olaf called out to him, 'Farewell, Berse!' Berse replied in kind, but soon found himself a prisoner in the hull of the *Carl's Head*, yet unbowed (as he later claimed) in morale.

With Svein's flight the rest of his force dispersed. Once out of danger, Svein called his ships' complements together for a meeting. Erling Skialgsson was all for sailing back north to collect another force for a second attempt at Olaf, but the other leaders were too shaken by their losses to agree. Most urged Svein to go to his brother-in-law, Sweden's King Olof Sköttkonung, to rest and re-equip. Einar Tambaskelfer was of the same opinion, and so the fleet was discharged and the nobles dispersed to their several fiefs.

Olaf was by no means certain that Svein had actually pulled out of the fight; he hoped that was the case, as he wished to avoid another battle. Sigurd Syr, on the other hand, counselled pressing the pursuit to destroy the enemy. He well knew Olaf's reflective character, which shunned impulsive actions, and chided him for naivete: 'I fear that someday you will be betrayed by trusting those great people [the nobles] for they are long accustomed to defying their sovereigns.' But Olaf's decision was made for him, as he saw Svein's fleet breaking up and dispersing. Stripping the slain and allocating the booty took up some days; Sigurd Syr and the other chief officers received generous presents, including a fifteen-bench yacht for Ketil of Ringanes. When Olaf's spies presently reassured him that Svein had gone from the region, he returned to Viken to reaffirm and formally claim his kingship. (The precise location of the Battle of Nesjar is not known; most authorities place it near the village of Helgeroa in Vestfold. In 2016, on the thousandth anniversary of the battle, the Nesjar Monument was erected on the presumed site.)

Chapter 6

Beware the Blinded Man

No-one has yet reconciled Christianity with government.

Will Durant

After his victory at Nesjar, Olaf was acclaimed king by a Thing convened at Viken. But that was nowhere near enough for him yet to exercise full *de facto* sovereignty over Norway. The south may have submitted, but his native Trøndelag was by no means secure as long as Earl Svein Håkonarson was at large and could still command considerable support in and around Trondheim. Moreover, Erling Skialgsson was a force still to be reckoned with. But the Thing at Viken is generally taken to mark the beginning of Olaf's kingship, as it was after the Battle of Nesjar that he emerged as the most powerful man in Norway and the only one with royal status. Olaf knew exactly what to do next, and that was to sail post-haste up the coast to Trondheim, where in September 1016 he was acclaimed king rather more officially. The charred embers of his previous home at Nidaros were cleared to make room for a new royal residence surrounded by a new town to consist of homes and business premises built by merchants and professional men.

In his new quarters at Nidaros Olaf could finally get down to some serious governing. Snorri gives us a positive yet surprisingly warts-and-all account of his character at this time (though, it must not be forgotten, at two centuries' distance): 'Olaf was a good and very gentle man, of little speech, and open-handed though greedy of money.' If this last trait brings us up short, we must also not forget that almost all saints, being human, have had their human flaws. It also adds a certain credibility to the saga as a whole. To be fair, the 'greed' for money could have been nothing more censurable than a preoccupation with funding, which was never very secure and which he needed for his grand aim. Besides, so far he had found it easy to buy off potential foes, which suggests that the 'greed' was not so much a personal failing as the need to pursue a practical financial policy.

Olaf's daily routine at Nidaros was fairly constant: after rising, dressing and washing his hands he would proceed to a meeting of the Thing assembly and be briefed on the state of the realm and any problems in its running. His aim, says Snorri, was 'to bring people to agreement with each other' and where the laws needed amending, he would order them amended. The heart of his new palace was the large throne room, in the centre of which stood the throne itself. Flanking the throne were seats for the senior clergy, and opposite it were the seats of the senior courtiers and a special place for any visiting dignitary. Discussions ended by the comforting glow of the fireside, no doubt with an adequate supply of alcohol to further warm the atmosphere and ease the process of deliberation. The royal staff was remarkably spare for the time: sixty full courtiers and thirty 'pursuivants' (attendants to the courtiers), thirty servants and 'many slaves' (rather to be described as unpaid servants).

At Olaf's side in the throne room sat his bishop, Grimkell, whom he had brought from Britain and who, apparently, had been with him throughout. Grimkell seems to have been a highly influential adviser. Little else is known of him, except that after Olaf's death he was the prime mover in his canonization and the preservation of his memory. Other sources, however, name Bishop Sigurd as the king's main spiritual counsellor; this cleric, of English origin, had baptized Olof Sköttkonung (later becoming Saint Sigfrid of Sweden) and by some accounts succeeded Grimkell in his post. Therefore, just who was the chief cleric at Nidaros, and at which time, remains uncertain. According to the author of *The Passion and Miracles of the Blessed Óláfr*, by now Olaf had undergone a thorough spiritual renewal:

> Forgetting what had gone before, passing on to things to come, this most perfect observant of the faith he had adopted walked in the newness of life. All vain pleasure seemed paltry to him, and the glory of earthly kingship grew vile in comparison with heavenly bliss. Although of royal rank, he was poor in spirit, and though involved in worldly affairs, he yet gave his mind to heavenly matters. Whatever divine law forbids he vehemently rejected; whatever that law commands he embraced with the most ardent love.

King Olaf kept a close eye on domestic issues, where consolidating the Christian faith in his domain was the number one priority. 'Not content with his own salvation', the *Passion* asserts, 'he strove with unflagging urgency to convert the people he was appointed by divine providence to govern.' The saga portrays Olaf as a new apostle – the equivalent of the Greek *isapostolos*, or equivalent-to-apostle, a status accorded to Late Roman Emperor Constantine I, an idea very likely imported from Byzantium. In this account, his graciousness of speech 'led not a few away from the abominable worship of demons' and into 'contempt of this world and love of the heavenly homeland'. Yet it was no walkover, for in the next sentence the *Passion* informs us that Olaf had to labour 'in the midst of a vicious and perverse nation' containing 'many strong and mighty enemies' who 'fought with all their might against the message and holy works of this most noble martyr'.

Olaf therefore felt he had to take a very tough line against the adherents of the old beliefs, though in the first stage of his reign we do not know of any actual instance in which the royal policy proceeded further than threats, which might well have been enough. Perhaps because of his firm stand, Olaf's prestige actually stood very high in the lower lands. Yet this was probably his first taste of the difficulties and hurdles that would rise against his evangelizing mission, against which he would have to take harsher measures.

One man who saw where events were leading was Erling Skialgsson, the independent lord who had allied himself with Svein Håkonarson in the Battle of Nesjar. Erling requested a meeting with Olaf at Whitings Isle; early in the conversation it became apparent that Erling's motives were less than pure: he imagined that the gentle Olaf, now he was king, might give him back the lands he said he had received from the late Svein and Olaf Tryggvason and thereby become the king's 'dutiful friend'. Olaf's right royal reply was blunt, and tinged with Machiavellian cunning:

> It would be no bad bargain, Erling, to get great fiefs from me... but even if I let you remain as the greatest vassal lord in Norway, I will bestow my fiefs according to my own will... and not as if I were obliged to buy your services.

In short, Olaf had to show who was boss. He did not want to appear to be haggling with potential rivals, or even buying them off; he was too straight for that. Erling smarted under the snub, and shot back: 'The service will be the most useful which I give with a free will.' He was at first inclined to stalk off and risk being in the king's black books, but his associates and relatives talked him out of it, and so Erling agreed to take orders from Olaf unconditionally.

Shortly afterwards Olaf moved south to Viken to check on affairs and collect his taxes, then travelled eastwards to the frontiers with southern Sweden, where at Svinesund he stopped to assess the situation. Near the coast he called a Thing at which a local lord named Brynjolf Ulfalde warned Olaf that his region faced a threat from Swedish pressures on all sides. He added that many locals would like to back Olaf but were afraid of the Swedes; as Olaf seemed to be concentrating on his northern domains, he said, he would do well to give a bit of encouragement and constructive advice to his southern supporters. One threat existed in the person of a powerful local chieftain, Eilif Gautske, who appears to have owed his position to the Swedes, though many of his own men seemed to favour Olaf. Eilif sent spies to see what Olaf was up to, but also consented to a form of shuttle diplomacy with him; the go-betweens ended up suggesting a direct meeting between the two men. Olaf, they told Eilif, was not one to be trifled with, and it might go badly for the latter if he decided to resist. The moral power that Olaf had gradually accumulated since becoming king was now attaining a critical mass of sorts; his fame, and reports of his calm determination to enforce his law over all of Norway, had surely by now percolated far and wide, and Eilif Gautske was about to experience it.

Seeing that Eilif was probably playing for time, Olaf sent seven men clad in armour beneath their ordinary apparel to persuade Eilif to come down from his highland refuge and talk things over. The tense meeting took place on a rocky promontory; Olaf's ships lay close by, while Eilif's force gathered on a piece of flat land, forming a human shield for Eilif himself. In Snorri's account of the meeting, after the king's chief emissary delivered a long and eloquent speech, and Eilif was rising to reply, one of Olaf's seven armed envoys, Thorer Lange, deciding to speed up the proceedings somewhat, drew his sword and sliced Eilif's head clean off. Such was the shock that Eilif's men began to flee; Thorer killed several, but somehow (Snorri does not say how), Olaf got the late Eilif's men to settle down again. A long parley followed, after which the potential rebels agreed to submit to Olaf.

With the border regions pacified, at the beginning of autumn 1016 Olaf sailed back to Viken. Sailing up the Raum River, he discovered a strategic spot where a spit of land juts out into the river north of a waterfall. He ordered a stone, wood and turf rampart to be built across the neck of the promontory, as well as a ditch. This was the start of a new commercial town he planned for the site, where he also intended to build his winter quarters far from the severe cold of Trondheim. As 1017 dawned Olaf celebrated a sumptuous Yule feast with the people he had gathered into the district to farm and trade. Here Olaf displayed the generosity typical of him by giving a large farm to Brynjolf Ulfalde, along with a gold-mounted sword. Not surprisingly, Snorri tells us, Brynjolf was henceforth 'the King's greatest friend'.

Olaf's overriding task, to which all others, including military ones, were subordinate, was to entrench the Christian religion and amend the laws accordingly in his domains. The work begun by Olaf Tryggvason was unfinished. Bishop Grimkell was given authority over all the churches in the land, and the people made responsible for providing for the clergy – this rule presumably to avert the possibility of the priesthood amassing independent wealth and prestige. Christian baptism and observance of the religious holidays was made compulsory, and marriage and funeral rites altered to conform with Christian ideals. Olaf replaced the heathen time-frames with the Julian calendar and rigidly enforced fasting days, such as every Friday, and Sunday rest. As a form of crude encyclical, the new annual schedule was inscribed on a wooden plaque to be carried from farm to farm so that the people could presumably make copies for themselves.

By any estimation it was a huge task. Olaf found it somewhat easier in Viken than in the Trøndelag, where in the winter of 1017 one of his earls was killed in a cross-border raid by Swedes. The people of Viken, and in general in the south, were better acquainted with Christianity than those in the north; the ports of the region were busy with Anglo-Saxon, Flemish and Danish traders, and even some Viking raiders had been tamed, as it were, by wintering in Christian lands.

In the winter of 1018 Olaf started out to inspect Uppland, the extensive region between Viken and the Trøndelag, where every third year a king was expected to make an extended stay in order to keep in touch with local problems and issues and, in an age before mass media, keep himself visible and accessible to his people. Here, according to Snorri, we perceive a rather unexpected side of Olaf, at first glance far from the idealized portrait the *Passion* paints of him. In the remote and heavily wooded area of Vingulmark, where he stopped first, Olaf's overriding concern was whether its inhabitants had become Christians or not; beside that, all other issues paled. And when he found that some of the locals remained stubbornly heathen, '[He] took the matter so zealously that he drove some out of the country, mutilated others of hands or feet, or stung their eyes out; hung up some; cut down some with the sword; but let none go unpunished who did not serve God.'

This, it must be remembered, was many centuries before the appearance of the modern doctrine of 'freedom of religion' familiar to us now. The Christian faith was just too important and vital to be left to the whims of individuals. Harsh measures were necessary, in Will Durant's words, 'to prevent fools from destroying the moral edifice built upon religious belief'. Olaf's approach was Hobbesian in that he believed 'the sovereign must also control the religion of his people, for this, when taken to heart, can be a disruptively explosive force.'

Olaf had with him 300 well-trained armed men to enforce his orders, and with these he proceeded to Raumarike, where he found, the farther he went from the coast and from the south, the more heathen the people tended to be. Though he made converts here, too, he also meted out harsh penalties to the heathen holdouts. Inevitably, the local lords (termed 'kings' by Snorri as they considered themselves independent rulers) became alarmed; daily reports reached them of Olaf's progress and the results of his proselytizing, which ran directly counter to their interests. It remains unclear whether it was Christianity *per se* they distrusted, or whether they feared losing power and influence to a centralizing national monarch; it was probably a bit of both. Five of these local rulers met at Ringsaker in Hedemark; their line appears to have been that Olaf was going around killing, mutilating and exiling their subjects, and that it just had to stop.

One of the rulers, Hrorek, gave an I-told-you-so speech: he had warned of this very thing before, but had not been heeded. His view was that it was now too late to stop Olaf, as he had an elite force with him; others, however, disagreed and urged a fight. Then Gudrod, described as a 'valley-king', remarked sarcastically that five rulers, 'none of less high birth than Olaf', couldn't get up the resolve to oppose him. Had they not helped him gain power in the past? True, their own 'kingdoms' were essentially Olaf's gifts, but if he were to trample over them, 'we shall never bear our heads in safety while Olaf is alive.' This energized the assembly, which agreed to stay at Ringsaker to coordinate action while sending out agents to spy on Olaf's movements in Raumarike.

However, security among the conspiracy was atrocious, as 'everyone has some friends even among his enemies'. One of those who attended a conference of the 'kings' was one Ketil of Ringanes, who after returning home at Lake Miosen thoughtfully ate his dinner, then gathered twenty of his trusted servants into a boat that Olaf had given him; after rowing all night they disembarked on the other side of the lake, and a short walk took them to where Olaf was staying. When Ketil delivered his message that the local lords were up in arms against the king, Olaf wasted no time in ordering a mass requisition of all the available riding horses in the region and all the boats on the lake. He then spent some time in church, and after his midday meal the commandeered boats were rowed up. Late in the afternoon, Olaf and about 400 men began rowing over the calm water to Ringsaker, which they reached just before dawn the following day.

The 'kings' were still asleep as Olaf and Ketil, evading the sentries, quietly had their quarters surrounded; when the sleepers awoke, they found themselves prisoners of the king. Olaf's vengeance was swift: Hrorek had his eyes gouged out, and Gudrod his tongue cut out; three others were banished from Norway. Olaf treated some of the lords' followers leniently, while others he 'mutilated'. Ottar the Black could now exult in verse:

> The king who dwelt most north
> Tongueless must wander forth…
> King Olaf now rules o'er
> What five kings ruled before.

The suppression of the five 'kings' cemented Olaf's royal authority over most of Norway, and would have made him feel rather more secure in his movements. After exacting tribute from Hedeland he returned to his territory in the west, where his mother Åsta held a lavish banquet for him.

Olaf's stepfather, Sigurd Syr, had just died. During Olaf's visit to his mother, we are told, she brought out her three young sons by Sigurd Syr

– Olaf's half-brothers. The king took the two eldest on his knees and pretended to scowl at them, which made them cry. Then the youngest, three-year-old Harald, was brought before him; Olaf made a frightening face again, but little Harald was unfazed. Then, apparently to further test the child's mettle, Olaf pulled some of his hair; Harald responded by tugging the king's whiskers. 'You're going to be vengeful someday, my boy', the king said prophetically.

Snorri's account includes a description of the following day, when Olaf and his mother were strolling around the farm. His two elder half-brothers were busy playing at farming, building toy houses and barns; Harald, by contrast, was playing with chips of wood floating in a pool, and when he was asked what they represented, he said they were warships. There followed a talk between Olaf and the three boys, in which the two eldest dreamed of owning much land and livestock – the pursuits of peace – but Harald said he wanted servants, 'as many as would eat up my brothers' cows in a single meal'. That boy, Olaf said to his mother, was destined to be a king. There is definitely a biblical flavour to this story, calling to mind as it does the tale of Joseph and his brothers, and it would be legitimate to speculate whether it was directly inspired by that. On the other hand, it shows Olaf to be a shrewd judge of character.

Starting in 1019 King Olaf was able to reign over Norway, in name at least. In the words of the *Passion*: 'Idols were smashed, sacred groves felled, temples overthrown. Priests were ordained and churches built... In many parts of that land the host of unbelievers were silenced, nor daring to murmur.' From Gautelven in the south to Finnmark in the north, from the islands in the west to the Swedish frontier in the east, in the Trøndelag and Uppland Norway had a single effective monarch. In fact the model could well have been that of neighbouring Sweden. Olof Sköttkonung, notwithstanding his fierce hatred of Olaf Haraldsson, was himself a baptized Christian, though we remain unsure of why this could not reconcile him to the Norwegian. Right after describing Olaf's reunion with his mother at the farm, Snorri launches into an account of developments in Sweden, pointing out that already that country had several bishoprics as well as a more or less democratic local administration system.

Olaf sailed with an army to the north; with him also was Hrorek, the rebellious chieftain whom Olaf had blinded. It is unclear why Olaf kept Hrorek with him, making sure that he was well housed, served and fed; perhaps his essential good nature underestimated the threat from his enemies and he hoped somehow by kind treatment to keep Hrorek loyal. Hrorek himself made himself quite unpleasant in the court, growling at people and beating his servant boys. One day he would get roaring drunk and be the life of the party, while another day he would stay morosely silent for long periods of time. Olaf appointed one of Hrorek's relations, named Svein, to serve the embittered ex-chieftain. Hrorek complained to Svein that his life was hard to bear, being blind and forced to live on the mercy of him who had blinded him. Svein was swayed by the words and agreed to Hrorek's proposal to assassinate the king: Hrorek would be the brains, and Svein would be the hitman, to be rewarded with an earldom, with Hrorek as king.

The plan backfired badly. Svein, dagger concealed, waited for Olaf to emerge from his mansion to go to Vespers, but according to Snorri, 'he walked quicker than Svein expected'. Something in the king's manner must have totally unnerved Svein, for the would-be-assassin turned pale and stood paralysed. 'Will you betray me?' the king asked, indicating that he possibly knew something was afoot. Svein threw down his dagger and the cloak he was concealing it under and fell at Olaf's feet, crying, 'All is in God's hands and yours, King!' Olaf had Svein arrested on the spot, had Hrorek's sleeping quarters moved far away from his own, and set two courtiers to keep a close watch on him.

It is worth pausing for a moment at this striking scene from the *Heimskringla*, where Olaf suddenly takes on an almost Christ-like quality. It could almost have been taken from the arresting scene in the Gospels, where Christ is betrayed by Judas in the Garden of Gethsemane, and therefore it is legitimate to ask whether it actually was. Of course, the question is impossible to answer, though we may assume without too much risk that Snorri, writing in the thirteenth century, was certainly steeped in the Christian story. His sources, many unknown to us, must have transmitted the report of the occasion, which Snorri perceived as authentic. We cannot tell, however, whether Olaf Haraldsson at this stage actually emitted the beginnings of a saintly aura – witness the account of Svein's turning deathly pale when he gazed into the king's face – or whether Snorri, long after the fact, chose to put this interpretation on the occasion.

Hrorek had not given up. One of his unobtrusive hangers-on was a man called Fin the Little, probably a Finn, as his name indicates. Fin, described as a very fast runner and competent archer, often did errands for Hrorek, but always in a way that escaped the attention of the guards. In the spring of 1018 Fin would disappear for several days at a time, without arousing any suspicion. At that time Olaf moved to Tønsberg on the south coast, not far from where the Battle of Nesjar had been fought; a lot of merchant ships had just put in, and the people were merry. One evening Hrorek, quite drunk, staggered into his lodgings and was served a strong soup of 'mead with herbs' by Fin; this soup seems to have put everyone to sleep except Hrorek and Fin, who were now free to execute their plan.

In the middle of the night Hrorek said he wanted to relieve himself in the outdoor latrine, and woke his two guards to accompany him. What followed was an elaborate piece of theatre: as the guards waited, a voice came out of the darkness shouting, 'Cut down that devil!' followed by a crash like a body falling. Hrorek told both his guards to go and break up what sounded like a drunken brawl. The guards turned away from the latrine to investigate, and were promptly cut down – the 'noise' had been a diversionary trap. Hrorek then assembled a dozen of his cronies, including Fin the Little, got into a boat waiting on the shore, and rowed away into the night.

Hrorek was not the only one who got up in the night to relieve himself. Sigvat the skald was another. He and his boy servant were just descending from the raised latrine when he slipped on the steps, put a hand down to steady himself, and found that the steps were wet. He chuckled, thinking that it was urine from all the others who had imbibed a little too much that night. Back in Sigvat's quarters, his servant gave one look at him and said, 'What's all that blood? Have you hurt yourself?' By the light of the room, Sigvat saw that the wetness on his hand was blood. He roused the king's standard-bearer, Thord Folason, and went out with him with a torch; they found the trail of blood from the latrine and the bodies of the two guards. The king, of course, needed to be told at once, but no-one would dare wake him. Thord said it would be better if the king were informed of the killings in the morning, but Sigvat feared that the killers would be too far away by then.

A compromise solution was decided: Sigvat went to the church and told the bell-ringer to toll the bells for the souls of the slain. The bells woke Olaf, who wondered why it was time for Matins already; Thord told him what had happened, and Olaf called an immediate meeting of the court, sending out search parties for the killers. One of the parties, consisting of thirty men headed by Thorer Lange, set off by boat and at dawn spotted Hrorek's two boats. A mad chase ensued; Thorer gradually caught up with Hrorek, whose boats turned towards the shore. Hrorek's men leaped ashore but the blind Hrorek himself had no choice because of his condition to remain in his boat and be captured.

Of the men on shore, Fin the Little shot an arrow at his pursuers, hitting Thorer in the stomach and fatally wounding him. Thorer's body was rowed back to Tønsberg, as was Hrorek, who was placed under close custody. Hrorek was reportedly in good spirits for some days or weeks afterwards, and his intentions became clear on Ascension Day, when Hrorek was seated next to Olaf in the church (one wonders how even then the king could trust him); Hrorek at one point put his hand on Olaf's shoulder, remarking how finely dressed he was for the occasion. In fact, Hrorek wanted to find out whether the king was wearing armour, and apparently he wasn't.

'The festival is in remembrance that Jesus Christ ascended to heaven from earth,' Olaf reminded him. Hrorek retorted that he didn't understand much about Christianity anyway. At the close of the service the king stood and bowed before the altar, his cloak hanging down behind the shoulders. As he did so, Hrorek sprang up and slashed at him with a short sword; but as he was blind, he missed, only ripping the cloak. In a fury, Hrorek struck again blindly, but he was quickly overpowered and seized. Naturally, Olaf's courtiers asked him why he was taking such a mortal risk by keeping this murderous dissident alive in his company and called for his immediate execution.

Olaf disagreed on the grounds that as Hrorek was in fact a distant relation of his, he didn't want to sully his reputation by putting him to death; and besides, he was still one of the five Uppland 'kings' whom he had overcome. If we accept this explanation, then it indicates that Olaf was very concerned about his reputation; he didn't want to be known as an arbitrary tyrant, even when sorely provoked. Perhaps he had in mind the fate of Olaf Tryggvason, whose foes had multiplied and cut short his reign and life. He may have believed that if he continued to show a degree of magnanimity to Hrorek, he might somehow earn the ex-chieftain's loyalty. But it was clear that something had to be done about this man.

In Olaf's court at the time of Hrorek's attempt on his life was an influential Icelander, 'a far-travelled man' named Thorarin Nefiulfson, described by Snorri as remarkably misshapen and ugly, though of good social manners and a sound mind. Snorri inserts a humorous episode in which Thorarin, who was in Tønsberg fitting out a merchant ship and a guest of the king, slept alongside other royal guests in the king's sleeping quarters. Early one morning Olaf awoke before the rest and noticed that one of Thorarin's feet stuck out from his bedclothes; it was a fascinatingly ugly foot and he stared at it for some time, musing to himself, 'I don't think an uglier foot can be found in this merchant town.' At that point Thorarin, awoke, said he would wager that there was. A friendly bet was thus made, so Thorarin simply pulled his other, equally ugly, foot (which also lacked a toe) from under the blankets. But Olaf said that wasn't fair, as the first foot had five toes, thus possessing more of a quota of ugliness than the four-toed one. So Olaf won the bet, and by that was entitled to ask a favour of his guest. The favour was:

'Take Hrorek and deliver him to Leif Eirikson in Greenland.'

'I've never been to Greenland', Thorarin said.

'You're a well-travelled man. Now's your chance to go there.'

By his albeit reluctant obedience to the king, Thorarin was made an official courtier. Hrorek was bundled onto Thorarin's ship when it was ready, and there must have been huge sighs of relief in Tønsberg. The ship sailed around the south coast of Iceland to make for Greenland, but storms blew the ship off course, with the result that it put in at Breijafjord in Iceland in the early autumn of 1018. For about three years Hrorek was passed among various leading households until he sickened and died; even then he earned some renown as 'the only king whose bones rest in Iceland'.

Chapter 7

The Swedish Princess

While Olaf was busy maintaining order in his kingdom he also had to give some thought to foreign policy, which in his case meant maintaining relations with neighbouring Sweden and keeping a cautious eye on the doings of King Cnut in England, who never ceased to consider himself the rightful sovereign of Norway.

Sweden was the refuge of Svein Håkonarson, holed up in the court of Olof Sköttkonung and chafing at the bit. Olof suggested that Svein stay in Sweden to live a life of lordly leisure as his vassal, and enjoy the fruits of large estates that could be his if he wished. But Svein preferred to claw back his Norwegian patrimony; he had a scheme to infiltrate himself and his men over the mountains into the Trøndelag, but before he could do that he needed money and resources, and so decided to employ the rest of the summer raiding the Baltic coasts. But after a few successful weeks raiding Russia in the summer of 1016, he had sickened and died on his return to Sweden in September.

The good news of Svein's demise reached Olaf as he was rebuilding his base at Nidaros. Though Svein's supporters continued to trickle into the region, the much-vaunted support for him among the locals appeared to evaporate almost overnight. The locals wanted a leader; if it couldn't be Svein, then it had to be Olaf. The speed of the switch in allegiance could argue for the fact that Svein's supporters had likely feared rather than liked him, and Olaf's generous reputation made it easy for them to accept Olaf as king, which they did en masse when Olaf toured the Trøndelag in the autumn and returned to winter, now more confidently, in Nidaros at the end of 1016.

Then there was Cnut, always something of an unknown quantity. The motives behind Cnut's decision to become a Christian remain unclear, though sources such as Adam of Bremen assure us that the conversion was sincere. Just twenty-two years old when he became king, he was given the baptized name Lambert, though he rarely if ever used it. He conspicuously

Olaf pulls down London Bridge, woodcut by Morris Meredith Williams in Eleanor Means Hull, *The Northmen in Britain* (1913).

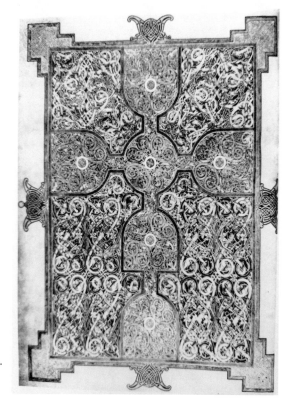

Title page of the *Lindisfarne Gospels* (c.700). (*British Museum, reproduced in H.W. Janson,* History of Art)

The iconic Oseberg ship, the prime restored example of a Viking longship, Viking Ship Museum, Oslo. (*Author's photo*)

Animal-head stern post from a Viking ship, Viking Ship Museum, Oslo. (*Nike Morgan*)

Left: St Anskar. Copy of painting by Hans Bornemann (1457), Church Trinitatis, Hamburg. (*Public domain*)

Right: St Edmund. Anonymous medieval depiction. (*Wikipedia*)

Olaf Tryggvason statue, Trondheim, by Paweł Szubert. (*Wikipedia*)

Wooden statue of St Olaf at Austevoll, Norway. (*WikiCommons*)

Coin of Olaf II dated to his reign.
(*Wikipedia*)

Images on church door at Hardemo, depicting key
moments in St Olaf's life, including Stiklestad, lower
right. (*Wikipedia*)

Håkon the Good (seated) being attacked by an unknown assailant. Canvas by Peter Nicolai Arbo.
(*Public domain*)

Geiranger Fjord near Valldal. (*Adobe Stock*)

St Olave stained glass window, St Olave's Church, Hart Street, London. (*John Salmon, WikiCommons*)

Olaf falls at Stiklestad. Painting by Peter Nicolai Arbo, 1860. (*WikiCommons*)

St Olaf's monument (*Olafsstøtta*) at Stiklestad.
(*Siri Iversen/public domain*)

Greek Orthodox icon of St Olaf
(Olavios). (*saintsfeastfamily.com*)

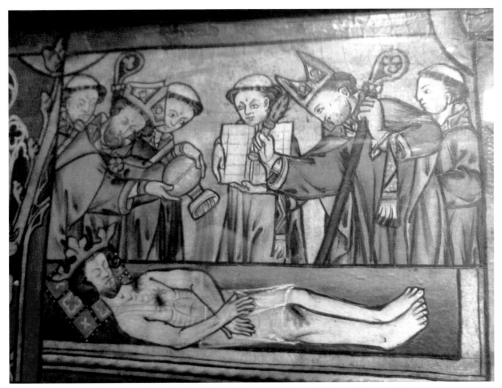

Bishop Grimkell proclaims Olaf a saint. Nidaros Cathedral panel. (*WikiCommons*)

Nidaros Cathedral at Trondheim. (*DXR via WikiCommons*)

St Olaf and the sea monster. Painting by
Pius Weloński, 1893, in San Carlo al Corso,
Rome. (*Abobe Stock*)

The Norwegian royal coat of arms, with
lion holding King Olaf's axe symbol.
(*Public domain*)

helped fund the rebuilding of churches destroyed in the recent conflict, in both Britain and France. On his accession he retained Wulfstan, the Bishop of York, in his post as a spiritual (and perhaps political) adviser. Inheriting the Danish throne in 1019, Cnut solidified its Christian character – which incidentally helped curb German political influence connected with the Hamburg-Bremen archbishopric. Under Cnut the Christianization of the Norse peoples was given a strong push forward.

The progressive Christianization of Britain, however, was never a risk-free process. People quickly tire of moral preachings if the rewards are not immediate, and thus there was always the risk that old heathen practices would again raise their heads. Especially in the Danelaw, and among the more recent Danish settlers, those practices persisted, despite severe measures by Cnut to outlaw them. Wulfstan himself preached sadly that faith in Christ was already waning among the English, apparently because He did not at once appear with flaming sword to vanquish the Vikings.

The climax of the resistance to Cnut's rule in England had occurred on 18 October 1016 at Ashington in Essex, where Edmund Ironside, Ethelred's successor, and Eadric Streona were put to flight by the Danes in a hillside encounter. Though Eadric was severely censured by the *Anglo-Saxon Chronicle* for leading his Herefordshire and South Shropshire men in flight from the battle (the implication of treachery is strong), we find him at Edmund's side during truce negotiations on the isle of Alney in the Severn estuary. Possibly Edmund wanted to preserve Eadric as having influence with Cnut. Edmund, whose cognomen of Ironside had been earned by his fighting qualities, did not have long to enjoy the peace; on 30 November he paid a common penalty of defeat by being murdered – according to tradition while sitting on the toilet – in London (some accounts say the west bank of the Severn).

Through 1017 Cnut consolidated his kingdom, financing its organization, and that of his large army, by fearsome taxation. To underscore his dominance, and symbolize a supposed continuity with the defunct old regime, he moved his seat of government to Wessex, appointed Eadric Streona his vassal ruler of Mercia, and handed Northumbria to his brother-in-law Eirik Håkonarson, the brother of Olaf's arch-foe Svein; thus Trondheim and its environs never ceased being of interest to Cnut, who could not help but see a potential rival in Olaf II Haraldsson for hegemony over the Norse peoples and territories.

Eadric Streona's time of triumph was brief. The wily noble may have helped Cnut win power by his treachery at Ashington, but a traitor was a traitor, and there was no telling if and when his new chief of Mercia would turn on Cnut. Therefore the king had Eadric beheaded, both as a precautionary measure and a salutary lesson for nobles henceforth to be faithful to their sovereigns. Another security measure was to get rid of two of the late Ethelred's grandsons; he sent them to King Olof Sköttkonung in Sweden with instructions for them to be quietly eliminated (but Olof sent them on to the Hungarian court for safety).

Cnut was well aware that he had not succeeded naturally to the English throne but had usurped it, and accordingly he took care to gather about him a strong praetorian guard, the *Thingalid*, made up of reliable men mainly from Denmark and Sweden. Yet he was sagacious enough to realize that though the Anglo-Saxon and Viking elements in the British population had assimilated into each other in large part, the mixing was not yet thorough enough if he was to consider himself a legitimate English king. He signalled his intentions in that direction in a most dramatic way: Ethelred had not been a year in his grave when Cnut summoned the late king's widow Emma from Normandy and married her. The power aspects of the marriage were enhanced by the fact that Emma was the sister of Duke Richard II of Normandy, himself a member of a Norse line. Though we are not told what Emma herself thought of the arrangement, with her Cnut had a son, Harthacnut, and a daughter, Gunnhild, who would wed a German emperor. (Cnut also had children via his longtime Northumbrian mistress Aelfgifu.)

Cnut knew Olaf well from the time when the teenaged Norwegian had lived at court. And what he knew did not make him comfortable. A hagiography issued by the Orthodox Church hints that Olaf showed signs of unusual greatness even then, when Cnut's bishop Sigfrid (later Saint Sigfrid of Sweden) called Olaf a king and appeared to rate him above Cnut himself. When the bishop received a severe dressing-down, he replied, according to Snorri:

> It is true, my lord, that [Olaf] has no land here, and he wears no crown of gold or silver. Nay, rather he is chosen and crowned by the highest Lord and Ruler, the king of all kings, the one almighty God, to rule and govern that kingdom to which he is born... All the

people of Norway, and the lands tributary to it... shall have reason to remember and keep in mind this pillar and support of God's Christendom, who will root out all brambles and weeds from God's field and vineyard.

Cnut, as young and ambitious rulers would be wont to do, bridled at this; his own feelings of insecurity came out as it seemed to him that he was definitely second fiddle to this precocious Norwegian youth. What rankled also was that Olaf dressed himself more sumptuously than the king at table and always seemed to have the best food and wine automatically served him.

When told all this, Sigfrid retorted that such an image was merely surface, and that Olaf was really a decent fellow:

It is true, my lord, that Olaf wears a shirt of silk, but he wears a hair-cloth under the shirt... You will always see that when King Olaf takes his seat and the choicest foods are brought before him, there is a mound in the place where he is wont to sit. There is hidden a cripple, and it is he that eats the dainties, but Olaf eats salt and bread. There is also a vessel of water, and this Olaf drinks, but it is the cripple that drinks out of the wine-cup.

What are we to make of this story? There is, admittedly, a credibility problem here. If it were literally true what Sigfrid said, that a poor cripple was hiding under the seat where Olaf was placed, it surely would have been noticed by everyone including Cnut. We may surmise that the bishop spoke metaphorically, meaning that under the sumptuous surface of Olaf lay a humble and selfless soul. Literal or not, all the words did, of course, were enrage Cnut, who banished first Olaf and then Sigfrid.

One of the matters Olaf gave his mind to incessantly, as a key principle of what we now would call foreign policy, was the state of the Christian faith in the other Norse lands, such as Iceland, the Orkneys, Shetland and the Faeroes, whose relative isolation put their fledgling Christianity at risk from heathen recursion. In the words of the *Passion* he 'strove with unflagging urgency to convert the people he was appointed by divine providence to govern'. What he heard from those territories was far from encouraging, but he never could forget that his prime objective was to consolidate the faith in Norway itself, where the opposition was considerable.

Early in Olaf's reign Olof Sköttkonung of Sweden sent the brothers Thorgaut and Asgaut and two dozen attendants over the mountains into the fuzzy frontier area, where the delineation of royal authority on either side was uncertain, to claim back taxes from some of his communities. These communities agreed to do so only if they were not already paying tax to Olaf. This refusal of double taxation appears to have been uniform wherever Thorgaut and Asgaut went, with the result that little, if anything, could be taken back to Sweden. At Stjørdal, not far north of Trondheim, the local assembly refused to even meet them. Asgaut suggested that they meet Olaf himself at Nidaros to talk out the issue.

The brothers called on Olaf as he was at table, and were told to return the following day when, after attending his usual morning service, Olaf heard them out. Olaf's reaction was to diplomatically inform the emissaries that he, not Olof the Swede, was the king of Norway, and that Olof would just have to accept that. Thorgaut replied by warning Olaf of his king's 'wrath' if he learned of Olaf's attitude. His proposal was nothing more or less than for Olaf to submit to Olof Sköttkonung's suzerainty, and be satisfied with that favour shown to him. The exchange, as told by Snorri, strongly suggests that Thorgaut and Asgaut were on an espionage rather than an ostensible revenue-gathering mission. Olaf's final words to the brothers were soothingly diplomatic: he advised them to inform Olof that in the spring he was willing to meet the Swede on the frontier and negotiate a peace on equal, rather than subject, terms.

Thorgaut and Asgaut returned to their lodgings, but apparently wished to make another try at changing Olaf's mind. The king, at table at the time of their second visit, refused them admittance. At this point Thorgaut decided to go home and admit failure, but Asgaut elected to move south through Norway to stir up some sedition. When Olaf heard of it he sent men to hunt down Asgaut and that portion of the entourage that went with him; discovered at Stein, they were bound and hanged on a cliff overlooking a fjord mouth 'so that they could be seen by those who travelled the usual sea-way'. Thorgaut heard of this on his way back to Sweden, and informed his king who, as befitted the son of Sigrid the Haughty, exploded in rage.

Olaf knew that he now faced a distinct threat from Olof, and in the spring of 1016 gathered together a force in the Trøndelag for a demonstration of strength in the frontier areas. This could well have been a feint, as Olaf himself moved in the opposite direction, by sea down the west coast. He found time to send a message to Iceland, via some Icelandic traders, for that land's rulers to align their laws with Christianity and revoke what was contrary. The tour proved largely successful, as we are told that the king called Thing after Thing in the districts he stopped at, ordering the laws of each to be stripped of their heathen and pagan elements that had lingered through the toleration of the local earls. Toleration was now no longer tolerated. There were mass baptisms by the sea. But Olaf had a tougher time dealing with the people of the mountainous hinterlands, who hewed to the old heathen culture, 'For', writes Snorri, 'when the common man is left to himself, the faith he has been taught in his childhood is that which has the strongest hold over his inclination.'

In spring 1017 Olaf contacted a wealthy trader named Gudleik Gerske who was familiar with Russia, and asked to go into a partnership with him in the hope of being able to import Russian luxury goods into the kingdom – and perhaps more than incidentally, earn him another increment of goodwill at home. Gudleik agreed, was provided with ample funds, and set out into the Baltic. As the summer progressed Gudleik bought a considerable quantity of luxury clothing for the king, plus furs and high-quality tableware. But word of his mission had leaked out to the Swedish coastal communities, and when Gudleik was on his way back, and delayed by contrary winds, he was met at sea by none other than Thorgaut, the Swedish king's emissary who had tried unsuccessfully to claw back tribute from some of Olaf's domains.

In the ensuing battle Gudleik was killed and his men scattered. Thorgaut seized the precious cargo and sailed off, intending to give the sumptuous clothing to Olof Sköttkonung in lieu of the tribute he had failed to collect earlier. News of the setback was quick to reach Norwegian territory; within a short time Eyvind Urarhorn gave chase with his own ships and overtook Thorgaut 'among the Swedish isles' (probably in the island complex east of Stockholm). Eyvind won that encounter, killing Thorgaut and most of his men, and retrieving the costly items which were duly delivered to Olaf in the autumn.

Despite the persistent hostility of Olof Sköttkonung, Olaf appears to have genuinely wished for peace with his Swedish neighbour. He had an ally in the person of Swedish Earl Ragnvald Ulfsson, who ruled a domain in the southern borderlands (Gautland) near the Gaut River, and especially the earl's wife Ingebjorg, the sister of Olaf Tryggvason. Snorri drops into his narrative a few tantalizing hints that Ingebjorg's liking for Olaf may have been more than merely political: 'She was quite zealous of giving Olaf every kind of help, and made it a matter of her deepest interest.' But we perhaps should not read too much into these lines, as Snorri goes on to say that Ingebjorg was keenly conscious that Olaf was a legitimate successor to the Norwegian royal lineage and by that fact could be expected to automatically give him her support. She had never forgiven Olof Sköttkonung for his role in her brother's murder. Olaf and Earl Ragnvald met at the Gaut River and discussed how Norwegian-Swedish relations could be restored, to the benefit of both the Viken and Gautland regions. Ragnvald appears to have had the authority to agree to a truce to last until the following summer, to allow trade to grow and underpin a degree of prosperity which, hopefully, would encourage a longer period of peace.

That was easier said than done. Olof Sköttkonung despised his Norwegian counterpart so deeply that he could not even hear his name without flying into a fury and insulting him in vile terms. One of the milder ones was 'Olaf the Thick'; the sobriquet appears often in Snorri's story, though it almost certainly referred to Olaf's body shape rather than his mental capacities. However, the majority of people in Viken appear to have sincerely wanted a lasting peace with Sweden, though no-one yet had the confidence to broach the subject with Olaf. Meanwhile, those of the king's entourage who had lands in the north chafed at having to stay in Viken and neglect their domains. Perhaps pressured by these, Bjorn the king's marshal one day got up the nerve in the king's hall, 'speaking in the name of the people', to suggest a more permanent settlement with the Swedes so they could all go home. Those present applauded him.

Olaf's reply to Bjorn, however, sounds curiously equivocal: 'Undertake the mission yourself and enjoy its benefits; and if it involves danger, then you'll share it.' Then Olaf stood up and went to church. Was this a shirking of royal responsibility, a buck-passing? Olaf probably did not wish to be seen as the initiator of an attempt at a rapprochement with Sweden; and after all, if the mission failed, it would not be his fault. Bjorn, for his part, did not expect that reaction. In fact he was distinctly unhappy at being given the mission, fearing the dangers it might involve.

An Icelander noble named Hjalte Skeggjason, recently arrived at court, noticed Bjorn's downcast face and asked him what the problem was.

'Well', Hjalte philosophically remarked after Bjorn told him, 'if you enjoy a king's honours, you might get respect, but then your life is often in danger.' But he added that he believed the mission would work as King Olaf always seemed to be successful in everything he did.

'Would you come with me?' Bjorn asked hopefully. Hjalte, already having formed a close friendship with Bjorn, agreed on the spot. A few days later, when the mission was ready and the horses saddled, Bjorn presented himself before the king to ask instructions about exactly what message he was to convey to Olof Sköttkonung. Olaf had carefully worded the message, avoiding all mention of conflicts of interests and stressing the benefits that peace and trade would bring to the Norwegians and Swedes in the borderlands. The heart of the proposal was that Olaf and Olof agree to a fixed boundary separating their domains, and quietly lay other claims to rest, such as reparations for losses in recent clashes.

As Bjorn walked to his horse the king handed him a gold-mounted sword that had been a present from Earl Ragnvald, and a gold ring that he was to give the earl, whose help he could thus count on. Olaf showed some surprise when Hjalte told him he was going, too, but agreed readily. At Earl Ragnvald's court the mission was cordially received, especially by Ingebjorg, who could count on a web of kinship and friendship ties connecting Olaf with Hjalte and going back to Olaf Tryggvason. There followed, says Snorri, some relaxation and feasting – until the moment Bjorn produced the gold-mounted sword and gold ring, explaining his mission. Ragnvald was aghast. 'What have you done, Bjorn, that the King wishes thy death?' Going to Olof Sköttkonung, he said, was tantamount to a suicide mission. Olof, he warned, was 'too proud for any man to speak to him in anything he is angry at'. Especially, he would have added, on the subject of Olaf Haraldsson.

Bjorn might well have gulped at this, but put on a brave face. The only encouraging factor he could cite, however, was the fact that Olaf so far had been generally successful in whatever serious task he tackled. Besides, he was now duty-bound to do the job and would 'not turn back before I have brought to [Olof's] ears every word that King Olaf told me to say to him'. Ingebjorg came to Bjorn's defence, encouraging him to take the risk. But Ragnvald still hesitated to place his own seal of approval on the mission, and asked Bjorn and his entourage to stay with him, which they did for some considerable time, as Bjorn seized on any excuse for not hastening to the king of Sweden.

But the mission could not be put off indefinitely. Bjorn knew that some time he would have to bite the bullet, and often spoke about it with Ingebjorg. At last Hjalte could stand it no longer, and suggested that he, rather than Bjorn, journey to Olof as Hjalte was not a Norwegian but an Icelander, with whom the Swedes had no quarrel, and besides, Olof was known to have among his entourage two Icelandic skalds who happened to be his personal acquaintances. 'From them', said Hjalte, 'I can find out what I can about the Swedish king, and based on that, might figure out a way of approaching him.' Ingebjorg promptly fitted out Hjalte for travel, giving him funds and two Gautland men as escorts and assistants.

At Olof's court Hjalte first met his Icelandic skald friends, Gissur and Ottar the Black, who at once informed the king. Curiously, however, according to Snorri's saga, Hjalte spent quite a long time at Olof's court without revealing his mission or who sent him; as far as Olof was concerned, he was just a high-ranking Icelander and friend of his skalds, who deserved hospitality. Some time passed pleasantly as Hjalte earned much respect in court circles, but still he kept his true mission secret, until one day he got up the courage to deliver Olaf's message in the company of Olof's skalds.

Hjalte seems to have thought that Olof needed sweetening up first, so he told the king he had brought with him the landing tax that, as an Icelander, he should have paid to the Norwegians on arrival at Norway but instead had kept to give to the Swedish king. The money amounted to ten silver marks, which he placed before Olof. The king, pleased at this, generously remitted the gift back to Hjalte. This was diplomacy of a very careful sort. Olof Sköttkonung still had no idea of Hjalte's real mission as he built up a friendship with him. Hjalte's next target was Olof's teenage daughter Ingegerd, who enters the story sitting at a table drinking 'with many men'. He conveyed greetings from Ingebjorg, and joined the drinking party. Ingegerd was taken by Hjalte's candidness – he seems to have been a genial and open-hearted character – and he quickly gained her confidence to be able to reveal, at last, his true mission: what was the chance, he asked, of her father agreeing to a reconciliation with

Olaf Haraldsson? Not a chance, replied Ingegerd, and for the time being, that was that.

Hjalte's next opportunity came during a meeting with Olof when the latter was rather the worse for alcohol. He casually mentioned that it was a pity that someone like himself, Hjalte, had to traverse the hostile land of Norway after an ocean voyage, with all its hazards, simply to enjoy the amenities of the 'most magnificent' monarch of the north. That was laying it on a bit thick, and then he took the plunge: 'Why is there no-one to bring proposals for a peace between you and King Olaf the Thick? I heard much in Norway, and in west Gautland, of the general desire that this peace should have taken place.'

Olof must have frowned here, but Hjalte was now too far into it to turn back.

'It has been told me for truth, as the words of the king of Norway that he earnestly desires to be reconciled to you... He feels how much less his power is than yours [and] it is even said that he even intends to pay court to your daughter Ingegerd, and that would lead to a useful peace.'

Hjalte here emerges as a first-rate diplomat: patient, tactful, economical with the truth when necessary, and always careful to cultivate the people he is among. But Olof Sköttkonung wasn't having any. 'That fat fellow shall not be called king in my court,' he retorted, and proceeded to harangue Hjalte to the effect that he, Olof, was the tenth king of his line in Uppsala; he continued with a long history of the relations among Denmark, Norway and Sweden, concluding that by rights Norway was a Swedish possession and any attempt by a king to proclaim it independent was ludicrous. 'So, Hjalte,' Olof snapped, 'don't mention that subject in my presence ever again.'

Like a good diplomat, Hjalte shut up but didn't give up, but consulted Ingegerd about what he ought to do next. Ingegerd agreed to make one last try to change her stubborn father's mind, catching him at a time when he was in a good mood. As we first saw her sitting drinking among the men of her father's court, we may surmise that she was of ready speech and sound mind, and fully able to conduct a serious conversation. Trying to dominate Norway wasn't really a good idea, she suggested to Olof: 'It is a poor country, difficult to reach, and the people dangerous, for the men there would rather have anyone for king but you.' Whether these words represented her own thoughts or were suggested by Hjalte is immaterial, as Olof's enraged response went beyond anything he had said before:

> I shall issue a proclamation to all Swedes to assemble for an expedition, and go to their ships before the ice is off the waters; and I will proceed to Norway and lay waste the land with fire and sword, and burn everything, to punish them for their infidelity.

Ingegerd delivered the bad news to Hjalte, who tried another tack. Making sure they were out of earshot, Hjalte asked Ingegerd how she felt about becoming engaged to Olaf Haraldsson. This was skating on thin ice indeed. But Ingegerd was intrigued by the proposal, and replied that if Olaf of Norway was as good a man as Hjalte always said he was, then she would have no objection to marrying him. She begged Hjalte to keep the idea under his hat, leaking it only to the skalds Gissur and Ottar. Hjalte sent a letter from Ingeberg back to Earl Ragnvald and Ingebjorg, who received it just before Yuletide.

Meanwhile, developments were occurring on the diplomatic front. The messengers whom Hjalte had sent westward with the encouraging message from Princess Ingegerd reached the estate of Earl Ragnvald. Encouraged by the message they bore, Bjorn, the king's marshal who had been most reluctant to travel to Sweden and who was still staying with Ragnvald, now appears to have gathered together his resolve to carry out the promise he made to the king to go to Olof's court. Ragnvald accordingly got together a sixty-man mission, including Bjorn, which set off over the snowy wastes to Uppsala, the seat of Olof's kingdom. After crossing the frontier Ragnvald arranged for a message to be sent to Ingegerd at her own farm at Ullraker.

Having received the message, Ingegerd secretly prepared for her trip to Ullraker. Hjalte wanted to go with her, but for this he had to justify his sudden departure to Olof. He did it with a burst of flattery, indicating that he had stayed long enough at this brilliant court, and that he would always treasure the experience and sing Olof's praises everywhere. Snorri's account of the exchange, however, leaves a great deal in the air. 'Why are you leaving in such haste and where are you going?' Olof asked.

'I'm riding out to Ullraker with your daughter Ingegerd,' Hjalte truthfully replied. And that, it appears, was that. We have no sign that Olof suspected anything amiss; on the contrary, he may have assumed that his daughter intended to marry and live with Hjalte on her farm, and his final words to Hjalte strongly suggest it.

At Ullraker Ingegerd laid on a lavish feast for Earl Ragnvald and his entourage. There was a discussion lasting several days, in which Ingegerd ruled out any Swedish-Norwegian rapprochement as long as her father kept up his hard line. Ragnvald asked Ingegerd delicately what her reaction would be if Olaf Haraldsson 'paid his addresses' to her – an unmistakable euphemism for a marriage proposal.

'Do you think that would be advisable?' she asked the earl cagily, although she very likely had already made up her mind. Absolutely, said Ragnvald, who went on to tell of Olaf's recent success against the five rebellious chieftains. We are told nothing more of this meeting at Ullraker; when it was over Ragnvald and Hjalte continued on their way to Uppsala. On the way they put up for the night at a local Swedish lord named Thorgny:

> In the high seat sat an old man; and never had Bjorn or his companions seen a man so stout. His beard was so long that it lay upon his knee, and was spread all over his breast... the man, moreover, was handsome and stately in appearance.

Thorgny was also good-natured, and received his visitors with all the hospitality demanded by his class. As was usual, a few days needed to pass before anything as indelicate as a practical purpose could be mentioned, but at length Ragnvald took Thorgny aside and informed him of the purpose of his trip: to mend fences between the Norwegian and Swedish kings, for the benefit of the peoples of both nations. But, suggested Ragnvald, as Olof Sköttkonuing was dead against anything of the sort, the wise Thorgny might be useful as a sounding-board. Thorgny must have furrowed his brow. He quite understood the mission, and probably had nothing against it personally, but he would need to go to Uppsala, consult the Thing, and hopefully soften Olof into at least agreeing to see Ragnvald. In the company of Thorgny, Ragnvald and Bjorn and the rest of the entourage rode on to Uppsala, where the Thing was in session and Olof present.

Snorri gives us a fascinating word-picture of the Thing, where Olof sat 'on a stool' encircled by the members. It appears to have been held in the open air, as some spectators 'stood upon hillocks and heights' to be able to follow the proceedings. When the ordinary business was despatched Bjorn rose and in a loud voice delivered the essence of Olaf's message that the king of Norway was prepared to settle any issues outstanding between him and the king of Sweden, along the lines of the old boundaries. Barely had the words escaped his lips than Olof stood up in a rage and in effect ordered Bjorn to shut up. After some moments of noise and confusion Earl Ragnvald took up the appeal, citing the serious problems that the West Gautlanders, for example, were having – and concluded by revealing Olaf's desire to marry Ingegerd. Olof, intransigent as ever, responded with a long tirade heaping scorn upon Olaf, Ragnvald, and anyone associated with them.

In the stunned silence that followed, Thorgny rose to speak. At first he could hardly make himself heard above the shouts and clangour of weaponry that broke out as listeners rushed closer to hear a most respected elder statesman. Thorgny began by recalling his grandfather's days when King Eirik Eymundson conquered the adjacent lands but 'was not so proud that he would not listen to people'; in Thorgny's father's time there was King Bjorn, who also expanded his territory but at the same time 'it was easy and agreeable to communicate our opinions to him'. Then from family flattery he swung to the attack:

'The king we have now allows no man to presume to talk with him, unless it be what he desires to hear... He wants to have the Norway kingdom laid under him, which no Swedish king before him ever desired, and therewith brings war and distress on many a man.'

There was more. Thorgny directly accused Olof of laziness, declaring outright that it was the will of all the subject nobles that Olof make his peace with 'Olaf the Thick' and give him Ingegerd in marriage. If Olof would agree, the country would be behind him in any eastbound military campaigns he would wish to mount. Lastly, Thorgny went straight for the jugular: 'But if you do not do as we desire, we will now attack thee and put thee to death; for we will no longer suffer law and peace to be disturbed.' Perhaps only someone as old and respected as Thorgny could put his neck on the line like this.

If Olof Sköttkonung had any idea of fighting back, it would have been nipped in the bud by the approving clamour of the entire assembly. Olof admitted defeat; conferring with Thorgny and Ragnvald, he gave the latter the authority to arrange the royal marriage and terms of the peace treaty. Ingegerd, when she received the news, gave Bjorn a fine, gold-embroidered linen cloak to take to Olaf. The momentous result of the Uppsala Thing indicates that Olof Sköttkonung was very much alone in his hostility to the Norwegians, and that once the views of his subjects were aired, on the occasion of Bjorn's and Ragnvald's mission, he realized that they were overwhelmingly against him and had no choice but to back down. The alacrity with which he did back down suggests that subconsciously, perhaps, he had been hoping for a resolution of the issue which his pride alone had prevented him from acknowledging – or, more likely, he was simply playing for time.

Olaf could now proceed in peace with the preparation for his nuptials – though Ingegerd would not be a part of it. Olof Sköttkonung was nothing if not persistent in his malicious obsession with Olaf; despite his being openly threatened with death by Thorgny and a considerable portion of the Swedish nobles, he stalled as long as he could. In the summer of 1018 Olaf and a magnificent retinue sailed along the south Swedish coast to Konungahella, where he expected to find Olof and his own retinue awaiting him. But no-one was there, and no-one could give him any information at all. As Olaf waited, he sent a message to Earl Ragnvald to see if he knew anything; Ragnvald said he would try to find out, speculating that Olof might simply have been too busy with his own affairs to meet the Norwegian king.

Olof had indeed been busy, plotting. Having no intention of giving Ingegerd to his arch-foe, he picked Astrid, one of his three illegitimate daughters by his slave-mistress Edla, to take her place. Astrid had spent her childhood in West Gautland as Olof's wife had behaved badly to all four of her stepchildren (Ingegerd being the only legitimate child). The Swedish nobility knew nothing of this, and fretted at the delay in the wedding arrangements. And so did Ingegerd herself, who quite refused to speak to her father for any reason whatsoever, on account of his harshness. But the canny princess, barely out of her teens, had the wit to guess what was going on. In Snorri's narrative one day when Olof was returning on horseback from a hunt with five game-birds in his catch he joked to his daughter: 'Do you know any king who captured so much game in such a short time?'

Ingegerd's answer came quick and cutting: 'It was better when one morning King Olaf of Norway took five kings.'

Olof jumped from his horse and confronted his daughter: 'However great your love for this man is,' he snarled, 'you will never get him and he will not get you. I'll marry you to some chief who can be my friend.'

Ingegerd promptly sent a mission to Earl Ragnvald with the news that her father had all but broken the peace he had agreed with Olaf. Ragnvald was placed in a very difficult position; he himself was a cousin of Olof Sköttkonung, and moreover, if renewed hostilities should break out, his own region of West Gautland would bear the brunt of the damage. Ragnvald relayed all this to Olaf, who was plunged into a depression. After some days of seclusion he called a high-level conference. An attack on Gautland was considered but rejected on the grounds that the army was not in the required state of readiness; Olaf decided to wait till the following summer, when he would call a general conscription for an offensive against Olof, and be able to enlist more and younger men for the enterprise. With that he disbanded the army and retired to winter quarters at Viken.

During the winter months Olaf would often speak longingly of Ingegerd, who had been denied him by the treachery of his Swedish opposite number. He also must have occasionally wondered, along with a good many of his senior men, on whose side Earl Ragnvald actually was – he was, after all, Olof's kinsman. It was Sigvat, the eager and loyal young skald, who had the idea of putting these concerns to rest by travelling over the snow-covered mountains to Gautland to try to obtain some intelligence from Ragnvald. With two companions he set off in the depth of winter, after composing a poem:

> Sit happy in thy hall, O king!
> Till I come back, and good news bring.

It was a hazardous journey. Besides the bitter weather conditions, they were at constant risk of being waylaid and robbed. When they arrived in Gautland four homesteads, assuming them to be outlaws, refused to admit them on various pretexts before they arrived at Ragnvald's house. The earl gave Sigvat a gold ring for his trouble. We have here a brief mention of Sigvat's 'coal-black' eyes, unusual for Scandinavia and a subject of comment in Ragnvald's household. It was probably during Sigvat's stay in Ragnvald's – a long one, according to the hospitality customs of the time – that the earl received letters from Ingegerd to the effect that Grand

Prince Yaroslav I of Russia had asked for her hand and that her father would most likely agree. As this was being digested Olof's illegitimate daughter Astrid arrived on the premises to great feasting. This of course, was more than mere coincidence. Twenty-year-old Astrid, it was now clear, had been sent as a substitute bride for Olaf in Ingegerd's place, and Ragnvald's task, it appears, was to broker the deal. When the subject was broached, Sigvat could come up with no objection. Astrid, we are told, was all in favour, and so all Sigvat had to worry about now was how to return home and tell King Olaf.

Shortly after Yuletide, Ragnvald Ulfsson and Astrid, accompanied by a force of 120 armed men, rode north to meet Olaf, who in the meantime had prepared a triumphal banquet for them. After the obligatory few days of merriment, Olaf, Ragnvald and Astrid arranged the marriage settlement: Olaf was to receive the same dowry that he would have gained from Ingegerd, and Astrid would receive the same gifts that the king had destined for her half-sister; only the bride would be different. The wedding was duly celebrated, and Earl Ragnvald returned home with the laurels of a difficult diplomatic mission successfully concluded.

But what of Ingegerd? Olof Sköttkonung had decided to give her to Grand Prince Yaroslav, whose realm of Novgorod and Kiev was a strong trading partner of Sweden. Ingegerd had little choice but to agree, albeit reluctantly (as emerges through the lines of Snorri), though in recompense she demanded the district of Ladoga. She also demanded that the trustworthy Earl Ragnvald, who had done so much to push forward the plan for her marriage to Olaf, accompany her to her new home. Olof at first bristled, accusing Ragnvald of treason and threatening to hang him, but in the end gave way to his daughter's entreaties on condition that Ragnvald not set foot in the kingdom again. The earl fitted out a ship with which he took Ingegerd to Novgorod, where she was duly married to Yaroslav to become Grand Princess of Russia. She handed the administration of Ladoga on to Ragnvald (which she had probably intended to do all along) and proceeded to live an admirable life, changing her name to the Greek Irene (Peace). Ingegerd Olofsdotter, the precocious royal Swedish girl whom we first met happily drinking with the men, would live for at least thirty more years with Yaroslav I (the Wise) and produce at least seven members of European and Russian royal houses. She, the granddaughter of Sigrid the Haughty, would end her life in 1050 as Saint Anna of Kiev in the Greek Orthodox Church. In the words of a hymn dedicated to her:

> Disdaining all allurements of vanity and donning the coarse robes of a monastic, O wondrous and sacred Anna, thou gavest thyself over to fasting and prayer, ever entreating Christ thy Master, that He deliver thy people from all want and misfortune.

Her feast days are 10 February and 4 October.

Chapter 8

'Hit it as hard as you can'

King Olaf's marriage to Astrid may have settled the bulk of the differences with Sweden, but some people in the southern borderlands, especially West Gautland, still worried about the effects of a possible conflict. They felt that Olaf was too far away in the north to be able to effectively intervene in time of need. One of the local chiefs, Emund of Skara, travelled to Uppsala to try to divine Olof Sköttkonung's thinking on Gautland. Snorri describes a curious meeting between the two, in which Emund, wanting to lay his case for a more enduring peace before Olof, apparently shies away from being too explicit and speaks in riddles. After Emund left one of Olof's advisers, Freyvid the Deaf, revealed the hidden essence of Emund's speech: namely, that the provinces had now had quite enough of Olof's high-handedness and constant friction with Norway – and moreover, Freyvid added, word had already gone out for the convening of a *Refs-Thing*, something resembling a high-level criminal court, to examine the case against the king.

Freyvid set out for the *Refs-Thing* at Ullaraker, taking with him Olof's twelve-year-old son and heir, Jacob. At Ullaraker Freyvid listened as the delegates appealed for Jacob, 'noble-born and of the Swedish race on both sides', to be acclaimed king alongside his father. Jacob was ceremonially renamed Anund (as Jacob was deemed to be too 'foreign'-sounding, although he remains in history as Jacob). Olof had no choice but to accept the decisions of the *Refs-Thing* and this time he gave every sign of intending to maintain the peace with Olaf Haraldsson, with Jacob in the wings to replace Olof if the latter should renege on the deal.

Olaf then made another peace overture to Olof, meeting him at Konungahella to fix a solemn pact. Olof's manner struck those present as 'remarkably mild'. The one outstanding issue to be resolved was the status of the disputed area of Hising straddling Norway and Gautland. As both sides were intransigent, the kings decided to resolve the issue in the simplest way possible, by throwing dice. In Snorri's description Olof threw first, coming up with a double six and smirking; Olaf also threw a double six. Olof again came up with a double six (one must wonder here whether the dice were loaded). On Olaf's second throw one of the cubes split, revealing a total of seven eyes as the two parts separated. Hence Hising went to Norway. It's a pretty tale, but its sheer improbability makes it suspect. Some such game of chance between the two kings may well have taken place, however, the story being embellished in the telling from one source to another.

By the end of 1019 Olaf, having seen off domestic and foreign foes, could now have no real worries about any challenges to his position as king of Norway. But there was one ruler who never accepted that arrangement, and that was Cnut of England and Denmark. We can be reasonably sure that, in theory at least, Cnut considered himself the nominal sovereign of Norway on the grounds that his grandfather Harald Bluetooth, having converted the Danes to Christianity, had inscribed the claim in stone on a monument in Denmark (the Jelling Stone, dated to about 965). By 1019 the news from the Scandinavian peninsula got worse for Cnut: Olaf was now married to the Swedish king's daughter, forming an alliance that could not easily be broken. It was one more indication to Cnut that Olaf Haraldsson was acting a mite too independently for a vassal, and Cnut wrote to him with a veiled warning. Come to England, Cnut told Olaf, and be formally assigned vassal status.

Olaf of course refused. But he had enough on his plate as it was. One problem lay in the unruly state of the Orkney Islands. This archipelago off the northeast corner of Scotland had been plagued by political turbulence since Harald Haarfager had brought it under his control. Olaf Trgyggvason's introduction of Christianity had apparently failed to curb the bumptiousness of the quarrelsome earls who ruled the Orkneys, which were always important to Norway as a way-station between the Scandinavian peninsula and the British Isles. Five years after Olaf assumed the throne, the islands had come under the control of Earl Einar, whose reported harshness was responsible for great upheavals, during which a promising young noble, Thorkell Amundason, exiled himself to Scotland, from where, in early 1020, he sailed to Norway to King Olaf's court. He was soon joined there by Earl Thorfin, who had royal Scots blood in his veins.

These two men gave Olaf the chance to eliminate a potential crisis point in the west, and create a buffer between him and Cnut. Thorkell and Thorfin sailed to the Orkneys in a longship in the autumn to challenge Einar. In Snorri's account Thorkell cornered Einar in a room and killed him with a blow to the head. The slaying stunned the people of the Orkneys enough to allow Thorkell to sail unhindered back to Norway and report to Olaf that his mission had been accomplished. The king 'expressed satisfaction' at the news – a strong indication that Einar's elimination could have been a royal command and not a spur-of-the-moment action.

However, as turmoil in the Orkneys continued, Olaf annexed the islands, citing the precedent of Harald Haarfager who had made clear that the local earls were not independent but owed allegiance to the crown of Norway. This was not to Thorfin's liking, however; citing his royal Scottish blood, Thorfin told Olaf he would not be his vassal. Olaf was adamant: it was his way or nothing. Thorfin asked for some months to think things over, but was eventually persuaded by Thorkell Amundason to step into line. Olaf, however, was irritated by Thorfin's high attitude. As Thorfin was about to leave for the Orkneys, and was in his ship enjoying a drink, he was accosted by Thorkell who feared that Thorfin might exclude him from the power structure at home. He was reassured on the spot, and both men sailed together. As if domestic turmoil were not enough, the Orkneys were also plagued periodically by independent Viking raiders who carried off cattle and foodstuffs. Thorfin, however, seemed to spend most of his time at Caithness, across the strait in Scotland, to be near his maternal relations, leaving the running of things to his brother Earl Bruse. Yet Thorfin did manage to make a decent job of administration, according to Snorri; he ruled more than sixty years and died peacefully. Olaf, therefore, could rest confident in the knowledge that the Orkneys, as well as Shetland, were safe within his realm.

Soon after his marriage to Astrid in summer 1019, Olaf moved back to his ancestral headquarters in Trondheim, staying at his Nidaros residence through the following winter. He still had his concerns about how the hinterlands were adapting to Christian laws. Officials informed him, in fact, that the situation was very shaky. There happened to be a wealthy man named Hårek, whose father had appropriated the island of Thjøtta, one of the myriad outcrops that dot the fjords and west coast of Norway.

As the family had some blood connection to Harald Haarfager, Hårek was on good terms with the king. Olaf must have asked Hårek's advice about a major expedition he was planning for the far north of Norway, to Halogaland, for the following spring. Reports would have been reaching the king of the potential hostility of the Halogalanders to Olaf's Christianizing mission. He knew, not least from the experience of Olaf Tryggvason, that it was one thing to convert the coastal regions, but quite another to spread the word among the hardier folk of the mountainous hinterlands. In the spring of 1020 he fitted out five ships and a force of 300 men and sailed north along the inhospitable windswept coast of North Trøndelag and Nordland.

Wherever he went he played political hardball, forcing the people to adopt Christianity, threatening them with the severest penalties, including execution, if they resisted. 'Severe punishments' were meted out to opponents, according to Snorri, while Adam of Bremen claims he ordered the burning of witches. However, most of the leading men of the regions welcomed Olaf and treated him to banquets and feasts (though no doubt some were not quite sincere). One of these men was an elderly noble, Grankell, whose son Asmund Grankellson joined the king on his tour, where we are told that he baptized many before returning to Nidaros in the winter of 1021.

Yet there were stubborn heathen holdouts even in the Trøndelag; Olaf received regular reports that the old rites, including the sacrifice of cattle and horses in times of poor harvest, were still being carried out. He was told that many people of the region attributed bad harvests to Olaf's turning the people away from the old gods. One nobleman who was accused of having indulged in the old rites, Olver of Eggja, denied all involvement in such things when ordered to appear before the king, although, he commented, 'I cannot hinder drunken or foolish people's talk.' It was a glib excuse, which Olaf indulged by merely sending Olver home with the warning that he had better stay in the faith. Rather more serious was a report that a great many people – including Olver – had held a mid-winter assembly at Maerin and performed the old banned sacrifices to bring a good spring season. When Olaf summoned them to him, only Olver had the courage to go, with the old excuse that the occasion was actually just a big party and that some people could be forgiven for inebriated heathen comments. Olaf 'looked angry' at this, as well he might. 'Some time or other I'll discover the truth you are now hiding', he told Olver, 'and in such a way that you won't be able to deny it.' Again, he let Olver go with a warning, but did not forget the incident.

At Easter 1021 Olaf readied his fleet and sent a message to Thoralde, his farm manager in Verdal. Summoned before the king and questioned, Thoralde admitted that a great many inhabitants of the Trøndelag had not abandoned their heathenism, even though some had been baptized just to stay within the law. He specifically named Olver of Eggja as the organizer of some of the thrice-yearly sacrifice rituals, adding that Olver was at the moment in the process of putting together the latest one. At that, Olaf ordered the fleet lying at readiness to sail, with the standard 300 men-at-arms on board; the ships made good time at night up the Trondheimsfjord to Maerin, surprising Olver in his house. Olver and several others were at once put to death, while all the provisions and other goods that had been assembled for the heathen feast were confiscated; others in Olver's company were arrested and put in chains, though a few escaped. At a specially-convened Thing Olaf imposed his will on the intimidated assembly. There followed a second wave of executions, maimings and banishments, after which Olaf returned to Nidaros, ordering that teachers be sent to the region and churches built there. Incidentally, Olver's widow, 'young and handsome, of great family and rich', was given to a young retainer named Kalf Árnason, who Snorri relates 'became a great chief and was a man of very great understanding'. He would also turn out to be one of Olaf's most fateful foes.

Through 1021 Olaf continued strong-arming his recalcitrant nobles, threatening them with death if they continued to resist, burning the houses of the hold-outs and taking their sons hostage. By contrast, when Olaf saw that he could employ milder forms of persuasion, he did so. Snorri cites the case of Dale-Gudbrand, a local lord in the Gudbrandsdal valley of Uppland whose reaction to the news of an impending visit by the king was: 'A man called Olaf has come [who] will force on us another faith and break in pieces all our gods. He says that he has a much greater and more powerful god.' (It is unclear whether Dale-Gudbrand was the man's actual name or simply meant a native of the Gudbrandsdal; for clarity we will assume the former.) Dale-Gudbrand gathered a large force of followers at Breida in the Sil valley. Olaf rode out to meet the leaders, inviting them to repent and embrace Christianity. 'We'll give you something else to think about today than to mock us', came the defiant reply. But as soon as Olaf's men charged, the rebels took to their heels in panic.

Dale-Gudbrand's eighteen-year-old son was captured, but Olaf set him free to return to his father to try to persuade him that further resistance would be useless. Dale-Gudbrand scoffed at what he saw as his son's lack of spirit, but according to Snorri, that night he dreamed that 'a man surrounded by light' came up to him with the dire warning: 'You and all your people will fall, wolves will drag you off and ravens will tear you into strips.'

The dream (also dreamed by another chief, we are told) convinced Dale-Gudbrand to give some consideration to Olaf's teaching, 'to know if there was any truth in it'. The implication in Snorri's saga is that Dale-Gudbrand was impressed by the king's magnanimity in sparing his son, most unusual in a violent culture. He therefore sent the son (who is never named) with a dozen men to Olaf. Both sides agreed to convene a Thing to discuss a mutually-acceptable peace. The Thing met under a heavy rain; Olaf opened the proceedings by describing how many communities had destroyed their old heathen sacrifice-houses and accepted 'the true God who had made heaven and earth and knows all things'.

Dale-Gudbrand then spoke: 'We know nothing of him of whom you speak. You call him God, whom neither you nor anyone else can see? But we have a god whom we can see every day, although he is not out today, because the weather is wet... But since you say your God is so great, let him make it so that tomorrow we can have a cloudy day but without rain, and let's meet again.'

Olaf may well have smiled at the image of Thor shrinking away from a bit of rain, but the exchange shows what a tenacious hold the heathen religion had on the country environment. Dale-Gudbrand's opposition is here revealed on purely practical and superficial grounds; the more metaphysical aspects of Christianity were beyond the capacity of his rugged disposition to perceive.

Olaf took Dale-Gudbrand's son as a hostage with him, and in the course of the evening questioned him about what his father actually believed. Did the king sense that his opponent's resolve could be wavering? The boy replied that Thor carried with him a large hammer and stood on a high pedestal when outdoors; he had plenty of gold and silver, and 'never went a day without meat and four loaves of bread'. All that night the king spent in prayer; in the morning he went to the scheduled Thing – the rain, meanwhile, having stopped – and listened as his bishop delivered a persuasive address to the suspicious attendees. There was some mockery of the bishop, 'a horned man with the staff in his hand crooked at the top like a ram's horn'. One man rose and issued a rather confusing challenge: if Olaf's God was the real thing, then he can prove it by making the sun shine the next morning, and if it does, we will either agree with you or fight you. Thus ended the second Thing.

The morning of the third Thing dawned overcast, not giving much encouragement to the king, who had again spent much of the night in prayer. As he approached the meeting place he saw 'a huge man's image glittering with gold and silver' set up in the middle, and Dale-Gudbrand's men bowing down to it. Encouraged by the cloudy sky, Dale-Gudbrand rose and mocked Olaf: 'Where is your god now?... Our god, who rules over all, is come and looks on you with an angry eye... Throw away your opposition.'

Olaf, uncowed, turned to one of the men in his entourage, Kolbein Sterke (the Strong) who was in the habit of carrying a sword and a large cudgel wherever he went. 'While I'm speaking,' he whispered to Kolbein, 'make sure that all those people's eyes are turned away from their idol, and when they are, hit it with your club as hard as you can.' Olaf then rose and began to speak, mocking his opponents, who 'would frighten us with thy god, who is blind and deaf, and cannot even move about without being carried'. As he was speaking the sun rose, dispersing the grey clouds and Kolbein brought his cudgel down on the Thor idol with a mighty blow: '[S]o that the idol burst asunder, and there ran out of it mice as big almost as cats, and reptiles and adders. The [men] were so terrified that some fled to their ships.'

Those boats couldn't get away as Olaf had ordered that the hulls be holed during the night. Those who ran for their horses, it is said, couldn't find them.

With some trouble the Thing reconvened, and Olaf, with some sarcasm, pointed out how the much-vaunted deity that had stood there had proved to be nothing more than the abode of reptiles and vermin (the idol had probably been kept in unhygienic storage).

Take now your gold and ornaments that are lying strewn on the
grass, and give them to your wives and daughters; but never hang
them hereafter on wood or stone.

The king then reminded all present of their resolution of the previous
day: to accept Christianity or risk a battle. Dale-Gudbrand, according to
Snorri's account, appeared to have been convinced of the former course,
and was promptly baptized, along with his son, by the bishop whom he
had earlier slighted as 'the horned man'.

Everywhere Olaf went he met opposition that, initially appearing to
be determined, would melt away with little trouble. The ease with which
the fight went out of his apparently implacable foes after even a single
encounter, to the point of accepting baptism, might strike the reader as
far-fetched. The key may lie in the essentially superficial and materialist
nature of the heathen beliefs. Overcoming the naysayers' resistance was
Olaf's spiritual rather than temporal authority, and the self-confidence
that comes with it. As the local lords' stock of spirituality was rather
low, their corresponding regard for personal power and prestige was very
high. When they therefore were confronted with a strong personality
who combined both worldly and spiritual power, instead of mere political
authority, they didn't quite know how to handle it and, realizing suddenly
on which side their bread would be buttered from now on, gave in quickly.

Olaf's next objective was Hedemark, not known as a friendly territory,
where he nonetheless consecrated churches and appointed preachers. At
Raumarike Olaf's force met a hostile formation at the Nitja River, but
the enemy fell back after the first clash and, if Snorri is to be credited,
consented to become Christian forthwith. Snorri hints that a food
shortage in the north of Norway could have contributed to the unrest. It
was at about that time that the Swedish skald Ottar the Black came to
find Olaf; Olof Sköttkonung had died in that year (1021), to be succeeded
by his son Jacob-Anund, though why the skald wanted to leave the
Swedish court is unclear. At the close of winter 1022 Olaf sailed south to
the warmer and more prosperous Viken where he remained through the
summer. One of his first acts there was to ban all exports of corn, malt
and flour in the northern districts, apparently to bring supplies of those
vital provisions up to normal and reduce the effects of the food shortage.

The death of Olaf Sköttkonung also had the effect of turning the
eyes of Einar Tambaskelfer, until now a fixture of the Swedish court, in

Olaf's direction. Einar, it will be recalled, was the rather arrogant Lade earl who had fought Olaf at Nesjar and was forced to flee to Sweden. Now Einar made overtures to Olaf, who negotiated with him by letter; at a meeting between them Einar agreed to travel north to Trondheim in the king's name and take over a considerable estate. Olaf appears to have placed complete trust in his old foe, as he subsequently did with another one, Erling Skjalgson. So far Erling had ruled the roost in South Hordaland, but his abrasive manner towards other nobles resulted in a summons to Olaf at Tønsberg to explain himself. Erling did not deny the charges, but claimed that he was forced to act autocratically to keep in place other arrogant men of lesser status than he. Nevertheless, he pronounced himself willing to 'bow the neck' to the king. Friends of both sides begged them to reconcile, which they did, apparently by simple gentlemen's agreement.

There were those, to be sure, who paid lip service to Christianity while conducting the old heathen rituals which involved heavy eating and drinking three times a year. In the lean years of 1021–22, however, keeping up the banquets became somewhat of a problem. It is not clear whether Olaf's ban on food exports applied to all of Norway or just to southern trade with the north. Erling was one of those local chiefs who chafed at the restrictions; despite his promises to Olaf, Erling seems to have gone back to his bad old ways.

Another disgruntled man was one Asbjorn, whose banqueting style had been cramped and was spending the winter sulking at home. In the winter of 1023 he slipped into his ship along with ninety men and sailed to Agvaldsnes, where he probably heard that the king had planned an Easter feast. Disembarking incognito, he wormed his way unnoticed into the banqueting hall where, we are told, he saw one of his inveterate foes, Thorer Sel, and what is more, overheard Thorer bad-mouthing him to others present. Whereupon Asbjorn sprang forward and decapitated Thorer with one sword blow, 'so that the head fell on the table before the king, and the body at his feet, and the table-cloth was drenched with blood from top to bottom'.

Olaf, keeping his temper under control, had Asbjorn immediately arrested. Would there be no end to these heathens' bloodthirsty habits? Once the gore had been cleaned up Olaf demanded to know why Asbjorn, who was sitting on the doorstep under guard, had not been hanged forthwith. But Thorarin Nefiulfson, who appears to have been some sort of security chief, told him it would not be proper to deprive a man of life after nightfall; Olaf accepted that explanation and deferred the execution until the morning. When dawn broke, as he was on his way to Mass, the king asked again why Asbjorn's neck still not had worn the noose. Thorarin in reply quoted Bishop Sigurd to the effect that a leader should be merciful like Christ and not give way to vengeful wrath. Olaf eyed the official, conceding the point, but ordered that Asbjorn be kept under strict arrest until the following day. Thorarin, he warned, would pay with his life if his prisoner should escape.

Thorarin was obviously reluctant to hang Asbjorn, for some reason unknown. Very likely they were kin of a certain degree, as was not uncommon among the chieftains, hence the procrastination. For the next day or so they acted like good friends, eating and drinking together. In fact, he bribed the priest of the local church with two silver marks to ring the Sabbath-bell at the moment Olaf had finished a long meal with plenty to drink. When the bell tolled Thorarin told the king it wouldn't be proper to execute a man on the (false) Sabbath, and again, Olaf gave way. Asbjorn, ordered to attend Mass, was not exactly reprieved, but could entertain hopes that the king's wrath against him might simmer down. The episode, again, brings out Olaf's willingness to see the good in people despite overwhelming evidence to the contrary before his eyes. After the bloody murder at the high table he could hardly not have ordered Asbjorn's hanging, but why he let himself be swayed from it repeatedly by Thorarin's excuses is a mystery perhaps explicable by a growing realization that eye-for-an-eye chains of violent justice in the end are futile, and that a Christian administration should avoid such practices when it could.

Yet at no point, it seems, could Olaf rest on any laurels, as there was always some domestic threat. The news of Asbjorn's deed and detention reached the ears of his kinsman Erling Skialgsson who, pressed by affronted dignity, assembled 1,500 men and descended on the mansion at Agvaldsnes, arriving on a Sunday while the church service was in progress. Olaf was present along with his prisoner Asbjorn. Erling's mob burst into the church and broke off Asbjorn's shackles, causing something of a tumult. But only the king, it seems, remained completely unperturbed, concentrating on the scripture lesson being read. By the end of the service Erling's guard had formed a double file flanking the path to the mansion, and between the files Olaf walked calmly and confronted Erling at the front door. There followed a tense exchange which, paraphrasing Snorri, we can summarize without losing too much of the flavour.

Erling opened the conversation:

I hear my kinsman Asbjorn is guilty of some great wrongdoing, King, and I'm here to request that you spare his life and let him continue to live here in his native land.

Do you think you have the power to make the decisions, Erling?' Olaf replied. 'You want to offer terms? It looks to me that you really brought this force here to settle accounts with me.' Erling, flushed with emotion (or embarrassment), denied that was so, and reiterated that he just wished to mend fences with the king – otherwise, they would part on bad terms.

Olaf's suspicions were not allayed. 'And you came here with such a large force to tell me this? Do you think you can scare me? No way is that going to happen. I'm not going away.

At this point Bishop Sigurd interrupted the tense exchange to suggest that Asbjorn's life be spared, though he could submit to any other punishment the king might decree. Olaf assented; Sigurd proposed that Erling deposit a guarantee for Asjborn's life, Erling in his turn agreed, and Asbjorn kissed the king's hand in gratitude. After Erling and his men had left (sullenly, without saying goodbye), Olaf took Asbjorn aside and appointed him bailiff of the Agvaldsnes estate, the position that Thorer Sel had at the time of his murder. Asbjorn asked for an interval to go home and put his affairs in order.

He never went back to Olaf, and probably never intended to. Back home, Asbjorn was swayed by the advice of a relative who reminded him that if he returned to Olaf's Agvaldsnes estate he would simply be 'a king's slave' and besides, he would be taking the place of a man whom he had despised enough to kill. Asbjorn saw some logic in this, and stayed put on his farm. It must have been at about this time that he acquired the sobriquet Selsbane, or 'bane of [Thorer] Sel'. Erling did a slow burn over his failure to have Asbjorn pardoned but could do little about it.

In the spring of 1023 Olaf travelled to Hordaland to enforce his policy, and at his first Thing he was challenged to a battle. When the sides were drawn up for a clash, Snorri reports, the king's opponents got cold feet and accepted baptism en masse. If this sounds just too easy, it might have been a sign that by now Olaf was slowly being transformed from earthly king into something more, and we may surmise that wherever he went he had begun to emit a certain aura that had the effect of cowing his foes, at least temporarily. Yet Snorri records a curious incident: while Olaf was riding along singing psalms, he halted his horse in front of some hills and said he wouldn't advise any Norwegian king to travel through them. We are not given any explanation of this strange geographic aversion; perhaps he feared the location as a potential ambush spot or had some other issue in mind unknown to us. (And in fact most later monarchs did avoid the place.)

Among the fjords there were plenty of challenges to the king's Christianization drive. At Valders near the Ostrarfjord he found himself up against yet more determined opposition; at a specially-called Thing the crowd threatened him loudly and clashed their weapons in his face. Realizing he was outgunned on this occasion, he changed the subject: religion aside, were there any issues among them, he asked, which he as king was willing to settle? It was a good stroke of diplomacy, as he found he had touched a raw nerve – there were, indeed, countless quarrels among the locals. There followed a contest to see who could promote each particular dispute, and the whole Christianity issue seemed to have been forgotten.

Still Olaf was by no means out of the woods; a Thing was held at Valders, where Olaf surmised that the menfolk would be there, leaving the surrounding district unprotected. His next move was to lead his ships across the adjacent lake by night and proceed to ravage the land and burn all the houses he could find. The local men at Valders, probably seeing the flames and smoke, dispersed in a panic; some fled to the king and begged him to show mercy, which he promptly gave, and, we are told, 'nobody refused to accept Christianity'. As one skald wrote:

> Against the Uppland people wroth
> Olaf, to most so mild, went forth;
> The houses burning,
> All people mourning:
> Who could not fly
> Hung on gallows high.

After this incident Olaf wintered at Nidaros (1024). It would have been a pleasant interlude, as at this point Snorri surprises us with the news that Olaf had a slave-mistress, 'a remarkably handsome girl' named Alfhild, who became pregnant in the spring; only Olaf himself and his closest circle knew who was responsible, though one suspects that it was an open secret at best. The birth was a very difficult one, and almost cost the lives of mother and child. Among the few people present was the skald Sigvat; a priest believed the newborn infant to be lifeless until it drew a very weak breath, and told Sigvat to wake the king. That was easier said than done; one of Olaf's well-known pet hates was being roused in the middle of the night and his staff walked in terror of having to do so for whatever reason.

Sigvat flatly refused to face the dire consequences of shaking the king out of sleep. Besides, few of those present thought the child would live for more than a short time. Sigvat said he would rather risk the king's displeasure by baptizing the child at once, in view of its frailty, and give it a name into the bargain. Thus was Magnus Olafsson brought into the world of Norwegian royalty, where he was destined to fill his father's Christianizing shoes. Sigvat's choice of name for the royal baby was inspired by Charlemagne – Karla Magnus in Norwegian – and since shortened to history as simply Magnus.

As was to be expected, after the king got up in the morning he was quite indignant that no-one had woken him up to give him the news! Sigvat soothed him and tactfully explained that the baby needed to be baptized at once in case it died 'a heathen'.

'But why did you call him Magnus?' Olaf asked. 'That's not a name our people use.'

Sigvat defended his choice, as in his view 'King Karla Magnus had been the best man in the world.'

Olaf would have had his poker face on. 'Foolish men sometimes get lucky, Sigvat,' he said. But of course he was overjoyed.

Snorri inserts the detail that Olaf had an attractive mistress rather casually in view of the king's marriage to Astrid of Sweden. He informs us, moreover, that Olaf had a definite weakness for concubines, though the assertion is made without any trace of censure. Obviously we are not meant to be terribly shocked by this, as the tradition of royal concubinage reaches far back into the Old Testament, and includes popes and European royal families up to the nineteenth century, without it seeming amiss. Olaf's marriage to Astrid was a clean political one, without any romantic ribbons tied to it, as have been so many royal marriages over the ages; hence, a king (or a queen) could legitimately (if not *de rigueur*) have a romantic-sexual consort on the side to make up for the limitations of the spouse foisted upon them by the exigencies of state. Besides, a Christian chronicler such as Snorri apparently saw no conflict of morals between a vigorous sex life and a saintly mission.

In that same year of 1024 Hårek of Thjøtta, whom we have met as a distant blood-descendant of Harald Haarfager on general good terms with Olaf, began to fret that the king was infringing a little too much on the precious degree of autonomy that he held. Hårek reluctantly conceded the post of sheriff of Halgoland to a royal emissary, Asmund Grankelson, who recruited a farmer, known to us as Karle, on Langey island. On a ship manned by thirty men, they sailed southwards; on the way they learned that Asbjorn Selsbane was on the way north with a ship of his own. The two vessels encountered one another in a sound; Karle said he recognized Asbjorn's ship by its high bulwarks, red and white hull, and coloured sail. 'If I know my ships,' Karle said, 'that's Asbjorn's, and you'll finally get a chance to see him.'

Asbjorn was indeed on the ship, sitting at the helm in a blue cloak. When Karle pointed him out, Asmund said he would dye that blue cloak red. Asmund's gold-mounted spear hit Asbjorn with such force, in Snorri's account, that it went clean through his body and stuck in the stern-post. Asbjorn's mother kept the blood-stained spear and gave it to one Thorer Hund with the instruction that it be administered to King Olaf in the same manner as it killed her son. Thorer, blind and speechless with rage, took the spear on board his vessel and kept it until he could find the opportunity to use it. Asmund, meanwhile, arrived at Trondheim where he told Olaf what had happened.

Olaf employed the summer of 1014 in touring his domain, rectifying abuses, stiffening the faith of the people and generally encouraging law and order. He oversaw the marriage of his half-sister Gunnhild to a leading man of Ringanes. He regularly sent messages and donations to his outlying territories, such as Iceland, the Orkneys and the Faeroes. The process, in Iceland at least, was not friction-free. A monarchy, after all, inevitably raised concerns about the succession. Voices were raised that, though Olaf was undoubtedly a great and good ruler, who could tell what his successors would be like? What rubbed many the wrong way also was Olaf's request for the ownership of a rocky islet at the mouth of Eyfjord; this could well be the thin end of a wedge of growing demands over time. And what could be the use of that barren outcrop to Olaf anyway? The sage Einar of Modruvellir pointed out the potential danger: 'Although [the island] can grow no food, yet it could be the base for a great longship force, and then, I don't doubt, there will be distress enough at every poor peasant's door.' That decided the issue: no giving in to the Norwegian king.

This was about the time that Olaf extended an official invitation to five of the leading men of Iceland, an invitation which, though politely worded, was actually an order. After some deliberation the five decided to play it safe and send five substitute negotiators; but even that was delayed, and no-one sailed that summer. Olaf, meanwhile, had also invited several of the chiefs of the Faeroe islanders, who on arrival at his court were informed in no uncertain terms that they would have to submit to tighter Norwegian rule and pay tax. The delegation set off for the Faeroes, and that was the last anyone saw of them, as they most probably perished at sea. A second ship, sent after the first, also vanished without a trace.

Chapter 9

Cnut's Gold Ring

[H]e had many trials and tribulations to endure from the people, until at length he could not oppose the multitude of evils (*The Passion and Miracles of the Blessed Óláfr*).

When Olof Sköttkonung switched brides on Olaf Haraldsson, giving him Astrid when Olaf had preferred Ingegerd, the Norwegian king, like a true Norse ruler, might have been expected to react in a rather more spirited manner than he did. That he accepted the crafty switch calmly indicates that it was not merely the desire to have a queen share his bed and give him an heir that motivated him. After all, he had access to any concubine he wanted; the real motive was probably strategic: to forge a blood alliance with neighbouring Sweden in case any threat should arise from the southwest.

A potential threat was certainly there, in the person of King Cnut of England, who by 1024 had all but decided that Olaf had become a tad too powerful in the Norse world. After all, was not Cnut himself also the king of Norway, a title he inherited as a descendant of Harald Bluetooth? As long as Cnut was busy with issues closer to home, and his vassal (technically speaking) Olaf Haraldsson was putting Norway in order, he was prepared to stay his hand. But undoubtedly Cnut would have had a steady stream of intelligence arriving at his court not only from the Scandinavian peninsula but also from Iceland and the island chains northeast of Scotland. He would have known that Olaf was encountering difficulties in his drive to Christianize Norway and build up a centralized kingdom. He would have known also that some of the earls in Iceland and elsewhere were hesitating to accept Olaf's rule because they feared the possible reaction of the 'real' king, Cnut. Therefore he had a vested interest in encouraging the independence of the Norwegian earls.

Since 1016, when Cnut finally overcame the last of his domestic foes and settled down to rule England as king, most of his prodigious energy had been taken up with Christianizing the country and overhauling its laws and administration – ironically, precisely what Olaf was doing in Norway. Questions have been raised, however, about just how pious a Christian Cnut was; it has been suggested that much of it was designed to assuage any ill-feeling among the English clergy who could potentially have sparked revolts at any time. He also yearned to be accepted by the European establishment, as evidenced by a much-publicized pilgrimage to Rome in 1027. In 1019 he had inherited the throne of Denmark, adding another stone to his edifice of rule.

Cnut's bad blood towards Olaf would have gone back to at least 1014 or thereabouts, when the young Olaf's princely bearing at Canute's court earned the English king's jealousy. Ten years later, writes the English monk Florence of Worcester in his early twelfth-century *Chronicon ex Chronicis*:

> Since it was intimated to Canute [sic], king of the English and Danes, that the Norwegians greatly despised their king, Olaf, for his simplicity and gentleness, justice and piety, he sent a large sum of gold and silver to be certain of them, requesting them with many entreaties to reject and desert Olaf, and submit to [Cnut] and let him reign over them.

A fairly constant stream of truculent Norwegians appeared at Cnut's court to load themselves with money and presents and return to Norway enriched and encouraged. In the words of L.M. Larson, Olaf 'found his throne completely undermined by streams of British gold'.* Did Cnut have pangs of conscience at this covert attack on a fellow Christian monarch by subsidising his enemies? In Larson's view he consciously suspended his spiritual inclinations in favour of cold political strategy. Cnut himself was at the apex of his power and popularity, as evidenced by the pomp and splendour of his court and by the general peace which his kingdom enjoyed at this time. Thus in the spring of 1025 Cnut decided to turn the first screw in a progressive pressuring of Olaf to acknowledge Cnut's suzerainty over all of Norway.

A delegation from Cnut's court turned up at Tønsberg without warning, somewhat to Olaf's consternation. He stalled them for a few days before agreeing to hear their case, which was that 'King Cnut considers Norway

---

* 'The Political Policies of Cnut as King of England,' *American Historical Review*, July 1910, Vol. 15 Issue No. 4, pp. 720–743.

as his property' on the basis of hereditary possession, and therefore Olaf would have to come to Cnut and 'receive his kingdom as a fief from him and become his vassal', as well as pay the necessary tribute. The ultimatum was accompanied by a veiled but distinct threat to invade Norway if Olaf refused.

And refuse he did, quite sharply. Is Cnut aiming to dominate the whole of the Norse lands? Are not England and Denmark enough for him? No way will he, Olaf, bow the knee to Cnut. He dismissed the delegation with a Leonidean challenge: 'I will defend Norway with the battle-axe and sword as long as life is given me.'

That noble sentiment was not shared by all the court. Sigvat the skald had the occasion to confer with Cnut's diplomats and gained the impression that they were baffled at the king's reaction. 'We don't know,' they said, 'to whom he trusts in not becoming King Cnut's vassal.' They made a point of what a basically nice fellow Cnut actually was, a ruler magnanimously inclined to forgive slights. Sigvat was not taken in, and sang (presumably later):

May [Olaf], our gallant Norse king, never... be brought as ransom
to a living man for the broad lands his sword has won.

Cnut reacted badly to his envoys' news. That same summer he received the sons of Erling Skjalgson and gave them extensive fiefs in Norway.

The summer of 1025 was a tense one for Olaf, who spared no effort to obtain information about Cnut's plans. Merchant seamen, a prime source of intelligence, reported that Cnut was assembling a large army; other sources appeared to doubt that. Staying in Viken, Olaf sent out spies to Denmark to see if any of Cnut's forces had gone there as an advance guard. By the autumn he was convinced enough to notify his ally King Jacob-Anund of Sweden that he was now facing a real threat from Cnut, and that if Norway were subdued the turn of Sweden would come next. Norway and Sweden together, Olaf suggested, would be strong enough to resist Cnut. Jacob-Anund agreed, and scheduled a summit meeting with Olaf in the winter. By now, however, Cnut himself had arrived in Denmark to stay the winter. He somehow learned that Olaf and Jacob-Anund had been in contact and suspected correctly that an alliance was in the offing. Soon envoys from Cnut turned up at Jacob-Anund's court with a full complement of diplomatic gifts and flattery. But they failed to sway the Swedish king, who heard them out and that was about all. The envoys left discouraged, and informed Cnut that he had better write off the possibility of any help from the Swedish king.

Olaf remained at Sarpsborg through the winter, amid his army and great numbers of supporters, awaiting the expected arrival of Jacob-Anund. As he waited he sent Karle, the ex-farmer whom he had recruited into his entourage, into the north on a raiding expedition to gather revenue. There he fell in with Thorer Hund, still nursing vengeance for the killing of Asbjorn Selsbane; Thorer lured Karle to a meeting, ostensibly to divide the booty they had gathered, and ran him through with what Snorri indicates could have been the same spear that killed Asbjorn. Shrugging off these violent little sideshows, Olaf and Jacob-Anund agreed to a further meeting at Konungahella in the spring of 1027, allowing an interval to pass during which they hoped to glean more intelligence about Cnut's plans. In fact, Cnut had decided to winter back in England, leaving his son Harthacnut in charge of Denmark.

At Konungahella the two kings conversed long and earnestly. Olaf returned to Viken to plan a voyage northwards to Jadar, where Erling Skjalgson, oiled by Cnut's gold, was gathering a considerable force. For some days, however, the desired south-westerly winds declined to fully cooperate, and Olaf hesitated to put out until one of his courtiers quipped that they would have moved soon enough if Erling had been preparing a feast for them instead of a hostile reception. When the winds turned favourable Olaf's force sailed past Jadar and landed on the Hordaland coast (north of present-day Bergen).

Erling was not the only truculent chieftain the king had to put up with. Messages were constantly arriving from Iceland, the Orkneys and the Faeroes of incipient rebelliousness and disobedience – no doubt fuelled by Cnut's financial incentives. 'The king's enemies are walking about with open purses,' the faithful Sigvat fretted. 'Men offer the precious metal for the priceless head of the king.' In the summer of 1026 Olaf sent a leading Icelander, Geller Thorkelson, back to his country with orders to enforce the Norwegian laws, including an oddly-named 'nose-tax' that would have been equivalent to a poll tax, and a tax on woollen cloth. The Icelanders delivered a sharp snub to these demands, which Geller relayed to Olaf. One Icelander with poetic talents, Stein Skaptason, had turned a few uncomplimentary verses about Olaf, which the king one day demanded to hear. Stein, caught unawares, found some excuse and left. While fleeing, he murdered a farmer who had recognized him and went on to seek refuge with relations of Erling Skjalgson.

In the early spring of 1027 Erling felt strong enough to fit out three longships, in which were his sons Sigurd and Thord, to be joined by two more ships under Thorberg Arnason, Erling's son-in-law, and his two brothers. More of the Arnason family followed. This force sailed up the Trondheim fjord to Nidaros where Olaf was, arriving at night and presumably unseen. There followed a council of war; the younger members were all for storming Nidaros at once, but Thorberg suggested that a small delegation call on the king and see if any negotiation might be possible.

When Olaf saw the size of the force docked before Nidaros he commented sarcastically that this was not exactly a peaceful demonstration. Fin Arnason, one of Thorberg's brothers, disingenuously denied that the show of strength outside Nidaros had any hostile intent; Fin added that they had really come to offer their services to Olaf, but if he remained intransigent in his policies, they would have no choice but to go over to Cnut. As related by Snorri, this exchange sounds more than a little vague. Thorberg and his brother Fin are now pictured as actually wishing to help Olaf after gathering their longship force against him. Was it all an audacious front? Did the dissidents get cold feet in Olaf's presence, or was there some uncertainty about the whole project from the beginning?

The threat to go over to Cnut was a piece of pure blackmail that misfired at once. Olaf counter-proposed that Thorberg and the others take a solemn oath to follow him wherever he might go, on domestic or foreign campaigns, 'and not part from me without my leave and permission'. If that was done, he said, he would be prepared to consider the dispute closed. When Fin relayed the king's terms to the others, Thorberg made his stand, and it was an unexpected one: 'I have no wish to leave my property and seek foreign masters, but on the contrary I will always consider it an honour to follow King Olaf, and be where he is.' His brothers Arne and Fin Arnason ranged themselves on his side; all three then returned to Nidaros and swore their oaths to the king. The rebels were, in effect, pardoned – except for the audacious poet Stein Skaptason, who was given to understand that henceforth he had better not show his face in the court again.

By now Olaf knew he would, sooner or later, have to go up against Cnut. 'I know he's not joking', he told Fin Arnason. He sent Fin to recruit men in Halogaland and issued orders for similar leveés in the Trøndelag and southern areas. Fin found a willing audience in Halogaland, including Thorer Hund, who fitted out a ship at his own expense. Thorer, of course, presented a problem in that officially he was a wanted man for murdering the king's friend Karle. When Fin confronted him on the issue with a posse of armed men, he was ordered (on the king's behalf) to pay a heavy blood-fine. Thorer protested that he could not possibly pay it on the spot, but Fin insisted, adding that it would be a good idea if Thorer also gave back a 'great ornament' that he was believed to have stripped from Karle's body. Thorer denied ever having such an object, but changed his tune when the point of Fin's spear pricked his chest and he hurriedly took off the ornament, which he had been wearing all along. There was some delay while Thorer scraped together some of the fine from various sources; Fin, impatient, said he would suspend part of the debt for the present and got ready to lead the flotilla south to Olaf. But when Thorer finally got his own vessel, laden with liquor and furs, he steered it westward out of sight of land and voyaged all the way to England, where he joined Cnut. When Olaf learned of Thorer's desertion he remarked that it was better to have this enemy at a distance than near, where he could do more damage.

King Olaf's emissaries often risked life and limb when they travelled to outlying regions to enforce the royal orders. Snorri gives an extensive account of one of them, the Icelander Thorod Snorrason, who volunteered to go to Jamtland, one of those ill-defined regions straddling Norway and Sweden east of the Trøndelag, to collect taxes. Jamtland, however, was claimed by Sweden and its people were by no means willing to pay tax to Olaf. When a Thing was called in the region, there were loud calls to hang Thorod and the eleven envoys with him. They were put under house arrest, which was not entirely unpleasant, since they seem to have been able to enjoy the Yuletide feasting and drinking with their captors. But as often happens when the drink is plentiful, the Swedes and the Norwegians got into an argument and harsh words were exchanged. That evening Thorod and his company fled into a nearby forest. But it wasn't long before dogs sniffed them out and they were brought back and put in a cellar.

The servants assigned to guard them lost no time in getting drunk, allowing Thorod and the others to fashion crude ropes from their undergarments and use them to haul themselves out of the cellar hatch. With the guards still out cold, they made rudimentary sandals out of reindeer hides and tied them to their feet 'with the hoofs of the reindeer feet trailing behind'. This time they used the cover of night to get away successfully, as the sniffer dogs that were employed the following morning were said to have been misled by the odour of the hoofs. The emissaries at length came upon a peasant cabin where they were able to get some food and warmth. It turned out that the owner of the cabin had picked a remote spot to live because he was wanted for murder. During the night Thorod and the others were woken by the peasant's brother-in-law, a huge man by the name of Arnljot Gelline, who urged them to flee and gave them skis for the purpose. This Arnljot had the reputation of being a notorious brigand, but he was also a proficient skier and had soon left the others behind. The party was able to progress, we are told, only by standing on the sides of Arnliot's broad skis – probably more like snowboards – and hanging onto their guide's belt.

They came to a travellers' inn to stay the night, but when they had settled down to sleep in a loft, Arnljot became uneasy and warned them against making a sound. Even more unusually, he had warned his companions against throwing away even the smallest leftover scrap after their evening meal; he himself refused to eat out of the inn's plates but used a silver plate that he carried on him. Soon afterwards a party of a dozen travelling merchants arrived and made a great deal of merry noise as they ate and drank, carelessly tossing away all the bones and scraps. Here the story becomes definitely grotesque. In Snorri's telling, 'a huge witch' entered and devoured all the scraps, then seized the merchants one by one, tore them to bits and threw them into the blazing fire to eat their flesh after it had roasted. As the sole surviving merchant called for help, Arnljot took up a long, gold-mounted halberd that he carried with him and struck the witch 'between the shoulders so that the point came out at her breast'. Far from dying, the witch gave 'a dreadful shriek' and ran off with the halberd still transfixing her. Arnljot advised Thorod and his companions to move off immediately and follow the incoming snow-track the merchants had made. 'Take my salutation to King Olaf, and say to him that he is the man I am most desirous to see.' He also drew out his personal silver plate, polished it a little with a cloth and asked that it be given to the king with his compliments. When Thorod told Olaf what had happened, the king thought it a pity 'that such a brave hero [Arnljot] and so distinguished a man, should have given himself up to misdeeds'.

This horror story involving a man-eating witch in the snowy wastes of Scandinavia may elicit a disbelieving grimace in a modern reader, and it is true that we have no way of knowing whether Snorri intended it to be taken seriously or not. Yet the tone is matter-of-fact throughout, and though it is merely marginal to the main story of Olaf, its very weirdness invites speculation. Was it an exhausted dream of Thorod, which he related later? Was it the result of inebriated delirium tremens? Was it a way of 'laundering' what could have been a mass murder and robbery by Arnljot, who had a reputation for criminality (and who pocketed the items the hapless merchants had left behind)? We have little doubt that Olaf himself would not have dismissed it as narrated, as evidence that the satanic forces intent on his destruction were everywhere in evidence, and everywhere to be guarded against.

When the snows began to melt in 1027 Olaf decided to make a move to forestall Cnut's expected offensive against him. Gathering an army from the Trøndelag and districts to the north, he left Nidaros on a recruitment drive and heard out local opinion in the Things he called. His initial objective was to discipline the Faeroe islanders who were in arrears with their tribute; he got few takers to join him in that task until one 'remarkable-looking man', decked out in a red tunic and brandishing a halberd, got up and rebuked his listeners for being ungrateful to a king who had done so much for them. In the same speech he admitted to being 'no friend of the king', yet nonetheless volunteered to join him in his planned expedition to the Faeroes.

Olaf asked the man his name, and recognized it when it was told him: Karl Morske, known as an incorrigible brigand and inveterate foe. Often the king had sent out parties to capture or kill this man; now, however, Karl inexplicably was joining him. May we attribute this change of heart to boredom on Karl's part and a simple desire for a bit of adventure; or was there something in Olaf's demeanour that could automatically command respect? Karl Morske took a ship and twenty men and sailed to the Faeroes, where he seems to have been initially successful in negotiating for the delayed tribute money, but in a dispute he was killed by an axe-blow to the head. The survivors of his party sailed back to Norway and informed Olaf, but he could do little about it, as by now he was fully preoccupied with the showdown with Cnut that he knew could not be long delayed.

Olaf set out from Trondheim with a fleet, whose large flagship, the *Visund* (Bison), sported a gilded bison's head on the bow. Sigvat sang: 'Olaf has raised a bison's head, which proudly seems the waves to tread.' The fleet sailed around the westernmost tip of the Norwegian coast at Stad to Hardaland, where he learned that Erling Skjalgson had defected to Cnut in England with a sizeable force. In an attempt to find out more he sailed around the south coast seeking intelligence; whatever sparse information he could glean indicated that Cnut was readying a strike on Norway. However, as to stay put and meet the expected invasion would be seen by his men as doing nothing, he gave the order to sail to Denmark, taking with him only his more reliable and better-trained soldiers.

Once landed in Denmark Olaf reverted to classic Viking tactics, plundering the land and villages, killing and capturing those unlucky enough to be in his way. This was not mere cruelty; the Danish landscape simply had to be made unfit to support Cnut. At the same time he was joined by his brother-in-law King Jacob-Anund of Sweden, who engaged in similar rough tactics. When both kings met up they proclaimed their intention to wrest Denmark from Cnut's hands. Snorri tells us that many Danes, apparently intimidated by the display of brute power, went over to the kings' side.

Cnut, meanwhile, continued his preparations, appointing Earl Håkon Eiriksson of Lade as his second-in-command. This was the Håkon who as a teenager had been pardoned by Olaf after an abortive showdown in 1015; now, as an earl of Lade, he had a vested interest in Olaf's overthrow. At some point during the summer of 1027 Sigvat the skald arrived at Cnut's court on a merchant voyage from Normandy. We are not told the reasons for, or details of, this trip; most likely Sigvat saw the opportunity for a little bit of profit through seaborne trade, as presumably a skald's pay was nothing special. He also could simply have wanted a bit of a change of scene. But when Sigvat reached England he found that Cnut had banned all outbound sailings (presumably to prevent any leakage of information about the military preparations, as sea merchants were prime providers of intelligence) and he found himself trapped with Cnut. Thus he was able to observe everything that was going on, though of course unable to inform his master.

Cnut and his fleet sailed for Denmark before the summer of 1027 was out; he himself had what Snorri calls a gilt-prowed 'dragon-ship' propelled by sixty pairs of oars, while Håkon commanded a smaller one of forty banks of oars. The fleet must have been an impressive sight, with sails of blue, green and red stripes, and painted hulls. Sigvat was impressed enough to compose a poem about it that sounds oddly strange to our ears, as it appears to praise Cnut's power and prestige; however, it may well be that the skald was pressed into composing for the man who gave him food and shelter. The force arrived at Limfjord, to find a large number of allies. There was a brief snag when local Danish nobles elevated Cnut's son Harthacnut to the kingship of Denmark without Cnut's express consent, but that issue was quickly smoothed over.

Cnut's arrival in Denmark had the effect of crystallizing massive support for him there, which is not surprising in view of the depredations of Olaf and Jacob-Anund. Learning of the arrival of Cnut's army, the two kings sailed eastwards and round the southern tip of Sweden to Skåne, chased by Cnut. Olaf halted at the Helga (or Holy) River where it flows out of a lake in a forest (near the modern town of Kristianstad), while Jacob-Anund stationed his ships off the river mouth. Olaf dammed the river, drying out a section of its bed in which they placed timber logs. It was not long before Swedish pickets spotted Cnut's ships approaching; Jacob-Anund sounded the battle-horns and sent couriers to notify Olaf, who abandoned his attempt at a fortification and sped to the river mouth. That evening Cnut reconnoitred the scene; as his fleet was too large for such a small space as the Helga River mouth afforded, and as there was not much wind, he decided to allow his crews and men some shore leave. Without warning, a wall of water came bearing down on them from the river – Olaf had broken the dam. The deluge drove before it the logs that Olaf had put in the river bed. These logs acted like primitive torpedoes, staving in the hulls of many of Cnut's ships in the harbour while many men ashore perished.

In Snorri's account it appears that Olaf's military engineers had come up with this stratagem in precise anticipation of the arrival of Cnut's force at the mouth of the Helga. It sounds like an extraordinarily long shot, but adding credibility to the account is that Cnut's own dragon-ship was caught in the watery onrush and driven into the midst of Olaf's and Jacob-Anund's ships waiting offshore. Cnut's ship came under attack from all sides, but as it stood high in the water it proved impossible to board, defended as it was by a choice crew. Shortly afterwards Cnut's chief lieutenant in Denmark, Earl Ulf Sprakalegson, turned up with reinforcements. After some indecisive fighting, both sides broke off the engagement; Olaf and Jacob-Anund had attained the immediate tactical goal of stalling the Danish attack, while Cnut, his initial plan in disarray and having lost men and ships to the flood, needed to reorganize his fleet.

Extant accounts of the battle at Helga River differ. While the *Anglo-Saxon Chronicle* records it as a definite victory for Olaf and Jacob-Anund, the bard Ottar the Black claims the Anglo-Danes were the victors, and the Norwegians and Swedes suffered heavy losses. Surprisingly, the skald Sigvat also credits Cnut with victory; however, if at the time Sigvat was with Cnut, he may not have had much choice in what he composed.

The two kings, though, could not afford to wait; when Cnut reorganized, they would be greatly outnumbered. There was another complication in that many Swedish crews, reportedly homesick, sailed right on to their homes. This desertion left Jacob-Anund with no more than 100 ships out of the 350 he had started out with; together with Olaf's mere 60 or so, they would not be enough to stop Cnut. Jacob-Anund suggested that Olaf err on the side of caution and stay in Sweden for a time, and is credited with a piece of homespun wisdom: 'It's always good to drive home with the wagon safe.'

But Olaf was not ready to withdraw. True, he replied, he was left with just sixty ships, but their crews were the best that could be recruited; moreover, the Swedish crews that had deserted were because of that fact pretty much worthless anyway. He saw around him, he said, many splendid men and officers. Besides, Cnut would be having problems of his own: if he chose to pursue, Olaf and Jacob-Anund could elude him indefinitely along the Swedish coast; if he chose to stay, his own crews would want to go home. 'But let us first find out what decision he makes.' Spies were duly despatched to infiltrate Cnut's forces.

There were spies from the other side, too, who were sent ashore in Sweden to monitor the progress of the Swedish-Norwegian fleet while Cnut pulled his own fleet back to the Øresund separating Denmark from Sweden. He had already learned about the Swedish crews' desertion, but somehow that did not lighten his mood. Attending a banquet in Roskilde hosted by Earl Ulf, his chief administrator in Denmark, Cnut was sullen and uncommunicative; Ulf attempted to cheer him up by suggesting a game of chess. In Snorri's account Cnut cheated, at which Ulf upset the chessboard and stalked off in a huff. When Cnut taunted him for being a coward Ulf stopped, turned round and retorted: 'You would have run farther at the Helga River if you had actually come to battle there. You didn't call me a coward when I rushed to help you as the Swedes were beating you like a dog.'

The next morning Cnut casually ordered his servant to find Ulf and kill him. The boy found Ulf in church but shrank from carrying out his task in that sacred surrounding. So Cnut gave the order to his Norwegian-born chamberlain Ivar White, who had no such compunctions and did the job without hesitation. Ivar went to the king, 'the bloody sword in hand', and received a rather casual royal thanks. The monks in charge of the church closed it, but Cnut ordered it reopened, and in fact, he later endowed it with considerable wealth. The murder of Earl Ulf, who was supposed to be Cnut's governor in Denmark, suggests that Ulf was suspected of aiming at the kingship himself. The recent mini-crisis over the precise status of Harthacnut may also have had something to do with it, though we know nothing more than what Snorri's somewhat sketchy account tells us. Cnut's moodiness at Ulf's banquet, and Ulf's cutting remark about Cnut's alleged inaction at the Helga River, could indicate a certain amount of pre-existing bad blood between them. And Cnut's deliberate cheating at chess could well have been a way of picking a quarrel with Ulf in order to get him out of the way.

With winter approaching, Jacob-Anund discharged his army, leaving Olaf with his fleet. Some Anglo-Danish prisoners appear to have been taken in the recent battle, who 'lay bound on the shore at night' and were in audible distress. Two of Olaf's aides decided on their own initiative to set free the unfortunates, and no doubt thought they were doing the charitable thing. But the king was furious and for a long time refused to even speak to one of the aides, the high-born Egil Halson. However, when Egil later fell ill and was in pain, Olaf laid his hands on the painful side of his body while chanting a prayer, and 'the pain ceased instantly, and Egil grew better'. The episode again illustrates a certain complexity of Olaf's character; though he could heal with a touch and a prayer, he was very angry when similar charity was shown to his suffering prisoners. We may speculate that in the case of the prisoners he wanted to keep them as potential bargaining counters, but when he could perform a direct individual healing he did not hesitate to do so.

All this time Cnut's spies in Olaf's army were doing their work diligently. They recorded the disagreements over strategy among Olaf's chief advisers and, according to Snorri, offered plentiful bribes to leading men to switch to Cnut's side, for 'every man who came to [Cnut], and who he thought had the spirit of a man and would like his favour, got his hands full of gifts and money'. We are therefore not surprised to learn that Olaf's advisers were split, counselling opposing courses of action. One piece of advice was for Olaf to sail back to Norway via the Øresund – advice which, if followed, would have exposed Olaf's force to an attack from Denmark. Olaf correctly rejected the suggestion as potentially (if not actually) treasonous and decided to return to Norway overland via Gautland and leave the ships for Jacob-Anund to take care of. The king's decision was not unopposed; Hårek of Thjøtta complained that he was too old to trek over the mountains, and besides, he valued his ship, in which he had invested a great deal of work and care. Olaf offered to have Hårek carried for some of the way, but the old sea-dog would have none of it:

> Forests and hills are not for me –
> I love the moving sea,
> Though Cnut block the Sound,
> Rather than walk the ground,
> And leave my ship, I'll see,
> What my ship will do for me.

As Olaf and his army prepared for the long march Hårek sailed westward around the southern tip of Sweden, and by the time he came within sight of Cnut's fleet, probably in the Øresund, he had taken down his red, white and blue sail and mast and disguised the decks and gunwales with grey canvas to make it look like a scruffy trawler. Only a handful of men manned the oars, the rest of the crew hiding inside the hull. Only when Hårek was safely past the Anglo-Danish fleet did he re-hoist his sail while still in sight. Some in Cnut's fleet saw it and thought Olaf himself had sneaked through by employing a stratagem, but Cnut doubted it. Hårek arrived home at Halogaland safely, but Snorri inserts a germ of a doubt about the alleged successful trickery. He cites a view held by many at the time that Hårek was actually in cahoots with Cnut, hence his insistence on going by sea around the Øresund: he knew he would be unharmed. The theory tends to be strengthened by Snorri's reference to a later 'friendly understanding' between Cnut and Hårek. Then why the trawler-disguise in the first place? There is no clear answer to this problem. Olaf himself trekked over Gautland and into Viken to take up winter quarters in Sarpsborg.

The suspicion surrounding Hårek well illustrates that no friendship or alliance, it seems, could be taken for granted – especially as about this time a question mark was even hovering above the figure of Sigvat the skald, who had been promoted to marshal in Olaf's court. As we have seen, Sigvat took advantage of a trading voyage to sail to Normandy and then to England, possibly in the hope of earning a bit of extra money. We have also seen how he composed verses putting Cnut in a good light and praising his war prowess. At some point, probably after the battle at the Helga River, he returned to Norway and went directly to Olaf at Sarpsborg. And we are not exactly surprised when Snorri relates that the king received him with an indifferent silence. As they were dining the skald came out with an impromptu song to the effect that he was done with roaming the seas and desired henceforth to stay by Olaf's side.

Finally the king spoke. 'I don't know if you are still my marshal, or have become one of Cnut's men.' Whereupon Sigvat emitted an oratorio of fidelity:

> Cnut, whose golden gifts display
> A generous heart, would have me stay…
> Two masters at a time, I said,
> Were one too many for one bred,
> Where truth and virtue, shown to all,
> Make all men true in Olaf's hall.

The words were enough to melt Olaf, and very soon Sigvat was back in his favoured position as marshal. Yet we cannot help wondering whether events occurred as Sigvat claimed. Did he indeed say those words to Cnut? Was he offered a choice of allegiances, most likely accompanied by lavish promises? Did he suffer pangs of conscience in England, or did something else happen to steer him back to Norway and the king he had served for so long?

When Cnut heard that Olaf had returned overland to Norway he disbanded his army for the winter but sent Erling Skjalgson to Norway with more lavish bribes that turned many local chieftains to Cnut's cause. It all got back to Olaf, of course, and there were many anxious hours as he and his court debated the dangers. After the Yuletide feasts, at the start of 1028, Olaf set out for Uppland to collect tax arrears, as his summer campaign had drawn heavily on the treasury and besides, he had left all his ships with the Swedes. In Uppland he was well received, but in the district of Osterdal he met a pair of young brothers named Sigurd and Dag, the latter of whom claimed to be clairvoyant and 'could see the misdeeds and vices or every man' he encountered. Intrigued, and we imagine with an impish sense of humour, Olaf asked for his own hidden faults to be detected. When Dag obliged, accurately (though we are not told what the particular faults were), and Olaf questioned him further, he revealed that a certain local official had been in the habit of stealing people's animals; when this, too, proved to be true the official in question was sent packing out of the country and Sigurd and Dag with their valuable abilities joined the king's retinue.

Dag's clairvoyance stood Olaf in good stead a little later when one Thorer Olverson, an eighteen-year-old influential relative of Thorer Hund, invited the king and his entourage to a lavish banquet. Dag, however, remained uneasily silent when Olaf remarked to him how excellent the treatment was. It took some time for Olaf to overcome Dag's reticence, but Dag eventually said he believed that Thorer was 'too greedy for money'.

'Does that mean he is a thief and robber?' Olaf asked.

'No, but to gain money he is a traitor to his sovereign. He has taken money from King Cnut for your head.'

When the king asked Dag what proof he had, Dag mentioned a thick gold ring that Thorer wore on his upper right arm where no-one could see it. That ring, Dag said, was a present from Cnut. So that was where the money for the big feast had come from. Soon afterwards, at the table, and as everyone was merry and tipsy, Olaf ordered Thorer to be called.

'How old are you, Thorer?' the king asked, in a dialogue that Snorri describes like a scene out of a thriller movie and deserves quoting here.

'Eighteen', Thorer replied.

'You're big for your age, and fortunate as well.' As the king spoke he put his hand around Thorer's upper right arm.

'Careful, as I have a boil on my arm', Thorer said, but Olaf had already felt something hard there.

'Haven't you heard that I'm a doctor as well?' Olaf said. 'Let me see that boil.'

Thorer could hardly refuse the king's order, and of his own accord slid the ring off his arm and put it on the table. After admitting that it was Cnut's gift he was seized and put in chains. So furious was Olaf that he shut his ears to all entreaties of mercy and had the young Thorer Olverson executed. But the execution did not sit well with many either in Uppland or in the Trøndelag, and it undoubtedly cost Olaf much popularity at a time when he needed it more than ever. Thorer's brother Grjotgard Olverson vowed to avenge his death and staged raids on royal supply depots. Olaf took a posse and surprised Grjotgard asleep in his house, killing him after a violent but brief scuffle.

When he arrived at Tønsberg Olaf sensed that his support in Norway was melting away in a sea of Cnut's money. His ships were still in the care of the Swedes, but the delegation he sent to get them back was delayed by bad weather in the autumn of 1028. More disheartening news arrived from Denmark: Cnut had collected a fleet of 1,200 ships crewed by men from all parts of his kingdom. ''Tis money that betrays our land', lamented Sigvat, correctly but helplessly. As Cnut in the well-known legend was said to be unable to halt the waves, so Olaf had proved unable to halt the waves of Cnut's gold.

'Let's not pretend that Cnut won't come here in the summer', Olaf warned his entourage and supporters. 'We have only a few men to oppose him, and as matters stand, we can't depend much on the fidelity of the country people.' There was talk of fleeing the country, with Sigvat in particular urging such a course. And that is where matters stood when in the summer of 1028 Cnut launched his grand attack on Norway.

Chapter 10

The Last Battle

Only fools hope to live forever by escaping enemies.

(*Hávamál*)

Olaf was in Tønsberg when the Anglo-Danish fleet was reported sailing across the mouth of the adjoining fjord. Cnut himself had already landed on the Norwegian coast – probably the west coast – where he gained a great many adherents and placed his own men in key positions 'and no man opposed him'. At Egersund he was joined by Erling Skjalgson, who was promised a large chunk of the country to rule as Cnut's vassal. From there Cnut proceeded straight to Trondheim, where he called a Thing at which he was proclaimed king of Norway. Thorer Hund and Hårek of Thjøtta, whose treachery to Olaf was now confirmed, were made sheriffs. Cnut, true to form, 'enriched all men who were inclined to enter into friendly accord with him both with fiefs and money, and gave them greater power than they had before'.

The speed with which Cnut is reported to have brought almost all the northern part of Norway to his side speaks much not only for the rivers of largesse with which he lubricated the country chieftains (remember that Norway was never a particularly rich country); the wealth might not have had such an effect had it not been for Olaf's own rigid and completely uncompromising attitude towards anyone or anything that would hinder his great Christianizing mission. Though of a good and charitable nature himself, he felt he needed to be merciless to the host of powerful and decidedly un-Christian enemies. It is a course that many national leaders, before and since, have felt compelled to follow. What the French were the first to call *raison d'état*, or 'reason of state' has generally nothing to do with personal morality tenets; when a ruler has an entire people to govern, he or she often must cast personal sensitivities aside in the interests of the greater good. It may not be fashionable in our present human-rights obsessed age to admit it, but in a fallen world force is often the only way to secure that good. Olaf was only one of many to realize this harsh truth. But like Olaf Tryggvason before him, it must have seemed to him that he was fighting a losing battle.

With a considerable part of Norway under his sway, Cnut appointed Earl Håkon Eiriksson to administer it. Håkon was the brother-in-law of Einar Tambaskelfer, who got back all the lands that Olaf had taken from him in the Trondheim area. Cnut seems to have gained a rather exaggerated idea of himself at this time, as Snorri records that he erupted in fury when an Icelandic skald in his court composed a poem of praise which he considered far too short for the purpose, and threatened to hang him for it. The hapless skald hurriedly inserted some more verses which included this couplet, which is of incidental interest for its classical allusion:

> Cnut protects his realm, as Jove,
> Guardian of Greece, his realm above.

Rewarded with fifty silver marks instead of a noose, the skald went on to compose a rambling account of the Norwegian expedition 'grander than saga can tell'. Cnut's behaviour here raises the question of how confident he actually was; did he really require long poems of praise to keep up appearances? It's not unreasonable to suppose that, as a Christian ruler himself, Cnut would have had some inner misgivings about hounding a fellow-Christian, especially one such as Olaf who had exerted himself so vigorously in propagating the faith and fighting heathenism.

Olaf, meanwhile, had retrieved barely a dozen of his ships from safekeeping in Sweden and with them he lay in wait in Oslo fjord for Cnut's expected return in that direction. But Cnut's fleet eluded Olaf, who subsequently sailed out along the Viken to get what funds and support he could from the coastal areas and outlying islands. It was now the autumn of 1028 and news was continually arriving from the north of the growing power of Erling Skjalgson. Olaf decided to go and confront Erling's force at Jadar. A few days before Yuletide Olaf's ships sailed past Jadar, braving the rain and cold winds; they were spotted, Erling sounded the 'war-horn' for a general mobilization, and a pursuit took place. Olaf was at a disadvantage from the outset. Besides being outnumbered, his ship timbers were waterlogged from standing too long in their Swedish refuge; together with their heavy loads, they were hard to manoeuvre. Olaf ordered the crews to furl their sails slowly and dismantle the booms. Erling saw this and urged his own crew to speed up to catch the king.

But Olaf had his wits about him. As he saw Erling's ships surging towards him, he ordered his own fleet to row into a narrow inlet, staying out of sight behind a rocky outcrop. Erling promptly sailed right into the trap; the next thing he knew, Olaf's fleet was bearing down on him. In Snorri's words (probably derived from Sigvat, a friend of Erling),

> Erling stood on the quarter deck of his ship. He had a helmet on his head, a shield before him, and a sword in his hand… [He] defended himself so manfully, that no example is known of one man having sustained the attack of so many men so long.

Such was the onslaught on Erling's vessel, with Olaf himself in the front line, that 'there was none who asked for quarter, or none who got it if he did ask'. We are told that in the midst of the fighting Olaf gained his adversary's fore-deck and called out to Erling:

'You have turned against me today.'

'The eagle turns his claws in defence when torn apart', Erling is said to have replied.

Then came a curious incident. The king asked Erling if he was prepared to abandon the rebellion and re-enter Olaf's service. Erling appears to have agreed, and laid down his helmet, sword and shield. Whereupon Olaf 'struck him on the chin with the sharp point of his battle-axe' and condemned him as a traitor to his sovereign. There is some doubt here about just what sort of blow Olaf delivered with his axe; was it a mere aggressive jab at the chin? Whatever it was, one of Olaf's men ran up and rammed his own battle-axe into Erling's skull. Olaf might well have been intending to spare Erling's life in the hope that he might abandon his revolt, as Erling himself had, apparently, just promised. Olaf was furious at his eager warrior for despatching Erling, as it were without permission, asserting that by his hasty deed he had dashed the king's hopes of recovering Norway. He ordered his men not to despoil the bodies of the slain – again to avoid creating any unnecessary hostility – and led his ships northwards just as the rest of the insurrectionists were sailing up. Discovering that Erling and his crew were all dead, they gave up the pursuit.

Olaf's victory, however, proved ephemeral; inevitably, the more he fought to preserve his throne and mission, the more opposition he engendered. The late Erling's sons, for example, in Trondheim and Hordaland, were bent on avenging their father's death. But he still could count on considerable support in the coastal districts and outlying islands. It was among a group of these that Olaf heard of a large force that Earl Håkon Eiriksson was building up at Trondheim. The king consulted his advisers about whether to attack or not; as their counsel (as usual) was divided, he decided to wait overnight. One of his ship captains, however, ran into an ambush by Erling's supporters and was killed.

In the morning Olaf received the news that Håkon's fleet, 'a great armament of many ships', was approaching. Though he had just a dozen ships himself, he sounded battle stations and ordered his crews to man the oars. However, the intention was not to fight but to elude the enemy. At this point some of his commanders deserted him and joined Håkon, leaving him with just five vessels. Entering the long and winding Tordar fjord (probably near present-day Ålesund), he landed at a place called Valldal and set up bivouac quarters there, taking care to put up a cross on a headland. The local chieftain proved friendly but doubted whether Olaf and his dwindling force would be able to make it over the inhospitable terrain inland to Lesjar (modern Lesja?) that would serve as an overland route to Trondheim. Olaf replied that he really had no choice but to try.

One of the curious legends of Olaf intrudes at about this point. According to an anonymous fourteenth-century writer, while Olaf was retreating from Cnut he passed a district where he knew the people were still heathen, and had a desire to stop there and preach the faith to them. He called on a particular family, wrapped in a grey cloak to conceal his identity, taking with him Fin Arnason and another companion. The daughter of the house, however, was not fooled and recognized the king, but was told to keep quiet. At dinner the girl's mother came in carrying a prized heirloom – nothing less than a horse's preserved penis, the revered *volsi*. A horse's penis, not to mention the rest of the animal, was very important in heathen practice as a symbol of strength and fertility. This she carefully unwrapped from its linen covering, preserved by an onion, and placed it in her husband's lap while reciting a ritual verse. It was accepted practice for each guest in turn to take the organ and utter the same phrase. When Olaf took it, however, he threw it straight to the family dog as a treat. Always according to this story, the *Völsa Thattr*, Olaf began forthwith to preach the Christian doctrine, which the husband accepted at once, though the wife, her precious object now a dog's dinner, took rather longer to follow suit.

Another curious story inserts itself here. Not mentioned in Snorri's saga is an alleged episode in which Olaf came on a sea-monster, presumably disporting itself in the fjord and threatening fishing-boats. In the tale, Olaf killed the beast and threw it bodily against the cliffside of the mountain Syltefjellet, on which the shape of a large serpent is still visible, and where Olaf set up the aforementioned cross. Why Snorri failed to record this event (if it happened) is a mystery. Perhaps he himself didn't believe it, thinking it too fanciful to insert into what for him was a serious chronicle.

The story appears in a skaldic poem, the *Glaelognskvida*, attributed to Thorarin Loftunga and written just a few years after the extraordinary event it describes. Thorarin, then, would have been an early hearer of the stories of Olaf's miraculous powers that very quickly circulated after his death. The start of his arduous trek from Valldal to Trondheim would appear to coincide with the first appearance of these powers that were witnessed and relayed far and wide, preparing the ground for the later cult of Saint Olaf. It was not a case of someone being endowed with saintly status only after death, but being vaguely recognized as such while still alive. The sea-monster story has persisted as a key part of the Olaf legend, appearing in a number of illustrations almost to the present.

On the way out of Valldal into the rugged terrain Olaf sat down on a hill to rest and gazed down at the tail-end of the fjord he had come through. Tired, he allowed himself a few pessimistic thoughts about whether his guides were really sincere, but rallied and remounted his horse until he came to what is mentioned in Snorri's text, untranslated, as an *urd*. This appears, in Old Norse, to mean a rocky scree, perhaps the result of an avalanche. (Urd was also the name of an Old Norse goddess of fate, and remains a woman's name in Norway.) Called the Skerfsurd, this obstacle was apparently impassable, according to scouts sent on ahead. A whole night Olaf spent in prayer. Then his chief cook warned of an impending provisions shortage – only two veal carcasses, he said, remained to feed the 500 men with the king. Olaf ordered that a small quantity of meat be placed in every cooking-pot and made the sign of the cross over each pot. Presumably while the meat was cooking he went himself to the Skerfsurd to see how his hard-working men were getting on trying to clear a path. In Snorri's account 'twenty men could now handle stones which previously a hundred men could not move from the place'. Within a few hours the Skerfsurd had been hacked through and the party could continue its journey.

It is therefore at this point in the *Saga of Olaf Haraldsson* that the reported miracles begin to appear. So far we have been given a largely politico-military account of his actions. Olaf's making the sign of the cross over the cooking-pots, reminiscent of Christ's feeding the Five Thousand, is the first such supernatural incident, closely followed by Olaf's washing himself in a spring after the hard work clearing the Skelfsurd. 'At the present day,' writes Snorri, 'when the cattle in the valley are sick, they are made better by drinking at this spring.' The king enquired about other possible obstacles on his route, to be told that there was a place haunted by evil spirits, where no-one wanted to be caught at night. In that case, Olaf replied, one imagines somewhat impishly, that it was just where he intended to be that night.

'Then the kitchen-master came to the king to tell him that he suddenly had an extraordinary supply of provisions, and he didn't know where it had come from, or how.' Snorri implies, but does not overtly state, that the sudden abundance was a direct result of Olaf's blessing of the pieces of meat in the cooking-pots. Moreover, that event is said to have occurred in the sinister place that everyone had feared; that night, we read, a 'dreadful cry' was heard in a cattle-shed: 'Now Olaf's prayers are burning me. I can no longer stay here. I must flee and never come here again.' Just who heard this cry is not made clear, as almost everyone would have been asleep at the time; it could have been the king himself, as the following morning, when the party prepared to continue its journey, he remarked that henceforth a farm would be cultivated at that spot and its crops would never suffer harm from frost or ice, even when other crops did.

After reaching Lesjar, the king moved on into the Gudbrandsdal valley. Now he could not help noticing that some of his less motivated followers were melting away. His support was dwindling fast. His harsh treatment of foes in Uppland, in whose territory he now was, had turned many against him. It would have been about this time that Olaf decided that, for the present at least, the game was up. He allowed those of his followers who had left families, homes and farms to return to them so as not to attract reprisals. He said he would travel first to Sweden as a temporary refuge, after which he intended to return 'if God should grant him longer life'. He expected that Earl Håkon would seize control of Norway, but hoped his rule would be a brief one; moreover, he said, Cnut himself had but a few years to live, after which his authority would evaporate.

Having made these reassuring statements Olaf said goodbye to those who needed to return to their homes, and suggested that they let him know of developments in Norway in his absence. Snorri says that with him were Astrid (no concubines now), their daughter Ulfhild, his son Magnus, the faithful Earl Ragnvald and a party of perhaps a few hundred followers. We can imagine the royal party trudging over the desolate, snowy fells and forests, rather in the manner of the biblical Flight to Egypt, not knowing what the immediate future would bring. They would have traversed the 100 or so kilometres between the southern end of the Gudbrandsdal and the Swedish border, north of present-day Lillehammer and Elverum, and entered the Swedish province of Värmlands Län. There, in the Nerike district, they stayed with an influential man named Sigtryg until the spring. At this time he is reported to have baptized many.

With the advent of warmer weather in summer 1029 Olaf reached the Swedish coast, fitted out a ship and sailed to Russia to seek refuge with Grand Prince Yaroslav I of Novgorod and Kiev and his consort Irene – the former feisty Ingegerd, daughter of Olof Sköttkonung. Yaroslav was a fitting ruler to seek aid from, as his father Vladimir (later Saint Vladimir) had succoured Olaf Trgyggvason in the same manner. Olaf had left behind Astrid and their daughter Ulfhild, taking with him only his son Magnus. In Russia Olaf could at last relax in the knowledge that he was, temporarily at least, no longer in danger of his life. Snorri and others say that his conduct at Yaroslav's court befitted that of his saintly reputation; however, being safe also meant being powerless, and he inwardly must have chafed at the uncomfortable fact that he was no longer in a position to extirpate 'the abominable superstitions of idolatry' from his homeland.[*]

---

[*] (Father Alban Butler, *The Lives of the Fathers, Martyrs and Other Principal Saints*, 1866. From CatholicSaints.Info)

He must also have engaged in a good deal of reflection on the causes of the widespread and growing opposition to him at home. One cause was outwardly obvious from the outset: the aggressive independence of the Norwegian chieftains, boosted and nourished by the endless gold flowing from King Cnut. Snorri inserts the story of Bjorn the marshal who was visited by a delegation from Cnut offering flattery and money to turn against 'Olaf the Thick'. Bjorn thanked them politely but declined. Then when the envoys pulled out a bag full of English money, Bjorn hesitated.

Now when the messenger saw that Bjorn's inclinations were turned towards the money, he threw down two thick gold rings and said, 'Take the money at once, Bjorn, and swear the oaths to King Cnut, for I promise you that this is a trifle compared to what you will receive if you follow King Cnut.' Dazzled by the wealth, Bjorn caved in. By then such scenes would have been common in Norway.

Besides the gold, the harsh measures Olaf often had to apply to enforce his own royal authority, quite apart from the overriding imperative to make Norway thoroughly Christian, did not improve his stock of popularity. He also had to accept the fact that Earl Håkon was by that time more popular in Norway than himself. He had all but abolished the Old Norse custom of seaborne Viking raids, and his administration of justice to keep it that way was correspondingly severe. In Sigvat's words, Olaf's 'just sword gave peace to all, sparing no robber, great or small'. Snorri himself does not ignore the excesses of Olaf's rough justice – 'he appeared hard and severe in his retributions' – but justifies them by saying they were in the main richly deserved.

Here we may leave Olaf, recuperating in Russia, for a while and trace the progress of his chief rival Earl Håkon, who after Olaf's flight had seized his fleet and based himself at Trondheim. One of his key allies, yet another who had deserted Olaf's cause, was Kalf Arnason, whose wife's first husband and two sons had been killed by Olaf's order. It was the woman's bitter complaints that apparently persuaded Kalf to join Håkon in the first place. While Olaf was still in Norway Kalf had sailed to Cnut, who promised him large estates in Norway if he should join the campaign to unseat Olaf. Also visiting Cnut's court was Earl Håkon, who used the occasion to purchase what was necessary for his impending wedding. After loading his ship with what he needed he set out for Norway rather late in the autumn of 1029. He was never seen again. It is generally believed that he and his crew perished in a storm north of Caithness.

When Bjorn the marshal, who earlier had succumbed to Cnut's bribery, heard that Håkon was missing he began to waver yet again. He comes across in Snorri's saga as a weak character, greedy for money yet stricken by conscience. He finally decided that Olaf had a chance after all; not wanting to be on the wrong side in case Olaf returned, he made a long trip by land and sea to Russia. From him Olaf learned of the fate of Håkon, which appeared to have left Norway without a ruler. Bjorn briefed the king and his entourage about conditions in Norway, and the number of rebellious chieftains at large. At one point his tormented conscience seems to have overcome him. He dramatically fell at Olaf's feet, admitting that he had taken money from Cnut and sworn fealty to him, 'but now I will follow thee, and not part with thee as long as we both live'. Olaf's reply was conciliatory, acknowledging that some of his former supporters might well buckle 'when exposed to the wrath of my enemies'. Or, for 'wrath' one might legitimately read 'money'.

Some more of Olaf's healing powers became evident at this time. We are told of a Russian widow whose son was dangerously ill from a neck infection that made him unable to eat. Ingegerd/Irene told her to go to Olaf who, however, to the widow's disappointment, dismissed her rather brusquely with the words that he was not a doctor. The story, however, intimates that Olaf could have been testing the woman's faith, as she boldly replied to Olaf that the queen had told her he was, in fact, the best doctor in town 'and you would use the remedy you understood' – a clear reference to faith healing.

Then the king took the lad, laid his hands upon his neck, and felt the boil for a long time, until the boy grimaced. Then the king took a piece of bread, laid it in the figure of a cross in the palm of his hand, and put it into the boy's mouth. The boy swallowed it down, and from that time all the soreness left his neck, and in a few days he was quite well.

Of course, in a secularist age the point can be made that phenomena such as auto-suggestion, and simply being in the mere awesome presence of the fabled Olaf, could have actually healed the boy. But that need not necessarily negate the factor of genuine faith on the part of both the boy's mother and the king. Either is quite possible. It was then, in fact, that Olaf's reputation as a healing holy man began to spread.

In Russia Olaf thought long and hard about his future course. One Sunday at dinner he lost himself in thought so much that he absent-mindedly whittled away at a piece of wood without realizing what he was doing. When a servant hinted delicately to the king that he was actually doing work on the Sabbath, he realized his sin and at once gathered up all the wood shavings into the palm of his hand and set them on fire with a candle, impervious to the burning. In his more discouraged moments he would contemplate giving up worldly power concerns altogether and retiring to a completely holy life, perhaps in Jerusalem.

That particular location, however, would not have been a good idea; the city was under Muslim rule and recuperating from the disastrous caliphate of mad Hakim II, and the Christian presence there was precarious indeed. Yaroslav would have told him of Constantinople but neither were political conditions in Byzantium very stable at that stage, with a weak emperor on the throne and continual problems with Muslims in the east and heathen Bulgars in the west. At one point, indeed, Ingegerd/Irene suggested that Olaf assume the kingdom of 'Vulgaria', which almost certainly was Bulgaria, to eliminate a major threat to Byzantine – and by extension Christian – security. Olaf mulled over the suggestion, but his advisers vetoed it. His heart, after all, was always with his homeland, but the more he thought of the alternatives open to him, the deeper his dilemma became.

One night when his thoughts kept him awake, and he finally nodded off in the early hours, he dreamed – or rather, as Snorri describes it, experienced a semi-waking trance – that a splendidly-attired man appeared by his bed. He had the idea that it was Olaf Tryggvason come to visit him. The apparition of Tryggvason spoke:

Are you sick at heart over which plan to take up? It seems strange to me… that you are thinking of laying down the kingdom which God has given you…

Go back to your kingdom which you have taken as your inheritance and have long ruled over with the strength God has given you… It is a king's honour to win victories over his foes, and an honourable death to fall in battle with his men… You will not act so as to deny your true right. You can boldly strive for the land, for God will bear you witness that it is your own possession.

Olaf jerked awake, thinking that he saw Tryggvason slipping out of the door, only his shoulders momentarily visible. That visitation, according to Snorri's saga, decided him; he would also have taken some encouragement from the news of Earl Håkon's disappearance and figured that Håkon's support would have taken a blow. The majority of Olaf's entourage keenly endorsed the idea of returning to Norway to fight for his kingdom anew. But Yaroslav and Ingegerd/Irene did their best to dissuade Olaf from his plan; to them it would be the utmost folly to return to the vipers' nest of his foes. They offered him any senior position he wanted, but he was adamant: after all, had no less an authority than Olaf Tryggvason urged him to go back, even if very likely to his death?

Just after Yuletide, in early 1030, Olaf set off from Russia with 200 followers, leaving his son Magnus safe at the court in Novgorod. The southern Baltic coast was icebound; it took some time to negotiate that stretch, and it was not until spring that the ice melted and the party could sail on to the island of Gotland. Here, Snorri relates, Olaf learned of Earl Håkon's disappearance. But the skald appears to contradict himself, as earlier in the saga he reports that it was Bjorn the Marshal who brought the news to Olaf in Russia. The earlier reference appears to be more likely, as Olaf had continually received intelligence of affairs in Norway and could hardly have been ignorant of Håkon's fate until arriving at Gotland; perhaps it was here that the news about Håkon was finally confirmed. The next stage of the journey was across to Sweden, to Lake Mälar, where Astrid and King Jacob-Anund came to meet him.

In Norway itself Thorer Hund arrogated to himself leadership of the northern part of the country, based on the considerable wealth he had gained in trading with the Laplanders, not to mention plenty of unearned income from Cnut. Thorer is said to have had special coats of tough reindeer skin made that would protect him as well as any armour. Having collected a force, Thorer went south to recruit Hårek of Thjøtta. In the Trondheim area Einar Tambaskelfer now assumed the reins of leadership in place of the late Håkon, who had been the last of the independent Lade earls. Einar made at once for England to beg Cnut to keep his promise to give him 'the highest title of honour in Norway' now that Håkon was no more. He was disappointed. Cnut had reserved that honour for his son Svein, but promised Einar that he would receive great advantages regardless. Somewhat miffed, Einar sailed for home.

Meanwhile in Norway, the chieftains were well informed by their spies of Olaf's arrival in Sweden. They sent what Snorri calls 'the war-message token' to all points of the compass, and this way amassed a large force mostly of peasantry. Olaf's allies also got organized, led by one of his half-brothers, fifteen-year-old Harald Sigurdson, who took some 600 men across the Swedish frontier to find out where the king exactly was and join him.

The messages that Olaf received from his own spies were not encouraging. His supporters almost unanimously told him that to re-enter Norway would be madness, given the influence of the chieftains. Even Jacob-Anund declared himself willing to aid an expedition with between 400–500 well-trained and well-armed men, but doubted whether the Swedes in general would care to invade Norway, given the fierce reputation of the chieftains. Olaf, however, was given the liberty to recruit whomever he could on his march. Leaving behind Astrid and Ulfhild a second time, he and his force trekked to Jarnberaland, where he met up with Harald Sigurdson and other supporters, giving the king something like 1,200 men.

A Norwegian exile in Sweden named Dag Hringson received a message from Olaf asking him to join his cause. Dag was a distant relative of Olaf's, a descendant of Harald Haarfager. He accepted the invitation with alacrity, eager to return to his homeland and reclaim the property he had been stripped of. It is not clear how Dag and his family were exiled, as Snorri intimates that he could originally have been driven out by Olaf himself. Nevertheless Dag, 'a quick-speaking, quick-resolving man, mixing himself up in everything', brought more men over to Olaf's side, bringing the total to about 2,400.

'King Olaf led his army through forests, often over desolate moors, and often over large lakes,' Snorri writes, 'and they dragged the boats from lake to lake.' His progress was preceded by messages promising land and booty to whomever should join him. Olaf's force marched in three separate columns: the king with his Norwegians, Dag's contingent and the Jamtlander Swedes. In this way he gained adherents, though some were of very questionable quality. Two of these, named Gauka-Thorer and Afrafaste, saw a chance for some profitable adventure as they had never before seen a battle. But Olaf demanded his own qualifications.

'Are you Christian men?' he asked when they approached him.

'I and my comrades have no faith but ourselves,' replied Gauka-Thorer in what he must have thought was manly pride. Olaf advised them both to be baptized, but they refused and were thus relegated to the rear-guard of the force. Crossing Jamtland the force traversed a ridge from where a large stretch of Norway was visible, about 150 kilometres east of Trondheim. At this point Olaf is reported to have become silent and uncommunicative, unlike his usual sociable self. A wave of nostalgia had come over him as he viewed the country in which he had been happy; he had some sort of mystic vision of not only his own and but also 'the whole wide world, both land and sea'. Bishop Sigurd, who heard his words, believed there was something clairvoyant about that vision.

Olaf had to watch himself every step of the way. While his men were passing through Verdal they trampled a wheat field – against the king's express orders – to the dismay of the farmer. When the farmer complained, Olaf rode around the flattened grain. 'God will make good your loss,' he told the farmer, 'and within a week it will be better.' Snorri says that the wheat indeed grew again, and was better than before. Olaf stayed the night with the farmer, whose two sons joined him after Olaf assured him they would return home safely. There was, however, a potentially serious personnel problem. Olaf's army contained several hundred heathens who might well melt away against serious opposition, and he decided he needed to do something about them. 'I will not mix heathen people with my own,' he declared; indeed, it would vitiate his very purpose of reclaiming his country for Christianity. When these men were pressed to make a decision for Christ, a little under half their number agreed to be baptized and the rest went home. Gauka-Thorer was in two minds, but in the end concluded that 'if I must believe in a God, why not in the white Christ as well as any other?' As for Afrafaste, he didn't care which side he was on, as long as he could get into a scrap. The newly-baptized were rewarded with assigned battle-stations under Olaf's personal banner.

When it became apparent that Olaf would soon have to do battle with the forces arrayed against him, he addressed his men on their tactics. The basic formation would be little changed from that of the march so far: Olaf, his banner, and his close entourage would be in the centre, backed up by volunteer contingents from Uppland and the Trøndelag; Dag Hringson would command the right wing, and the Jamtlander Swedes would make up the left. Olaf divided the force into manageable units based on kinship and friendship so as to reinforce morale and fighting spirit. Helmets and shields were to be adorned with a white cross – sixty years before the practice was adopted for the First Crusade. The signal to charge would be the battle cry: 'Forward, forward, Christian men! Cross men! King's men!' The lines would be spread out somewhat, to prevent outflanking by the enemy. With a final admonition to the men to stick to their units and banners, and to stay under arms around the clock, Olaf stood them down.

The king's wider recruitment efforts, however, were largely ineffectual; the great majority of able-bodied men in the region had either gone over to Cnut's minions or remained neutral, unwilling to take a risk either way. At a conference Fin Arnason was all for ravaging the uncooperative countryside with fire and sword, to 'leave not a hut standing for treason against the sovereign'. Such a deterrent, he argued, would be the only remedy against desertion. The suggestion drew warm applause, but Olaf demurred. True, he admitted, he himself had applied the fire and sword remedy often enough in cases where his adversaries 'rejected the true faith and betook themselves to sacrifices'. But in this case, he argued, it was not God the enemy was fighting against but his own power – a rather lesser offence. There would be no point in needlessly making more enemies. The first step would be an attempt at negotiation. Until then, however, the army would continue its progress, recruiting where it could, seizing forage and supplies where possible, but shunning any needless damage. Olaf also gave orders that any enemy spies caught should be executed.

At this point Olaf had something in the region of 3,000 men. In normal circumstances it might have been enough to fight a pitched battle. But against him a massive, if unruly, force of some 14,000 was massing – the biggest ever assembled in Norway to that time. Snorri calls it the Army of the Bondes, that is, made up largely of peasants and other bondsmen under the leadership of Cnut's bought chieftains. For his own personal defence Olaf assigned a squad of his best men to precede him with a wall of shields. Inside this wall for safety he placed his skalds, the bards who would thus experience the action at first hand and hopefully survive to tell it 'as it was' for later generations. (Was this the origin of what would become the war correspondent?) A noticeable absence was Sigvat, who could that moment have been on a pilgrimage to Rome (Snorri's text here is unclear); wherever he was, he was assumed to be praying for the king's success. Several skalds composed battle-ballads, which were taken up by the whole army. Sang Thormod Kolbrunarskald:

> Up, brave men, up! With Olaf on!
> With heart and hand a field is won.
> One Viking cheer! – then instead of words,
> We'll speak with our death-dealing swords.

As Olaf progressed down to the lowlands he received ever more frequent reports of the size of the Army of the Bondes. He would have had a growing presentiment, as we are told that at this point he gave a large amount of silver to a countryman to hand on to churches and priests – as well as payment for the souls of those of his enemies who should fall in battle, as 'the men who follow us to battle, and fall, will all be saved together'. That same night Olaf slept little, consuming hours in prayer; he awoke, however, before most of his army and called for the skald Thormod to sing a song, a kind of reveille, to rouse the troops. By way of reward Thormod received a heavy gold ring. But the skald was anxious for the king's life and blurted out that the king 'should never part from me either in life or death'. The scene here is strongly reminiscent of the Apostle Peter vowing eternal fealty to Christ, with Olaf the Christ-figure reassuring him: 'We shall all go together as I rule, and you will follow me.' Thormod, however, couldn't help making a snide remark about the absent Sigvat 'with the golden sword'. It was he, Thormod, who deserved to be the king's skald now:

> Your skald shall never be a craven,
> Though he may feast the croaking raven,
> The warrior's fate unmoved I view –
> To thee, my king, I'll still be true.

And so Olaf and his army approached Stiklestad, near the Trondheimsfjord some 25 kilometres south of the fishing and trading town of Steinkjer. This is the narrowest part of Norway today, squeezed by the sea on the west and a bulge of Swedish territory to the east. The countryside is gentle and rolling, alternating between low wooded hills and acres of lush grassland, studded with the occasional farmstead. Purple heather paints much of the vegetation in large brush-strokes, and on a clear day the northern part of the Trondheimsfjord is visible, sparkling in the distance.

But also visible by now were the hordes of Olaf's enemies in the Army of the Bondes. One of its leaders, Hrut of Viggia, took a squad of men up close to Olaf's army – perhaps a bit too close, as Olaf let loose his Icelanders, who killed him. When battle appeared imminent Olaf told his horsemen to dismount and take up positions. There was, however, an empty space on his left, where Dag's force should have been, and the king detached a contingent of Upplanders to fill the place. Among them was Olaf's half-brother Harald Sigurdson, still a mere fifteen. The king feared for his safety, but Harald said spiritedly that if a sword proved too heavy for him, he would tie the hilt to his wrist – 'I shall go with my comrades.'

> My mother's eye shall joy to see
> A battered, blood-stained shield from me.

A local farmer, Thorgild Halmason, offered to fight in Olaf's ranks. The king thanked him but said he preferred Thorgild to stay where he was to care for the wounded and bury the dead after the battle. 'And if I should fall, take the necessary care of my body.'

Olaf also had a visit from that strange Jamtlander Swede, Arnljot Gelline, who had delivered the king's emissary Thorod Snorrason from the man-eating witch. Arnljot is described as: '[S]o tall that none stood higher than up to his shoulders. He was very handsome in countenance and had beautiful fair hair. He was well-armed with a gold-mounted spear.'

This fine specimen of manhood reminded Olaf of his help for Thorod Snorrason's hazardous tax-collecting mission and asked to join his service. The first question Olaf asked him was whether he was a Christian. Arnljot said frankly no, that until now he had relied solely on his own strength, and successfully at that, but now he had decided to place his faith in Olaf.

'If you intend to place your faith in me,' Olaf told him, 'you must also place faith in what I teach you. You must believe that Jesus Christ has made heaven and earth, and all mankind, and to him shall all those who are good and right-believing go after death.'

Arnliot said that he had indeed heard much of the 'white Christ', but didn't know much else, 'but I will believe all you tell me and put my fate in your hands'. Arnljot was baptized, given as much Christian catechism as the shortness of time would allow, and placed in the front line under the king's banner, held aloft by Thord Folason.

With the army – or as much as could be assembled – in position, Olaf began his pep talk. In Snorri's description he cut an impressive figure: clothed in chainmail, his helmet glittering gold. In one hand he held his white shield with a gold-inlaid cross on it, and in the other his lance. His gold-handled sword, Hneitir, rested in its scabbard. He was well aware, he said, of the numerical superiority of the enemy, yet was not cowed, as 'it is fate that determines victory'. He vowed either to win this battle or die trying, leaving the result to God, Who 'must either protect us and our cause or give us a far higher recompense for what we may lose here in this world'. He promised his men in case of victory that they would receive adequate land. As for tactics, Olaf urged a sharp, shock advance on the enemy front line to drive it back against the rear lines for maximum confusion. The speech was received with cheers.

As the enemy was still some distance away, Olaf felt he could allow his army a little rest. He sat down in the centre of the assemblage and promptly dozed on Fin Arnason's knee. As he slept he dreamed that he climbed a ladder almost to the gates of heaven; but just as in the dream he was about to take the final step, he was jerked awake by Fin who had seen the entire enemy force advancing. Olaf looked, but judged that the enemy was still too far away, and upbraided Fin was not letting him sleep a little more, especially as he was having such an inspiring dream. But on hearing Olaf's dream Fin's heart sank; to him it sealed his king's doom.

The *Passion* adds that Olaf had another dream on the eve of the battle:

> The Lord Jesus appeared to him, soothing him with fair words, with words of solace. 'Come to me,' he said, 'my beloved. It is time for you to reap the most sweet fruits of your labours, and receive the crown of everlasting honour.'

In this account Olaf was 'elated beyond measure' and 'offered himself joyously to martyrdom'.

The Army of the Bondes arrayed against Olaf outnumbered his by at least four to one. But it was not so well-organized or disciplined. Subsequent accounts speak of a vast 'peasant army' and it is true that the great bulk of it consisted of farmhands and labourers, led by local nobles. Most of the men were from the Trøndelag, where opposition to Olaf was at its most intense, no doubt cultivated by the late Earl Håkon and his like. The army contained a hot-headed bishop, Sigurd, who seems to have been Cnut's puppet. (Historically, this cannot be the Bishop Sigurd who ministered to Olaf, but another, vaguer figure of Danish origin.) This Sigurd is reported addressing the troops to the effect that Olaf was nothing but a raider and plunderer by nature; naturally he made a great deal out of the savage punishments that Olaf had in the past inflicted on his foes. 'Do you think he will now be more merciful to you, when he is roaming about with such a bad crew?... Cast forth these malefactors to the wolves and eagles, leaving their corpses on the spot!'

Sigurd's peroration, as recorded by Snorri, makes no mention of religious issues, which might seem strange in a speech by a bishop. He could not have been unaware of Olaf's Christian beliefs, but it is striking that the knowledge appears not to have made him the slightest bit conciliatory. He himself made much of his allegiance to Cnut, whom he considered the authentic Christian ruler of Norway. In his eyes, then, Olaf was a mere usurper, a rival who had to be eliminated. Sigurd no doubt saw himself as the imminent archbishop of Norway, but what of more practical issues, such as who would be in command?

A conclave of army leaders suggested that Hårek of Thjøtta assume overall command, but Hårek declined on grounds of age; he would now have been nearing seventy. He also said it would look bad if he assumed too high a profile against Olaf, who after all was a relative in the bloodline of Harald Haarfager. After some inconclusive discussion, it was agreed that Kalf Arnason should raise the banner, with Hårek at his side and Thorer Hund's contingent in the vanguard. Flanking Thorer were squads of selected warriors; the men of the Trøndelag and Halogaland made up the central mass and the right wing, with Rogalanders, Hordalanders and other coastal levies on the left. In the front line was an aggressive character named Thorstein Knarrarsmid, a former shipwright and merchant who had once been fined a merchant ship by Olaf for manslaughter; he had hated the king ever since for 'robbing' him of his ship, and wanted to be the first to get in a blow at him in the field. In fact, anyone who felt he had a personal grudge against Olaf – and there were plenty – was encouraged to take up a position from which he could charge the king's banner directly.

Thus thoroughly stirred by thoughts of revenge, stoked by rabble-rousing speeches by Thorstein and others, the Army of the Bondes trudged towards Stiklestad, Kalf and Hårek in front, banners flying. It was actually a rather disorganized mass, as there was some delay in getting all the contingents to march in coordination. Bringing up the rear was Thorer Hund, whose task was to stop any desertions when battle was joined. By the time the army came in sight of Olaf's force, Dag had already come up to join Olaf, who still was far outnumbered. Sigvat the skald partly faults Olaf for not spending enough on more men:

> I grieve to think the king had brought
> Too small a force for what he sought:
> He held his gold too fast to bring
> The numbers that could make him king.

As the two front lines approached each other in clear summer sunshine on 29 July 1030, acquaintances on both sides called out greetings, rather in the manner of Union and Confederate officers in the American Civil War. Olaf noticed Kalf Arnason and called out to him to ask why he was fighting, as they had last parted as good friends and, moreover, four of Kalf's brothers were with the king. Kalf replied, rather lamely, that circumstances had changed, and if it were up to him there would be a reconciliation. Kalf's brother Fin warned Olaf that Kalf was insincere. The king replied that the force before him did not appear very conciliatory. At that point, reminiscent of opposing warriors haranguing one another in Homer's *Iliad*, Thorgeir struck a more aggressive note, warning Olaf that he was about to suffer the same 'peace' he had once meted out to his own foes. To Olaf, who had originally raised Thorgeir to his present exalted station, it was a mean statement, and he said so.

But the Army of the Bondes was getting impatient. 'Forward!' yelled Thorer Hund, to be echoed at once by Olaf's soldiers: 'Forward, Christmen, cross men, king's men!' There followed a confused melee on the Army of the Bondes' wings, which echoed Thorer's battle-cry that was mistaken for Olaf's; men on the same side butchered one another before the mistake was realized. Olaf ordered a charge on the enemy from high ground and at first drove the whole centre of the Army of the Bondes in wild flight. But the sturdier, armoured elements among the Bondes held fast and urged the fleeing men back into the fray.

A counter-attack by the Bondes resulted in a sharp close-quarters fight, the men in front slashing with swords, those behind jabbing with their spears, and the light-armed men in the rear shooting arrows and throwing stones and hand-axes. Newly-baptized Arnljot Gelline was one of the first to fall on Olaf's side, along with Gauka-Thorer and Afrafaste, who presumably had gone along just for the adventure.

Seeing he was suffering serious losses, Olaf ordered his standard-bearer Thord Folason to advance, himself following close behind his picked squad with its wall of shields. The king got right to the front himself, 'and when the bondes looked him in the face, they were frightened and let their hands drop'. Sang Sigvat:

> Clear as the serpent's eye – his look
> No Trondheim man could stand, but shook
> Beneath its glance, and skulked away...

This was Olaf's supreme moment. By all accounts he fought valiantly, drawing on all his military experience right back to his feat at London Bridge twenty or so years before. Coming on Thorgeir of Kvistad, he slashed him across the face, 'cut off the nose-piece of his helmet, and clove his head down below the eyes so that they almost fell out,' and addressed a few sarcastic words to him into the bargain. Thord Folason stuck the king's banner firmly in the ground, but that was the last thing he ever did, as he fell mortally wounded almost immediately afterwards.

At this hour, Snorri relates, 'the heavens and the sun became red, and... it became as dark as night'. We know now that a total eclipse of the sun occurred on that date (or the day after, 30 July). It was just as Dag Hringson was bringing up his own delayed column to join the fray, but in the sudden inexplicable darkness the men became confused. In the front line Olaf slashed at Thorer Hund across the shoulders, but Thorer's thick coat of multiple layers of reindeer skin protected him except for a wound in the hand. Olaf turned to Bjorn the marshal with an order to kill 'the dog whom steel will not bite'. Bjorn smashed a battle-hammer down on Thorer's shoulders, momentarily stunning him, but that was the last thing the marshal ever did, as he fell, transfixed by a spear. Thorstein Knarrarsmid, he who believed he had been 'robbed' of a ship by Olaf, struck the king on the left thigh with his battle-axe, to be immediately slain in turn by Fin Arnason.

The king after the wound staggered towards a rock, threw down his sword and prayed God to help him. Then Thorer Hund struck at him with his spear, and the stroke went in under his mail-coat and into his belly. Then Kalf struck at him on the left side of his neck.

Dag Hringson was in the fight and making headway until overcome by a concentrated counter-attack and forced back through a valley where 'men lay scattered in heaps on both sides'. By that time, King Olaf Haraldsson was dead.

One of his men, Thormod Kolbrunarskald, fell back wounded. As he paused for breath an arrow hit him in the left side; he snapped off the shaft and staggered to a nearby barn, where he met a man named Kimbe who said he had just been in the battle on the side of the Bondes. Kimbe noticed a gold ring that Thormod was wearing, realized he was one of Olaf's men, and demanded the ring in return for being taken to safety. When Kimbe reached out his hand to take the ring Thormod chopped off the hand with a single sword-blow.

Thormod went into a room where many wounded men were being tended by a young woman heating water over a fire. The first thing he noticed was that the girl seemed to be giving priority to younger men handsomer than himself. But the girl soon reached him and examined the wound. The iron arrow-head was deep in the abdomen and hard to get at; Thormod gave his gold ring to the girl, telling her it was King Olaf's, then took the pincers and wrenched out the arrow-head himself. The head itself was barbed, so that it came away with pieces of flesh and fat deposits. Thormod made a rueful comment that the king indeed fed him well, and then leaned back and died and joined his king.

When he fell mortally wounded at Stiklestad, Olaf Haraldsson was just thirty-five years old. He had been king of Norway for fourteen tumultuous years. And many at the time thought that was the end of the line for Olaf. King Olaf was finished. But the legend of Saint Olaf was only just beginning.

Chapter 11

The Saint

We have seen in previous chapters how certain divine attributes of Olaf would occasionally emerge in his earthly life and reign. From what we are told, early in life he probably acquired a certain charisma that stood out, for example, during his teenaged sojourn in the court of King Cnut, where he reportedly could not help but emit a royal aura, much to Cnut's chagrin. Then came the occasions where his enemies would somehow come under his spell, and potential assailants would be neutralized by a mere glance or sharp phrase.

Later the actual miraculous events came more into focus, as with the multiplication of the meat portions when he and his followers were about to tackle the Skelfsurd on their trek through the southern Trøndelag, or the restoration of the farmer's wheat field shortly before the Battle of Stiklestad. Some of these miracles he performed reluctantly, as if afraid of the temptation to exalt himself or be seen as a mere magician. This seems to have been the case with the Russian widow's sick boy, healed only after his mother's insistence. A true saint does not advertise the fact; he or she must suppress the ego more than anyone, so as not to become an idol and thus nullify God's mysterious mantle.

The miracles of Olaf, therefore, begin to appear for the most part after his death, the first such occurring just after he had breathed his last and Thorer Hund, his killer, had bent over Olaf's body and in what we like to think of as a gesture of respect for a fallen foe, spread a cloak over it. In Snorri's account, when Thorer wiped the blood away, it seemed to him that Olaf's face was as fair and fresh as if he were alive. Some of the blood ran between Thorer's fingers where he had been wounded, and the wound promptly healed without treatment – as Thorer himself later testified most earnestly.

The Battle of Stiklestad lasted about an hour and a half and ended practically with Olaf's death. Kalf Arnason of the Army of the Bondes retrieved his two brothers who had been fighting on the other side and had been wounded and took them back on his ship. The rest of the ragtag army melted away rapidly, as most of the men wanted to return to their homes and farms. As Snorri tells it, the development seems sadly anticlimactic, and lends an air of bitter futility to Olaf's loss. As the experience of Thormod Kalbrunarskald attests, the local farmsteads were full of wounded men being looked after, and where there were not enough buildings available, tents were set up. Thorer Hund and 600 men pursued some of the remnants of Olaf's army, including Dag Hringson's contingent, up through the mountains of Verdal towards Swedish territory, but gave up the chase as futile. Five days after the battle Thorer returned to Stiklestad, to find burial parties still at work and many wounded men still being treated. The first thing he did, writes Snorri, was ask where Olaf's body had been taken. No-one seemed to know. But one man said he heard that Olaf had been seen the previous night in the hills with a troop of men. Just how that rumour began is not known, but many seemed to place some credence in it. Thorer himself was in no doubt that he had killed Olaf, but thought no more about it and sailed off with a shipload of wounded men.

Olaf's body was in fact taken up by Thorgils Halmason, the farmer who had wanted to fight alongside the king but had been advised to stay put, and his son Grim towards evening, several hours after the battle ended. They took it to a small hut on the edge of their farm, removed the bloody and soiled clothing, washed it, wrapped it in linen and hid it under a pile of firewood. The battlefield may have been empty of warriors (except for the dead and wounded), but as usual in those times, swarmed with poor camp-following beggars eager for any scrap of food or shelter. Snorri reports a story that one of these poor fellows, who was blind to boot, was led by a boy to Thorgils' hut, where he felt for a place where he could lie down for the night. As he stooped his hat fell over his face, and when he tried to raise his hat he felt that his hand was wet. His fingers happened to touch his eyes, which began to itch furiously. Feeling most uncomfortable, the man exited the hut, to find that immediately 'he could distinguish his hands, and all that was near him'. He walked to the farmhouse declaring to everybody he met that he could see. Thorgils and his son guessed the truth: that the water they had used to wash Olaf's body and that had remained on the floor of the hut contained enough of Olaf's blood to have healing properties. The healing of the blind beggar is the first instance of a miracle manifesting itself after Olaf's earthly demise.

For Thorgils and his son, however, there still remained the very practical problem of what to do with the body. They had overheard his enemies looking for it and vowing to burn it or throw it into the sea. Making their task rather more difficult was a mysterious light that they saw hovering over where the body was hidden, and which could prove a giveaway. They therefore made two coffins, putting Olaf in one and filling the other with a man's weight in stones and straw. As by now night must have fallen, the father and son probably waited until the next day, when they loaded both coffins onto a ship in the Trondheimsfjord; the coffin with Olaf was stowed below decks and the other placed in full view above. It was evening when the boat docked at Nidaros and messengers were sent to notify Bishop Sigurd – the Dane loyal to Cnut, not Olaf's own bishop Sigurd – that the king's body had been brought to him. The bishop swallowed the deception and sent men to row alongside Thorgils' ship and take the weighted-down coffin to dump into the sea.

Thorgils and Grim, no doubt smiling grimly, tacked back up the fjord at night to a place called Saurhlid, where they deposited the coffin with Olaf's body in an empty house. This was probably not too far from Trondheim, as Thorgils is said to have returned to 'the town' to contact some of Olaf's friends about the proper burial of the body. Under an unfriendly regime none of the friends dared do anything to help, so Thorgils retrieved the coffin and rowed up the fjord some distance to a sandy hill where they buried the body and levelled the grave so that it would be inconspicuous. Day had not yet broken before Thorgils and Grim, their secret safe, returned home to their farm at Stiklestad.

With the demise of King Olaf, Cnut could now realize his claim to the real kingship of Norway. As a practical measure, in fact, he assigned the throne to his thirteen-year-old son Svein, with his English mother Aelfgifu as regent. At the time of Stiklestad Svein was already in Viken, no doubt poised to take over Norway if the Army of the Bondes proved victorious. Once installed in Trondheim, however, he began a rule that an authority such as Ferguson describes as a frank 'colonial exploitation'. Norway was treated as Danish-occupied territory. No Norwegian was allowed to leave the country without royal (that is, Aelfgifu's) permission. At Yuletide every household had to supply provisions to the palace; forced labour was levied to build the royal farmsteads. Women were taxed on the amount of flax they wove; such were the levies on produce that poor families were forced to eat cattle fodder in lean times. Every seventh young male was marked for conscription, while the legal system was so heavily weighted in favour of the Danish overlords that in court cases one Danish witness could overrule ten Norwegians.

Naturally, this unexpectedly harsh despotism shocked the great majority of people. 'You were promised peace and justice', Olaf's supporters taunted those who had opposed him. 'Now you have slavery and oppression for your great treachery and crime.' But few were in a position to do anything about it. Many families had given hostages to Cnut and were, of course, loth to endanger them in any way. Svein being but a minor, Aelfgifu must bear the responsibility for his harsh rule.

One of the bitterly disillusioned ones was Einar Tambaskelfer, who had refrained from fighting King Olaf but had been promised (or so he believed) the regency of Norway by Cnut. He was therefore in a receptive mood to hear the reports of miracles attributed to Olaf that were beginning to be heard in the Trøndelag, and to wonder if there was anything to them. The reports multiplied in the winter of 1031, and had great influence, we are told, even among those people who had most bitterly fought Olaf in the past. It was not long before their ire was turned against Sigurd the Danish bishop, who had done much to stir up anti-Olaf hatred and who came under such opprobrium that he was forced to flee to his master Cnut in England. In his place came Bishop Grimkell, whom Olaf had brought from England and who had remained quietly in Uppland after Olaf had moved to Russia.

On the way to Nidaros Grimkell fell in with Einar Tambaskelfer, who by now had placed full faith in the reports of the miracles occurring in Olaf's name. Once at Nidaros the bishop received a visit from Thorgils and Grim, who revealed to him Olaf's secret burial-place. Yet they had to be careful, as Nidaros was the seat of King Svein and his all-powerful mother, the despised Aelfgifu; permission, therefore, had to be asked of them to give Olaf's body a decent interment. Their agreement indicates that they either deemed the cause not worthy of their attention, or that they had begun to take notice of the miracle stories and deemed it unwise to upset the locals too much by denying Grimkell's request.

Olaf's coffin was disinterred on 3 August 1031, a year after the Battle of Stiklestad. Snorri says that it had in the meantime raised itself almost to the surface, and when it was unearthed it appeared as if new, without visible decay. When the coffin was opened in Grimkell's presence, the saga goes, a sweet smell arose. Olaf's face seemed as fresh and rosy as if he were alive, and his hair and fingernails showed a year's growth. Present were King Svein and Aelfgifu, who tried to play down the momentousness of the sight by commenting that bodies buried in sandy soil decompose very slowly, so there should really be no surprise.

When challenged by Grimkell to explain the growth of nails and hair, Aelfgifu retorted that she would believe in Olaf's sanctity only if his hair refused to burn. Grimkell thereupon snipped off some of the long hair. Then the bishop had live coals put into a pan, blessed it, cast incense upon it, and then laid King Olaf's hair on the fire. When the incense was burned the bishop took the hair out of the fire and showed the king and the other chiefs that it was not consumed.

Still Aelfgifu was not convinced, and demanded another demonstration, but Grimkell, with what must have been rare courage, 'silenced her and gave her many severe reproaches for her unbelief'. Svein himself seems to have been willing enough to recognize Olaf's sanctity – whether out of conviction or convenience cannot be known – and permitted the coffin to be taken to Clement's church in Trondheim, where it was deposited at the high altar and covered with expensive fabric.

The church quickly became a focal point, a shrine, for people seeking divine help. A similar spot sprang up at the sand-hill where Olaf was first laid to rest; a fountain of water emerged that was said to have healing powers and was preserved in bottles as holy. A chapel was built on the site, replaced by a larger church whose altar still stands over the spot where Olaf was buried or, according to another version of the story, where the hut where Olaf was first taken once stood and where the miracle of the bloodstained water took place. As for the deceased Olaf himself, according to Sigvat:

> I lie not when I say the king
> Seemed as alive in everything:
> His nails, his yellow hair still growing,
> And round his ruddy cheeks still flowing.

Bishop Grimkell, the story goes, found that he had to regularly cut Olaf's hair and nails.

Even in King Svein's brief five-year reign the cult of Olaf grew in intensity and breadth. One of his bards, Thorarin Loftunga, composed a song of the late king who had begun to exert such extraordinary power over the Norwegian people, a power greater than he ever could while alive:

> And crowds do come,
> The deaf and dumb,
> Cripple and blind,
> Sick of all kind...
> To Olaf pray
> To eke thy day,
> To save thy land
> From spoiler's hand.

Thorarin attested that 'vast numbers' of people were cured by visiting Olaf's shrine.

Small wonder, then, that within a very few years Svein and Aelfgifu were widely accused throughout Norway of having engineered the death of their holy king, aided and abetted by the treacherous people of the Trondheim area. The despotism of Svein, and the suffering it caused, were seen as divine punishment. The leading men of the Trøndelag, disturbed by the bad reputation the region was acquiring, began to wonder whether there was something to what was being said. The wonder soon turned to near-certainty, as leading lights such as Einar Tambaskelfer and Kalf Arnason began a process of painful soul-searching. Had they in fact been duped by Cnut? Neither Einar nor Kalf had gained any reward for their services in eliminating Olaf, as Cnut had promised. Kalf, in fact, had put his life on the line leading the Army of the Bondes and fighting at its head; he accordingly made peace with his brothers on the opposite side.

Svein faced a serious threat in 1033 in the person of one Trygve Olafson who claimed to be a son of Olaf Tryggvason and Queen Gyda of England (not to be confused with the Gyda who enchanted Harald Haarfager) and had raised a force in the west, probably from Denmark and England. When that force landed in Norway Svein called out a mass levy. Einar Tambaskelfer, in fact, pointedly ignored the call and stayed at home; Kalf

Arnason equipped a ship but instead of joining Svein he hastened south to consult his brothers, returning to an impatient king. To Svein's request to enlist his ship in the defence of the kingdom Kalf returned a flat refusal. 'I've done enough,' Snorri quotes him as saying, 'if not too much, fighting my own countrymen to increase the power of Cnut's family.'

Svein (still only about sixteen years old) sailed his fleet around the southern tip of Norway to Viken in search of Trygve, then retraced his route, colliding with Trygve's fleet probably somewhere north of Bergen. A fierce battle took place, in which Trygve distinguished himself by his prowess, strengthening his claim to be a son of Olaf Tryggvason, who he said had taught him to celebrate Mass by throwing spears with both hands at once. But his warlike talents were not enough to save him, and he was killed along with many of his men, the riddle of his paternity unsolved.

Svein's respite was short. At some point an order came from Cnut to Kalf Arnason to send him three dozen battle-axes, 'chosen and good'. The reason for this striking request is not given. Cnut certainly had no pressing need of such a small amount of military equipment; very likely he wanted to test Kalf's allegiance, as he would have heard of the growing unrest in Norway under his son's rule. There was no way Kalf would comply; he told the messenger who conveyed the order to relay to Cnut that he, Kalf, would 'bring his son Svein so many' axes that he wouldn't know what to do with them.

From that point on it was war between Svein and Aelfgifu on the one hand, and Einar and Kalf and the majority of Norwegians on the other. In the spring of 1034 Einar and Kalf prepared their campaign. Amassing as many men as they could in the Trøndelag, they trekked over the rugged Swedish frontier into Jamtland and to the Baltic coast. There they obtained ships that when the weather was warm took them to the Russian port of Ladoga, in the trail of Olaf six years before. At Ladoga they sent word to Grand Prince Yaroslav to allow Olaf's son Magnus, all of eleven years old and living with Yaroslav and Ingegerd/Irene, to return with them to Norway to be crowned the legitimate king and heir of Olaf. On receiving the message Yaroslav summoned Einar and Kalf to his court at Novgorod. That Magnus, as the son of Olaf's concubine Ulfhild, was technically illegitimate was no obstacle. There both men pledged allegiance to Magnus, as well as an uncertain number of others who accompanied the mission and had repented of having fought Olaf at

Stiklestad. Snorri informs us that Magnus (presumably aided by mature advice) agreed forthwith to be Norway's king when he attained his majority, and until then to live as a foster-son of Kalf Arnason.

At this point Snorri concludes his extensive saga of Olaf Haraldsson, to follow it up with the saga of Magnus, called the Good in subsequent annals. Magnus gained the throne of Norway with an ease that may not surprise us, given the general contempt into which the Svein regime had fallen, and mass repentance among many who had opposed Olaf in the past but now recognized his sainthood. From here the story of King Olaf becomes that of Saint Olaf; he is transformed from a warrior monarch who lost the battle for earthly power into the ultimate winner – a heavenly healer of bodies and souls, and eventually to his present status as the patron saint of Norway.

Just when Olaf was proclaimed a saint remains vague, but it was most likely on 3 August 1031, a year after Stiklestad, when Bishop Grimkell performed the beatification ceremony. Cnut, oddly enough, seems to have had no objection to recognizing Olaf as a saint. Perhaps, now that Olaf was no longer a physical threat to his power, he could afford to be charitable. In fact, churches dedicated to Saint Olaf were going up all over the Norse world, from Dublin to Novgorod, some forty of them in Britain alone. Before the century was out Olaf would have a church in Constantinople and be recognized by Byzantine Emperor Alexios I Komnenos as a saint of the Greek Orthodox Church (which he still is).

The canonical *Passion and Miracles of the Blessed Óláfr* goes into some detail of what happened in Byzantium when the Varangian Guard, an imperial body made up of Scandinavians, Anglo-Saxons and Russians, was very hard pressed in battle against 'a certain king of the heathens' and prayed to Saint Olaf to save them. This is likely to have been one of the many battles which the Greeks waged against the pagan Pechenegs and their chief Chaka, sometime after 1090. As Emperor Alexios I valued his Norsemen highly, he was at first reluctant to risk them in battle, but as the Pechenegs prevailed, and the Greeks fell back with heavy losses, an Icelander in the Varangian Guard named Thorir Helsing begged Alexios to let the guard 'leap into the fire'. In the words of the *Passion* the Norsemen called on Saint Olaf for aid, promising him a special church in Constantinople, and 'the martyr appeared to some soldiers and preceded the vanguard of the Christians as an illustrious standard-bearer'.

When that church of Saint Olaf was built is uncertain; the Vikings in Greek service are known to have had their own place of worship in an annexe to Haghia Sophia, and there are no reports of another. At the time it was famous for containing Olaf's sword Hneitir, which he had been carrying at Stiklestad and which had, according to the legend, been picked up by a Swede in his service and preserved as an heirloom for his descendants, one of whom took it to Byzantium. Emperor Alexios was said to have bought Hneitir for three times its weight in gold and had it placed reverently on the altar in Saint Olaf's church. The city also sent 'many precious things' to adorn Saint Olaf's church in Trondheim. Both church and sword disappeared in 1204 when the Fourth Crusaders sacked Constantinople.

That story describes one of some fifty miracles attributed to Saint Olaf after his earthly demise recorded in the *Passion*. Of these, eight involve restoring sight, eight deal with restoring distorted or broken limbs and eight more with multiple healings of various ailments in the same person. The dumb are made to speak in six instances, and mental illness is (including a case of epilepsy) healed in three. There are five cases in which invocation of the saint rescues someone from confinement or imprisonment, four where a dangerous fire is doused, two where an abundance of food (fish and livestock) appears after fervent prayer, two where victory in battle is granted, and one each for raising a person from the dead, helping a building go up, finding a lost boy and for a fragrance emanating from the saint's tomb.

It would be tempting in our secular age to dismiss these as mere pious tales, but such a stance would be historically irresponsible. The border between 'factual history' (whatever that may mean) and the mythological element has always been blurred and porous. In the case of Saint Olaf, one cannot separate the historical-political element from the divine; they are too tightly intertwined. It would be a foolhardy commentator who attempted to apply a scalpel to try to separate the two. The author of the *Passion* (if we assume, as is probable, that it is Bishop Eysteinn Erlendsson) takes great pains in his text to add touches of authenticity where he can, declaring that he and others were 'personally enlightened' by Olaf's miracles, 'as we have seen for ourselves or have learned from the testimony of truthful men'. And here he gives his own corroboration.

It was while Eysteinn, accompanied by a number of other people, was apparently inspecting some building or repair work on Saint Olaf's church when the scaffolding gave way under the combined weight and the bishop fell a considerable distance onto a mortar trough, breaking some ribs. He was carried away unconscious, and when he came to he realized that he would be unable to attend a ceremony scheduled for Saint Olaf's day three days hence, for which the church was being repaired. The realization pained him as much as his cracked ribs, and he prayed to Olaf for some solution.

When the saint's day dawned Eysteinn was still too weak to walk, so his attendants agreed to carry him to the church to which a great many people had flocked. Once there, however, he felt his strength slowly returning and asked for his sacerdotal robes. He had been originally scheduled to deliver a sermon during a halt in the procession; he had no real confidence he could do it, but attempted a small homily on the Pope's power to remit sins. Describing the occasion in the *Passion*:

> But when, in answer to my prayers, my strength grew even as I spoke, I drew out the exhortation in the usual – albeit unexpected – sermon. And I carried out the rites of mass, and of the whole ceremony, in such a way that the effort did not leave me fatigued, but rather the fatigue left me thoroughly refreshed.

He still experienced some pain for a time, but his broken ribs were soon fully healed.

This story, of course, is open to more than one interpretation. A secularist might say that the ecclesiastical environment combined with strong auto-suggestion, or some other superficially 'natural' process, could have been responsible for Eysteinn's healing. But that does not necessarily clash with the view that healing miracles are genuine. In the view of C.S. Lewis, for example, a miracle is a natural process speeded up and telescoped by divine intervention for a specific purpose. Eysteinn's ribs would have healed anyway, but the speed at which they seem to have done, and after prayer, impressed him so much that he attributed it to the saint's direct action.

Of the miracles restoring sight to the blind, one of the more dramatic deals with a blind Swedish woman who had made a long and difficult journey over the mountains to visit Saint Olaf's shrine on his feast-day, and during the mass received her sight, which she had been without for thirteen years. Other blind people are reported to have been similarly cured on the occasion of the saint's day. Another blind woman, possibly from the Stiklestad area, had been blind since childhood when, playing with another child, one eye had been pierced by a knife-point. The 'intervention of the martyr' restored her sight. A partly-blind young man travelled to Nidaros in supplication for a healing, and was cured after a few days. As he was not from that region he was at first disbelieved by many, but on Saint Olaf's day other out-of-towners confirmed the man's story.

As the eyes and tongue are two of the most valued parts of the body in terms of perception and communication, miracles involving them tend to be more common than for other problems. The *Passion* gives us a rather gruesome instance of a young boy who suffered the barbarous punishment of having his tongue cut out for a crime that we are assured he did not commit, 'as often the just bear blame for the wicked'. After travelling to Saint Olaf's shrine he spent some time there 'in prayer and tears' before falling asleep, exhausted.

He saw coming forth from the shrine a man of middle height, with a handsome countenance, who, approaching nearer and opening the youth's mouth with his hand, drew out the remaining part of his maimed tongue and stretched it out with such force that the youth, unable to bear the violence of the effort, was compelled to cry out in his sleep.

He awoke to find his tongue restored, and he returned home 'able to speak freely'. This last phrase has some significance, connoting a restoration of personal liberty as well as the physical tongue itself.

A similar adventure befell a man 'taken prisoner by the Slavs' who cut out his tongue. This man, too, journeyed to the shrine, and after fervent prayer was healed. Thereafter he dedicated his life to the saint's cause. There is the case of a young slave who was probably Russian, bought by a member of the Varangian Guard of Constantinople; the boy was dumb from birth, but was skilled in making weapons. After having a succession of masters he was bought by a merchant who out of piety set him free. He then went to live in Novgorod in the home of a woman who prayed to Saint Olaf around the clock. One night she saw (or dreamed) Olaf bidding her to bring the youth to the church. Once there the boy fell asleep, and as in the case of the boy whose tongue had been removed, awoke with the power of speech.

Some of the more remarkable instances of healing occurred with deformed limbs. The *Passion* cites more than one case of a curious deformity in which the legs were jack-knifed backwards so that the feet pressed against the thighs. One small girl who had this problem was brought into the saint's church as the saint's body was being raised from its place for the annual procession; 'a crackling of stretching sinews was heard' and the girl's legs were at once made straight. A young boy, an only child, with the same problem went with his father to the same church on Saint Olaf's eve; as the boy slept that night he dreamed that 'a certain man pulled his legs straight with such force' that the boy cried out in pain. When the boy awoke his legs were indeed normalized.

There are also notable instances of more general healing, involving multiple afflictions rather than a single physical problem such as blindness or deformed limbs. One dramatic story in the *Passion* describes two noble brothers who suspected their sister of having an affair with an English priest – possibly one of those brought over by Olaf. Having lured the unsuspecting priest to a secluded place, they broke his legs, gouged out his eyes and cut off most of his tongue, and left him for dead. A poor woman took pity on him and took him in. There the wretched priest lamented and prayed without rest. When he finally was able to sleep he dreamed that Saint Olaf came to him and touched his eyes and legs. Finally the saint 'pulled at the root of the tongue with such force that the priest gave a loud cry in exceedingly great pain'. He awoke fully healed of all that had been inflicted on him, with nothing to betray what he had suffered except a white scar on his eyelids.

Mental issues and at least one problem of a sexual nature were similarly dealt with. There was the case of a rather cocky and overconfident young man who treated all religion with contempt and was bent on securing all the material benefits this world could give him. This man attended the saint's feast day for no other purpose (we are implicitly informed) than to ogle the girls and see which one he might chat up. But when the saint's body was borne in procession, something stirred in this man. 'He began to weigh in himself the glory of the martyr, and to consider in his heart his own wretched state... and the terrors of damnation.' In floods of tears he knelt and sought forgiveness for his sins, and appeared to receive it. But that wasn't the end of the story. Lust still ruled his mind and heart, something he could not bring himself to admit even to himself. We are told that because of this he suffered 'a most grievous weakness' which ended only when he was able to make a full and sincere confession of his own moral weakness.

A fascinating story is told of a Danish deacon whose sex life was extraordinarily active, and which became a problem for him only when the number of children he sired became too great for his income to provide for. Realizing his basic plight, he sought help (presumably from the clergy), but in vain; he just liked sex too much. But something had to give, and it was his penis that erupted in a very painful swelling. So bad did the pain become that he could not stay still, and finally he fell down before the saint's shrine in wretched misery. He did this several times. Falling asleep in the church, he dreamed that Olaf came up to him 'in the guise of a physician' and pierced the painful organ with a hot iron. Jerked awake by pain and fear, the deacon felt as if his penis were engulfed by fire; trying to soothe it by a warm bath at home, he saw it quickly return to its normal condition, 'eased and unswollen... the power of sinning had left it'. Church elders later confirmed the story.

One more miracle which the *Passion* attributes to Saint Olaf deserves mention: the case of raising a man from the dead. He was a peasant wrongly convicted of theft and sentenced to be hanged. Despite his pleas and prayers, he did not escape the noose. 'One who was guiltless was hanged by those who deserved to be hanged' – a familiar enough miscarriage of justice in all ages. According to the narrative, just as his body dropped he had a vision of Saint Olaf putting a plank under his feet to support him. To others, however, it appeared that he was dead and he hung there for nine hours. Eventually his son got permission to cut him down from the tree on which he was hanged, but apparently fumbled the operation and the body tumbled down a steep adjoining precipice. 'He remained as one fast asleep, recalling his vision as in a dream.' His limbs gradually re-warmed and his consciousness returned, upon which he hastened to the saint's shrine and told the bishop what had happened.

Reports of such occurrences detailed in the *Passion* spread far and wide in Norway and beyond its frontiers. Two brothers are reported to have travelled from Chartres, France, after murdering their mother, her second husband and their baby brother in a bloody property dispute. Having repented, they got off with being bound by iron bands but otherwise were free; it also could have counted that one of the brothers was a priest. They called at the Holy Sepulchre in Jerusalem, where the iron on the non-priestly brother's arm broke off, apparently of its own accord (or perhaps it just rusted). After much wandering they arrived at Trondheim, where in front of the saint's shrine the iron bound around the priest's waist was also loosed. Rescue from grievous confinement, as well as mysteriously unlocking cell doors (reminiscent of Saint Paul in prison) was also widely reported as having been Saint Olaf's doing – again, indicating that a basic result of all miracles is the regaining of a certain freedom, whether from disease or death or fire or a cruel enemy or injustice of any kind.

Chapter 12

Mission Accomplished

It remains uncertain how far the reports of Saint Olaf's miracles helped consolidate the Christian faith in Norway. The contribution of Olaf as king has been called into question by some writers, who note that the Christianization process began long before him, even before Håkon the Good and Olaf Tryggvason. But though the basic faith was there, it was Olaf Haraldsson who took the vital step of aligning the laws of Norway and codifying them along Christian lines. Also, it is worth remembering that Olaf's war with Cnut, also a Christian, had no religious overtones; it was a pure struggle for hegemony. Cnut himself, remarkably, had no objection to the growing cult of Olaf, though how charitable this feeling actually was is open to question; Cnut may well have been more comfortable with the idea of Olaf safely up in heaven than on earth as a rival king. Contrariwise the cult that grew up around Olaf, moving him up from king to saint, had no political overtones at all; it was purely a spontaneous spiritual movement that took no account of borders or factions or allegiances – even Einar Tambaskelfer, one of the more aggressively independent of the chieftains, was quick to realize the other-worldliness of Olaf and became a devoted follower. And there were many others like him.

It has been suggested that even details of the Battle of Stiklestad might have been manipulated anachronistically to buttress Olaf's later sainthood. For example the *Anglo-Saxon Chronicle* entry for 1030 alleges that Olaf was 'murdered by his own people'. That may simply be a reflection on his death at the hands of fellow-Norwegians rather than a foreign foe. Several decades later Adam of Bremen and Florence of Worcester wrote that Olaf perished in an ambush. And since that kind of sordid demise would not square well with the image of the saint as a hero, the theory goes, the story was changed. Most learned opinion, however, accepts Snorri's account of Stiklestad as the most trustworthy (or least untrustworthy) as it is also the most detailed.

It is a moot point whether the end of Svein's rule in Norway was a factor in the rapid spread of Saint Olaf's cult, or vice versa. Certainly the growing number of miracle accounts eroded what little popularity Svein and Aelfgifu had. All they could do was rely on Cnut, away in England, as a backstop for emergencies. They also seem to have retained a core of support among some chieftains, though by now those chieftains would have been in a minority. Therefore when news filtered through to them in South Hordaland that Magnus Olafsson had arrived in Sweden from Russia with the intention of reclaiming his father's heritage, Svein imagined he could resist.

Magnus, meanwhile, was making rapid progress. Still only eleven years old, he had almost overnight become the living symbol of Norwegian independence, further hallowed by his status as Olaf's son. On arrival at the Swedish court Magnus was welcomed by his stepmother Astrid and King Jacob-Anund. At a specially-convened Thing at Hangtar, Astrid made a dramatic appeal for manpower and aid, adding that she intended to accompany Magnus and his army. Some Swedes, however, were unsure about the prospects of an invasion, mainly on the grounds of Magnus' extreme youth. They also remarked that the Swedes under Olaf's command had not really accomplished much in the run-up to Stiklestad, and there was no reason to suppose they would do any better this time.

Astrid would have none of this pusillanimity. As recorded by Snorri in the opening paragraphs of his saga of Magnus Olafson which follows that of Olaf Haraldsson, she rounded on the doubters: 'If any of you have lost people at the side of King Olaf, or have been wounded in his service, now is the time to show a manly heart and courage and go to Norway to take revenge.' Sang the ever-alert Sigvat, who was most likely present:

> And with the Swedes no wiser plan,
> To bring out every brave bold man,
> Could have been found, had Magnus been
> The son himself of the good queen.

Sigvat's poem claims that Astrid offered up all her jewellery to help finance her Magnus' campaign as if he were her own son.

Sigvat himself had a rather chequered career. In Rome at the time of Stiklestad, he learned of Olaf's death while on the way home. Arriving at Trondheim on a merchant ship, he was offered hospitality by Svein, but preferred to go home to his farm and family first. Adding to his grief over Olaf's death was his own guilty conscience in having been absent from his king at a critical juncture. Some people jeered at him for this and so, disillusioned, he crossed the mountains into Jamtland and thence to the Swedish court to stay with Olaf's widow Astrid and await news of Magnus.

> I ask the merchant oft who drives
> His trade to Russia, 'How he thrives,
> Our noble prince? How lives he there?'
> And still good news – his praise – I hear.

Even though very young, Magnus Olafsson displayed much of his father's spirit and resolve. He and Astrid and the large force they had gathered – distinguished by their dark red shields – took the well-trodden westward route across Jamtland and into the Norwegian Trøndelag, soon to be joined by Trondheimers with white shields. In Snorri's account any remaining supporters of Svein were thoroughly intimidated. Magnus and his entourage entered Nidaros where, at a specially-convened Thing, Magnus was proclaimed king over all Norway, the legitimate heir to Olaf II Haraldsson. After setting up a basic state mechanism, and waiting until after the autumn 1035 harvest so that men could be free for military service, young Magnus' army began to head south to Hordaland, where Svein was headquartered.

Svein, on hearing of the move, sent out the usual war signals, but without the success he expected. Though his Danish lords were enthusiastic, the same cannot be said for the Norwegians of the district, many of whom flatly declared for Magnus. His countrywide support melting, Svein thought it prudent to remove himself to Denmark to recruit men from his brother King Harthacnut. At about that time Cnut died, to be shortly followed by Svein, though the cause is not recorded; it is not inconceivable that he was eliminated.

Magnus had an elaborate, jewel-studded gold and silver shrine made for his father the saint. He established 29 July as the saint's holy day, a date that is still observed. But more practical problems loomed, as when Magnus had a visit from his father's arch-enemy Hårek of Thjøtta. It is not clear why Hårek took the trouble; most likely he merely wished to ingratiate himself with the new power structure. He was spotted by Magnus and Asmund Grankelson as he stepped off his ship. It was a golden opportunity for vengeance on Asmund's part, as Hårek had murdered his father. As Asmund fingered a small hatchet he had on him, Magnus suggested that he take his own, stouter, battle-axe. 'You need to know, old man, that man has hard bones.' Without losing a moment Asmund went down the path towards Hårek and brought down the axe on his head with such force that the brain was penetrated and the axe head bent back. The young Magnus seems to have been unfazed. 'If this axe is spoiled, would yours have done anything at all?' he remarked to Asmund.

Another instance of Magnus' hot-headed character occurred at the start of his reign, and momentarily threatened to derail it. The position of king having been thrust on him at a very early age, he let the status go to his head. There is an incident in the *Ágrip* where, barely had the first assembly gathered at Nidaros when the young king lambasted the elders of the Trøndelag for supposedly lukewarm support of his father. Only Sigvat, who was his godfather, had the nerve to rebuke Magnus for his disrespect. We are told that the following morning a chastened Magnus addressed the elders again, but in a much more conciliatory and respectful tone. Clearly, however, Magnus would require careful chaperoning, and we may assume that, in the absence of major incidents, he was thus chaperoned.

Magnus' youthful imperiousness showed itself to an old foe of Olaf's, his battlefield nemesis Kalf Arnason, who was sitting at table with Magnus and Einar Tambaskelfer when Magnus suggested to Einar that they ride out to Stiklestad to view the battlefield memorials. Perhaps craftily, Einar suggested that Kalf go instead. When Kalf tried to back out, young Magnus angrily ordered him to comply. Before setting out Kalf, rightly suspecting a trap of some sort, ordered his servants to go home and put all his movable property on his ship before sunset. On the battlefield Magnus asked Kalf to show him the spot where Olaf fell. Kalf marked the spot with his spear shaft.

'And where were you, Kalf?' Magnus then demanded.

'Right here', Kalf replied.

Magnus flushed. 'So your battle-axe could have reached him.'

Kalf, in panic, attempted a denial but moments later jumped on his horse and galloped off, not stopping until he reached his readied ship.

That night Kalf sailed down the Trondheimsfjord into the open sea to commence a new career of plunder in Ireland, Scotland and the Hebrides, which was probably well within his capabilities.

After this, Magnus cracked down hard on any remaining opponents of Olaf, seizing their property and exiling some. He seems to have overdone the severity somewhat, and it was Sigvat who channelled reports of growing discontent to Magnus; Sigvat's own suggestion – typically rendered in song – was for Magnus to be even more decisive, but without being too harsh. The king took the advice to heart and had a code of laws drawn up which did a great deal to restore his initial popularity.

When Harthacnut, who ruled Denmark and England, died about 1042, Magnus at once eyed the vacant dominions. He lost no time in assembling a war-fleet of seventy vessels and leading it across the sea – himself in Olaf's old flagship, it was said – and landing in Jutland. He appears to have had little difficulty in establishing his authority there, as the legends of Saint Olaf had already become well-known. At a Thing in Viborg, Magnus was proclaimed king of Denmark, returning to Norway in the autumn after reorganizing the Danish internal administration.

The Dane Svein Ulfson, the son of the murdered Ulf Sprakalegson whom Cnut had ordered eliminated after that tense chess game, had now grown up and was living in Sweden, an impressive young man in speech and physical prowess. Magnus made Svein a full-fledged earl, essentially appointing him viceroy in Denmark. When the announcement was made, Einar Tambaskelfer demurred, saying the post was too great for one so young. But Magnus, whose quick temper and impulsiveness were already noticeable traits of his character, handed Svein a shield and put a helmet on his head, confirming the appointment.

Stirrings of insurrection, however, were soon heard in Denmark, so in the spring of 1048 Magnus led a punitive force across the sea to Vindland, laying waste the country. Svein, meanwhile, with the assent of most Danes, took on himself the title of King. This was open usurpation of the position of Magnus (who may have remembered Einar Tambaskelfer's cautionary comments about Svein's youth). Hearing of Magnus' mobilization, Svein slipped over to King Jacob-Anund in Sweden, where he raised a considerable force. Magnus, who in the meantime had enlisted his brother-in-law, the Duke of Brunsvik, received intelligence that Svein's army far outnumbered his, but was determined to bring his enemy to battle. Snorri recounts that after spending most of a night in prayer, and dozing off towards morning, Magnus dreamed of his father Olaf, who told him not to be afraid of the heathen horde he faced, for 'I shall be with thee in the battle.' That morning Magnus' soldiers reported hearing a mysterious pealing of bells, identical to the sound of those in Nidaros church.

'Then King Magnus stood up and ordered the war trumpets to sound,' writes Snorri, endowing the young king with extraordinary powers of leadership. He is described as throwing off his chain-mail tunic to reveal a red silk shirt, and running ahead of the rest of the army brandishing Olaf's battle-axe, Hel. He 'hewed down with his own hands every man who came against him'. Magnus at this time would have been about twenty years old and his physical strength almost fully developed. This battle, at Hlyrskog Heath, was a stomping victory for Magnus, who is said to have taken on some of the attributes of his saint father by tending to his wounded and naming a dozen men with 'the softest hands' to act as medics; these previously inexperienced corpsmen were at once transformed into 'the best of doctors' – another miracle attributed to Saint Olaf.

There followed another battle at Re, in which Svein's army was smashed and Jutland saved for Magnus. But Svein did not give up, and confronted Magnus a third time at Aros, with a superior force. By now some of his father's aura had stuck to Magnus, who invoked 'our trust in God and Saint Olaf, my father, who has given victory' and ensured the devotion of his soldiers. A stiff naval encounter ensued, in which Magnus, throwing all caution overboard, personally boarded Svein's ship in a spirited assault. Svein himself escaped to Sweden and was able to get together a fresh force that attempted to strike Magnus off the Danish coast. The result was a repeat of the disaster at Re, after which Svein fled to Sweden once more.

Once secure in his rule over Norway and Denmark, Magnus eyed England. He wrote to the English king, Edward the Confessor, demanding that he give up the kingdom on the grounds that Magnus and Harthacnut had agreed that England should go to whoever lived longer. 'I consider myself now, in consequence of my rights by this agreement, to own England also.'

Edward returned a defiant reply: 'I have established my royal dignity and authority, as my father before me, and while I live I will not renounce my title.' He added by way of conclusion that Magnus would take England only over his own dead body. Magnus, on receiving King Edward's reply, seems to have admired his spirit and decided to let him be for the time being, though he still considered himself the lawful sovereign of England. Only one military consequence of this exchange is recorded: according to the *Anglo-Saxon Chronicle* Edward sailed to Sandwich with thirty-five ships. The reason for the expedition is not known, but it is generally assumed that it was a response to rumours of an imminent invasion by Magnus.

Another of Olaf's close relations, his half-brother Harald Sigurdson, had a rather more interesting and adventurous career. He shared the family's propensity for combat at an early age, being just fifteen when he fought alongside the king at Stiklestad and was wounded. Harald spent some time in the Orkneys recuperating, whiling away the tedium with dreams of future fame and glory. Later we find him in Russia, in the court of Grand Prince Yaroslav, and wooing the prince's daughter Ellisif (Elizabeth). As he wasn't considered quite worthy enough for that prize, he betook himself to Constantinople, where by all accounts the real action was.

'Micklegarth' – the Viking name for Constantinople (meaning 'Great City') – was full of opportunity for a capable mercenary like Harald Sigurdson. In Snorri's account nearly seven feet tall, with long fair hair and beard, he gained a reputation of something of a swashbuckler and ladies' man, rounded out with a taste for gold. The emperor of the time, Michael IV, gave him a company command under the Greek general George Maniakes. Called 'Gyrger' by Snorri, Maniakes led several successful attacks on Norman pirates in the Aegean Sea and as far as Sicily, during which Harald distinguished himself. The account of these campaigns has been painstakingly recorded by Snorri, but need not concern us here. However, being subordinate to anyone was not congenial to Harald's royal blood; he often quarrelled with Maniakes (himself a tough character), but was careful to stop short of outright insubordination. What saved his career were undoubtedly his military qualities which by now had earned him a new surname – Hardraada, or Ruthless.

There followed battles in the Byzantine Army against various Saracens, with Harald going as far as Jerusalem. Up to now, religion had not played a particularly large part in his personality make-up; to all intents and purposes, his life resembled that of a typical heathen, long on action, short on thinking. Yet he had fought with his half-brother Olaf at Stiklestad and must have heard plenty of reports of Olaf's saintly status. Snorri relates that Harald bathed in the Jordan River and 'gave great gifts to our Lord's grave, to the Holy Cross and other holy relics'. While doing this he eliminated sundry robber bands along the way. That proto-crusade over, Harald returned to Constantinople. But in the meantime he seems to have become homesick for Norway after hearing that Magnus Olafson had become king. This would have been about or after 1042.

He asked Empress Zoe for permission to leave, and gave up his command in the Greek service, but Zoe refused to let him go on the grounds that he was suspected of purloining money belonging to a previous emperor. There was also Zoe's attractive niece Maria, whom Harald wooed unsuccessfully. It was widely rumoured in the city that Zoe herself was eyeing the strapping Norwegian, all of which moved her husband, Emperor Constantine IX Monomachos, to consign Harald to a prison tower.

As Harald was being led to the tower, Snorri recounts, Saint Olaf appeared to Harald and assured him of help. Then, always according to the saga:

> A lady of distinction with two servants came, with the help of ladders, to the top of the tower, let down a rope into the prison and hauled them [Harald plus two comrades, Haldor and Ulf] up. Saint Olaf had formerly cured this lady of a sickness and he had appeared to her in a vision and told her to deliver his brother.

Who was this 'lady of distinction?' Might it have been Zoe herself, or Maria? What is certain is that all three prisoners escaped and returned to the Varangian Guard barracks. Snorri adds that they went to where the Emperor was sleeping, bound him and put out his eyes. This is frankly pure fantasy, as there is nothing in the Byzantine records about Constantine IX being captured or blinded or even anything close; the worst of his afflictions was arthritis that plagued him until his death in 1055. Snorri, in fact, at this point veers rather badly off course; it was not Constantine IX who was captured and blinded but his predecessor Michael V Kalaphates, an ex-shipyard worker and incompetent ruler standing in for Zoe. Michael's fall was the result of mass unpopularity rather than anything Harald did, though there is evidence to suggest that

Harald belonged to the special punishment squad that stabbed the hapless emperor's eyes out. The incident in Snorri's narrative is almost certainly a distorted reflection of that event, embellished and romanticized in the telling and re-telling to put a favourable spin on Harald. Shortly afterwards Harald slipped out of the city with Maria in tow, but left her ashore to go back and tell her aunt Zoe that Harald Hardraada, in the end, was not one to be trifled with.

Ten years in the Varangian Guard was enough for Harald to have amassed a considerable fortune, which he was keeping for his real objective – Princess Ellisif, whom this time he successfully purchased with his gold. He also would have heard of his nephew Magnus' successful rule over Norway, and conceived a desire to return, which he did in the spring of 1045. He stopped off at the Swedish court, where a kind of extended family reunion took place, as Ellisif was the daughter of Ingegerd/Irene, who was the sister of Sweden's King Jacob-Anund. Also there was Svein Ulfson, who had been chased out of Norway by Magnus. Harald saw Svein as a useful ally for his scheme to seize the rule of Norway; together they recruited a large force which sailed to Denmark to cut off that territory from Magnus' south-west flank.

Harald Hardraada's reputation as a formidable warrior preceded him, throwing Magnus into a state of anxiety. Cooler heads, however, prevailed in Harald's camp, pointing out that it would be most unseemly for two of Saint Olaf's close relations to 'fight and throw a death-spear at each other'. In Snorri's account Magnus secretly sent a party of envoys to Denmark in a small ship to propose a deal whereby Harald and Magnus would share half of Norway as co-kings, and Harald agreed. This, of course, was not to Svein's liking at all, and Snorri records a heated exchange between Svein and Harald which ended with the former attempting to assassinate the latter as he slept. Harald, however, had taken his precautions and had gone to sleep somewhere else, putting a log under the covers of his usual bed. A great axe found stuck in the log next morning revealed the truth. Harald at once got into his ship and set a course for Magnus, with whom he firmed the agreement in an elaborate ceremony. During the proceedings Magnus, as a token of good faith, offered his father's gold ring to Harald, saying it was all the wealth he had.

The truth may not have been quite so neat. The bond between Harald and Magnus was not a smooth one, which was rather to be expected between two powerful personalities. Busybodies, according to Snorri, were constantly trying to set them at odds – which probably means that Harald himself was playing off Magnus against Svein Ulfson. There was a near-quarrel during a joint expedition against Svein in the spring of 1047, when Harald intimated that Magnus, though now a grown man, still had childish traits, but that spat, as well as others, seems to have been settled without undue consequences. Harald, by far the abler and craftier of the two, almost certainly was playing for time; he is said to have cynically used Magnus' need to control Svein to put forward his demand for a co-kingship.

Shortly after this Magnus died, in disputed circumstances. As Snorri tells it, one night on campaign in Jutland Magnus claimed to have dreamed of his father who gave him a choice: either join him in heaven or, if he desired a long life, eventually commit a crime 'which you will never be able to expiate'. The meaning of this remains vague; did the saint foresee some foul deed that his son was fated to commit if his years were drawn out? We have no way of knowing what this is supposed to have been. In the dream Magnus told his father to arrange his fate as he thought fit. What Saint Olaf meant became clear not long afterwards, when Magnus fell ill and died, leaving Harald the sole ruler of Norway. Other sources, however, claim he fell in battle against Svein; either way it was most convenient for Harald, into whose lap Norway fell. Magnus the Good, as he was by now known, having apparently shed much of his youthful arrogance, was not more than twenty-three years old.

The rest of Harald Hardraada's story can be briefly told. In the spring of 1048 he resumed his ravaging of Jutland after marrying Thora, the daughter of Thorberg Arnason, with whom he would have two sons – Magnus and Olaf; this was in addition to his wife Ellisif, with whom he had two daughters, but that apparently caused few, if any, family problems; multiple political marriages were quite justifiable in most people's eyes, and the Arnason family, as we have seen, was influential. Harald spent a year or more fighting Svein's Danes and earning a general admiration which Snorri much later put in glowing terms:

> King Harald was a great man, who ruled his kingdom well... It is the universal opinion that no chief ever was in northern lands of such deep judgement and ready counsel. He was a great warrior; bold in arms, strong and expert in the use of his weapons beyond any others.

He seems to have reserved some reverence for his sainted half-brother and is reported to have donated a bell to a church in Iceland, for which Olaf had supplied the timber. He also, according to Snorri's saga, completed Saint Olaf's church at Nidaros left unfinished by Magnus and built a new one, the Mary Church, over the spot where Olaf's body had first been concealed after the Battle of Stiklestad.

With the passage of years, however, Harald grew more autocratic. Einar Tambaskelfer, a leading figure in the district, was unwilling to put up with it; when his independence began to border on outright rebellion, Harald had Einar and his son ambushed and slain. More depredations in Denmark followed, during which the miracle of the Danish official's serving-woman was reported. In 1062 the chronic conflict with Svein was still going on. At the Battle of the Nis River, Svein was thoroughly routed but retained his control of Denmark; two years later Harald and Svein, bowing to the general war-weariness after fifteen years of continuous conflict, finally agreed to talk peace.

England, however, remained a sore point with Harald. King Edward the Confessor had successfully warded off a hostile bid by King Magnus, but on Edward's death in January 1066, his brother-in-law Harold Godwinson claimed to have been given the succession. Harold's brother Tostig strongly disputed the claim and sought aid from Svein in Denmark, but Svein shied away from the prospect – especially after a long and wearisome war with Harald Hardraada – of invading England and Tostig sought the aid of Harald at Viken. Harald took the bait, though Snorri tells of gloomy premonitions as the king set out Ellisif and his two daughters, plus his son Olaf from Thora, with him. Leaving the queen at the Orkneys, he sailed south along the east coast of England, landed at Scarborough and burned the town, and proceeded up the Humber. At some point, Snorri reports Harald dreamed he met Saint Olaf in Trondheim, to be told by the saint that his lack of caution would result in his death – 'God is not to blame'. His army came up against that of Harold Godwinson at Stamford Bridge in East Yorkshire on 25 September 1066. The English attacked stoutly with powerful cavalry and placed the Norsemen in a difficult position. Harald threw himself incautiously into the thick of the fighting and took a fatal arrow that slashed his windpipe. The man who had packed more action into his first few decades than almost any other man of his time had fought his last fight. He was just over fifty years old. Less than a month afterwards, Duke William of Normandy, a distant descendant of the Vikings who raided England and France in the tenth century, landed at Hastings, eliminated Godwinson and whatever was left of the Anglo-Saxon royal house, and inaugurated a new chapter in world history.

In the fifty or so years between the accession of Olaf II Haraldsson and the death of Harald Hardraada, Christianity was finally consolidated not only in Norway, but also in Sweden and Denmark, despite the almost constant turmoil of war roiling Scandinavia. Olaf is generally acknowledged to have placed the capstone on this process, building on the painstaking labours of Håkon the Good and Olag Trgyggvason. Yet the exact value of his contribution is still a matter of debate. It can be argued that Christianity got started well before the turn of the eleventh century in the coastal areas of Norway that were open to sea-borne influences from Britain and Normandy.

Concrete evidence of the early Christianization of Norway is the so-called Kuli Stone (*Kulisteinen*) whose runes, however, are hard to interpret. The stone is unmistakably Christian, however, as it bears a large cross on one side. Its origin remains mysterious, and adding to the interest is that it includes the first mention anywhere of the term 'Norway' (*Nóregi*). For that reason the stone has been dubbed 'Norway's baptismal certificate'. It has been dated to about the reign of King Olaf, suggesting that he could have had it set up, especially as one decipherable portion of the inscription says that 'Christianity had been twelve winters in Norway'. (It is also the earliest known use of the term 'Christianity' in Norway as well.)

While much of the Christianization process in Scandinavia remains vague, what is unmistakable is the rapid spread of the cult of Saint Olaf in a mere few years after his battlefield death. The spread does not seem to be explainable by the ordinary processes of cultural acclimatization and transmission; the heathen beliefs and practices common in the Norwegian hinterlands, which had hindered Olaf so much in his mission, appeared to evaporate almost overnight. We have the example of a hard-headed character such as Einar Tambaskelfer, who had given King Olaf more than his share of trouble, turned into a worshipper of Saint Olaf without the slightest hesitation.

It was Olaf, then, who supplied the critical mass of Christian faith – enforcing it ruthlessly, sometimes brutally – that enabled Norway to slough off the dead skin of heathenism and prepare for eventual modern European nationhood. The course was not easy; Norway spent very long periods under first the Danes and then the Swedes, until 1905, when at last the independent Kingdom of Norway came into being. And it may not be too far-fetched to suppose that the popularity of the present king, Harald V, owes something to the example set by Olaf, the country's patron saint, whose axe now graces the royal Norwegian coat of arms.

Epilogue: Where is he now?

Somewhere in the south of England about 1060, relates Snorri Sturluson, a destitute cripple crawled along the roads and, exhausted, fell asleep by the wayside. He dreamed that 'a gallant man' appeared to him and told him to 'go to Saint Olaf's church in London, and there you will be cured'. On waking, the cripple asked for directions and eventually got someone to accompany him to the church gate. While the anonymous helper vaulted over the gate, the cripple crawled through, 'and rose up immediately sound and strong; when he looked about him his conductor had vanished'.

That is the earliest known legend surrounding one of the best-known of Saint Olaf's churches, Saint Olave's in Hart Street, London. Reputedly built near the site of Olaf's feat of pulling down London Bridge, it underwent several changes before taking its present form about 1450. Somehow Saint Olave's escaped the Great Fire of London, only to be severely damaged by the German blitz in the Second World War. Nonetheless, King Håkon VII of Norway, in exile in Britain at the time, regularly worshipped there, and in 1954 donated to the church a stone from Nidaros Cathedral in Trondheim.

As early as 1055 we hear of a Saint Olaf's church in York, while another Saint Olave's went up south of the Thames in Bermondsey. Though far more churches in his name were built in the Scandinavian countries, the English connection most likely came about through Bishop Grimkell, who after Olaf's death moved to England to become, by some accounts, Bishop of Selsey.

Farther afield, Saint Olaf became the chief symbolic figure of the Varangian Guard of the Byzantine emperors, with whom Harald Hardraada served. Probably during the reign of Alexios I Komnenos (1081–1118) or possibly earlier, the Greek Church as we have seen included Olaf (Olavios) in its list of saints, where he remains to this day. His church in Constantinople was named the Panaghia Varangiotissa

(Virgin Mary of the Varangians); there was some doubt about where exactly it was situated, but recent research by Bishop Ambrose von Sievers of the Orthodox Archdiocese of the Goths places it as 'almost touching' the western façade of Haghia Sophia. Saint Olaf himself was given a side-chapel in that church. Unfortunately, the tumult of centuries has ensured that no trace remains.

As the early cult of Saint Olaf received its first flowering just before the cataclysmic Schism of the Churches in 1054, when the Greek East and Latin West wings of Christianity irrevocably split, the Roman Catholic Church, too, holds Olaf in veneration. In Saint Mark's basilica in Venice there is a Byzantine icon of the Madonna Nicopeia (Victory-making) which is believed to have been kept in Saint Olaf's chapel in Constantinople when it wasn't carried to a battlefront. An impressive, if slightly over-romanticized, painting of Saint Olaf, by the Polish painter Pius Welonski, stands in the basilica of Sant'Ambrogio e Carlo squeezed tightly among the old *palazzi* on Rome's busy Via del Corso. It depicts the saint in flowing robes and gold crown standing on a rocky headland, orb and sword in hand, trampling the sea-monster which he supposedly encountered on the headland at Valldal.

The Vatican, however, seems to have been somewhat late in canonizing Olaf. Part of the reason could be that Olaf himself, in constructing the Christian legal system of Norway, nowhere made clerical celibacy a requirement; like the Orthodox priests, the Norwegian ones were free to marry. When the strong-minded Pope Gregory VII (1073–85) made clerical celibacy binding on the entire Western Church, the Norwegians simply ignored him. About eighty years later, however, Norway became a metropolitan province of the Church, forcing its clergy into line. It was not until 1164 that Pope Alexander III, who had his hands full with rival contenders for the papacy and needed allies, officially confirmed the 1031 canonization. Oddly enough, however, Saint Olaf under the Catholics has been given the duties of protecting carvers and difficult marriages!

The Protestant Reformation effectively dimmed the cults of sainthood in Scandinavia after the sixteenth century. The prevailing Lutheranism frowned on relic-veneration of any kind, but Saint Olaf was simply too important to be ignored. Interestingly the re-emerging national consciousness of the Norwegians was accompanied by a renewal of interest in Saint Olaf as having embodied their sense of separate nationhood. In

1847, while Norway was still politically united with Sweden, King Oscar I of both established the Norwegian Order of the Knighthood of Saint Olaf, who was now designated '*Rex Perpetuum Norvegiae*' – The Eternal King of Norway.

It was perhaps inevitable that over time elements of the older heathen beliefs would meld into the cult of Saint Olaf. For example, he was given some of the attributes of Thor as a quick-tempered and strong slayer of trolls. He also took on some of the fertility symbolism of his erstwhile foes in the inland farming districts, who adopted him as a patron saint along with fishermen and merchants. There is nothing inherently regressive about this; Christianity in general has recognized the positive elements in pagan religions such as that of ancient Greece and the Norse peoples as contributing in their way to the Christian milieu. The needs of people throughout the ages for food, shelter, health and love have been unchanged, and if the average farmer or seaman visualized Saint Olaf as like the powerful deities of old, there to call on when needed, then to all intents and purposes he was there.

But where are his remains now? Sadly, no-one quite knows. We do know that the incorrupt body was placed in the newly-built Nidaros Cathedral in 1075, and there it remained, a major pilgrimage destination, until in the sixteenth century the Danish authorities, acting under the radical influence of the Lutheran Reformation, destroyed the main parts of the shrine and looted its valuables. According to Father Alban Butler's classic *Lives of the Fathers, Martyrs and Other Principal Saints*, the ship carrying the loot sank on the way to Denmark, and what had been left was seized by robbers ashore. However, the Lutherans maintained a modicum of respect for the saint as they left the innermost coffin untouched. This, however, was taken to an offshore castle at Steinvikholm, to be retrieved by Swedish soldiers in 1564 and returned to Nidaros with great ceremony. But the Danish Lutherans were uneasy with the pilgrimages that resulted, and a few years later ordered the tomb to be filled in; it remains unclear whether or not the saint's relics were removed secretly to another grave.

Attempts continue to this day to discover where the earthly remains of Saint Olaf finally ended up. Some old graves were dug up during restoration work on the cathedral in the first decade of the nineteenth century and their contents stored in a wooden box in the crypt. Officials suggest there is evidence that the saint could be among them. Archaeological investigation continues, at this writing, under the cathedral floor, where one particular grave has aroused professional interest.

Elsewhere, a human calf bone in St Olaf Roman Catholic Cathedral in Oslo has been dated to about the time of Stiklestad; research indicates its owner had been in battle. The possibilities are intriguing, but further progress can be made only by investigating the mitochondrial DNA, a so far next-to-impossible proposition.

There is some controversy over whether the remains brought back to Nidaros Cathedral were authentic. For example, at the time the saint's face was observed to be bearded, whereas the same face thirty years before was seen to be hairless. Both descriptions, however, agree that the saint's body was whole and undecayed. Said one eyewitness:

> Olaf's face was completely intact with flesh and skin, his eyes somewhat sunken; the hairs of his eyebrows were clearly visible... His jaw was quite intact, but there was no beard on it. When touching his thighs, skin and flesh could clearly be felt. Also on his feet, skin, flesh and sinews were unspoiled... A good scent came from his body and there was no abomination to it. All who were present could clearly see this.

We may assume that this particular observer was not overtly religious, and moreover, he claimed that all present agreed with him.

All we know is that the mortal remains of Olaf Haraldsson must lie under the ground somewhere in Trondheim. Yet it is perhaps fitting that we know no more, as long ago the human King Olaf Haraldsson was translated somehow into Saint Olaf, putting him beyond the mere time-space limitations of human existence. Therefore, in a basic sense he is far more real than a mere worn name on a tombstone. The mystique persists, as it should. Otherwise there would be little reason for the arduous pilgrimage, the *Pilegrimsleden*, which many hundreds of people make each year over more than 600 kilometres from Oslo through Oppland and the Gudbrandsdal valley where Olaf led his faithful band on the inland march from Valldal, right up to the Pilgrim Centre in Trondheim. There may no longer be a visible shrine to the saint in Trondheim Cathedral where those who seek healing can still pray and stretch out their hands, but in a way there no longer needs to be one, as Saint Olaf's active spirit, for those who believe, has remained firmly in place.

Bibliographical Note

As the reader will have been quite aware, my main source has been the Olaf Haraldsson saga in Snorri Sturluson's *Heimskringla*, whose historicity and reliability I assess in the prologue. The entire work, translated into English and produced by Douglas B. Killings and David Widger, is available as an online e-book from The Project Gutenberg, though as pure text only, without critical comments or emendations, and that is the version I have used. In the excerpts I cite I have in places changed the language slightly to conform more to modern usage.

Equally important as a source is *The Passion and Miracles of the Blessed Óláfr*, generally credited to the pen of Archbishop Eysteinn Erlendsson of Trondheim (also known as Saint Øystein) and dated to the latter half of the twelfth century. This has been made available online recently by the Viking Society for Northern Research (University College, London) under the general editorship of Anthony Foulkes and Richard Perkins. I have used Volume XIII, 'A History of Norway and the Passion and Miracles of the Blessed Óláfr', translated by Debra Kunin and edited by Carl Phelpstead. I have also referred to an earlier chronicle of the miracles, the *Glaelognskvida* of the Icelander Thorarin Loftunga, which most likely would have been one of Snorri's sources. The *Anglo-Saxon Chronicle* makes frequent mention of Olaf, though it contradicts Snorri in a number of places.

One of Snorri's main sources was the *Ynglingatal*, or 'Genealogy of the Ynglings', a saga composed probably a century or so previously by an unknown author – though some attribute it to one Tjodol of Hvin in the tenth century, well before Olaf's time. Apart from the aforementioned *Glaelognskvida* we can cite the *Ágrip* that was penned a few decades before the *Heimskringla*, and Theodoricus Monachus' *Historia de Antiquitate Regum Norwagensium* of about the same time or possibly a little earlier. It has been argued that Snorri's chief source is the anonymous Icelandic

Fagrskinna (Fair Leather) which in turn is believed to have drawn on a work, now lost, by an Icelandic priest, Saemundr Frodi Sigfusson. Tracing the origins of the story of Saint Olaf in this way may bring us a little closer to authenticity, but at the cost of a consistent and interesting narrative. Having gone through the book at this stage, the discerning reader will be no doubt aware that I have preferred to keep the story going in a coherent and unified direction, even if some elements argue otherwise.

An insight into Viking culture and mentality is offered in a little book, the *Hávamál*, known also as *The Wisdom of the North*, which I have used in places as a source of vignettes. A handy edition is an English translation by Björn Jonasson with a foreword by Matthias Vidar Saemundsson titled *The Sayings of the Vikings* (London: Gudrun, 1992).

For a general history of the Viking era, with emphasis on the gradual transformation of Scandinavia from heathenism to Christianity, I have leaned heavily on Robert Ferguson's *The Hammer and the Cross* (London: Penguin, 2009). Ferguson includes a chapter on Olaf Haraldsson ('The Viking Saint') which places him in the context of the wider political and social events of the time – and incidentally compels any other author on the subject to come up with a different title! Also useful is *Olaf Viking and Saint* by Morten Myklebust (Oslo: Norwegian Council for Cultural Affairs, 1997).

There have been numerous articles and monographs written about Saint Olaf and his times, many of them in Norwegian. Among those in English is 'Martyr-King Olaf of Norway – a Holy Orthodox Saint of Norway' by Vladimir Moss, issued online by the Orthodox Church on www.orthodox.net. St Olaf's Catholic Church in Minneapolis, Minnesota, USA, has issued its 'St. Olaf, Patron Saint of Norway', available online at Wayback Machine. The story of the downing of London Bridge, and Olaf's role in it, is examined by J.R. Hagland and B. Watson in 'Fact or folklore: the Viking attack on London Bridge', in *London Archaeologist*, December 2005. Of course, the accounts are not all one-sided: an anonymous author has published an item on a Trøndelag website titled 'Olav den Heilige var en sadist', which does not really require translation. It does, however, throw light on the continuing awkwardness over Olaf's documented record for harshness in his mission to nail the faith firmly down in his homeland.

Index